Bullets, Ballots, and Rhetoric

Winner in 1976 of the
Mrs. Simon Baruch University Award by the
United Daughters of the Confederacy

Bullets, Ballots, and Rhetoric

Confederate Policy for the
United States Presidential Contest
of 1864

Larry E. Nelson

The University of Alabama Press
University, Alabama

Library of Congress Cataloging in Publication Data

Nelson, Larry E. 1944–
Bullets, ballots, and rhetoric.

Bibliography: p.
Includes index.
1. Presidents—United States—Election—1864.
2. United States—Politics and government—Civil War, 1861–1865.
3. Southern States—Politics and government—Civil War, 1861–1865.
I. Title.
E458.4.N42   324.973'07   79-27869
ISBN 0-8173-0037-6

For JaLene

121841

Contents

Baruch Awards
1927–1979

1927   Carpenter, Jesse Thomas. "The South as a Conscious Minority 1789–1861." New York University, Washington Square, New York, 1930. 315 pp.

1929   Whitfield, Theodore M. "Slavery Agitation in Virginia, 1829–1832." Out of Print.

1931   Flanders, Ralph Betts. "Plantation Slavery in Georgia." Out of Print.

1933   Thompson, Samuel Bernard. "Confederate Purchasing Agents Abroad." Out of Print.

1935   Wiley, Bell Irvin. "Southern Negroes 1861–1865." Yale University Press, New Haven, Connecticut, 1938. 366 pp.

1937   Hill, Louise Biles. "Joseph E. Brown and the Confederacy." Out of Print.

1940   Haydon, F. Stansbury. "Aeronautics of the Union and Confederate Armies." Out of Print.

1942   Stormont, John. "The Economic Stake of the North in the Preservation of the Union in 1861." Not Published.

1945   Schultz, Harold Sessel. "Nationalism and Sectionalism in South Carolina 1852–1860." Duke University Press, Durham, North Carolina, 1950. 259 pp.

1948   Tankersly, Allen P. "John Brown Gordon, Soldier and Statesman." Privately Printed.

1951   Todd, Richard Cecil. "Confederate Finance." University of Georgia Press, Athens, Georgia, 1953.

1954   Morrow, Ralph E. "Northern Methodism and Reconstruction." Michigan State University Press, 1956. 261 pp.
        Cunningham, Horace. "Doctors in Gray." Louisiana State University Press, Baton Rouge, Louisiana, 1958. 338 pp.

1957   Hall, Martin H. "The Army of New Mexico: Sibley's Campaign of 1862." University of Texas Press, Austin, Texas, 1960. 366 pp.

1960   Robertson, James I., Jr. "Jackson's Stonewall: A History of the Stonewall Brigade." Louisiana State University Press, Baton Rouge, Louisiana, 1963. 271 pp.

1969   Wells, Tom Henderson. "The Confederate Navy: A Study in Organization." The University of Alabama Press, University, Alabama, 1971. 182 pp.

1970   Delaney, Norman C. "John McIntosh Kell, of the Raider *Alabama.*" The University of Alabama Press, University, Alabama, 1972. 270 pp.

1972   Dougan, Michael B. "Confederate Arkansas: The People and Policies of a Frontier State in Wartime." The University of Alabama Press, University, Alabama, 1976. 174 pp.

1974   Wiggins, Sarah Woolfolk. "The Scalawag in Alabama Politics, 1865–1881." The University of Alabama Press, University, Alabama, 1977. 230 pp.

1976   Nelson, Larry Earl. "Bullets, Ballots, and Rhetoric: Confederate Policy for the United States Presidential Contest of 1864." The University of Alabama Press, University, Alabama, 1980.

1978   Franks, Kenneth Arthur. "Stand Watie and the Agony of the Cherokee Nation." Memphis State University Press.

Acknowledgments

The cooperation and support of many people aided me in writing this book. Special thanks to Robert F. Durden of Duke University, who provided encouragement and numerous kindly criticisms that led to important corrections and improvements. I am also indebted to Clarence L. Mohr, who generously subjected the manuscript to a critical reading. The many patient librarians and archivists who helped me find materials in the recesses of numerous depositories are owed a debt of gratitude. I am also grateful to the United Daughters of the Confederacy, who awarded my manuscript the Mrs. Simon Baruch University Award for 1976.

My deepest appreciation is to my wife, JaLene, and our two boys, Michael and Andrew. Without their patience and long-suffering, I could not have completed this project.

Preface

Jefferson Davis's conduct of Southern affairs during his tenure as president of the Confederacy has long been a subject of inquiry and a source of controversy. General and specialized studies have assessed various aspects of Davis's Confederate career, but the present monograph is the only full-length treatment of the responses of the Davis administration to the challenges for Confederate policy generated by the United States presidential election of 1864. This study also contributes to understanding the conflicts within the Confederacy caused by a lack of confidence in the chief executive and by an absence of consensus among Southerners on Confederate war aims.

The Northern political situation during 1864 presented both external and internal challenges for the government of Jefferson Davis. The external problem was first of all a matter of assessing the potential of the election. From the beginning of the war, reports had reached the Confederacy of tension and malaise in the North: fluctuations in the value of greenbacks, draft resistance and riots, cries of outrage and protests against the emancipation policy, political defeats suffered by the Republicans in the elections of 1862, and growing alienation and discontent in the border states and old Northwest. Davis expected that the canvass of 1864 would be particularly trying for the North and might result in election of a candidate amenable to Confederate independence. Another aspect of the external challenge was to devise and implement a stratagem that would intensify Northern distress and promote the election of an acceptable candidate. Davis drew upon personal observations and the suggestions of advisers to draft a scheme that he and selected subordinates labored to implement during the presidential campaign and election.

The internal challenge the Federal election created for Davis was to cope with the expectations the election inevitably aroused among Confederates. Weary of the long war, many Southerners took solace in the evidence of Northern distress and found strength to continue the fighting in the hope that somehow, some way, the election would bring an acceptable peace. The approach of the election gave additional stimulation to the already burgeoning peace sentiment in the Confederacy, and leaders of that movement were anxious that the South successfully influence the course of political events in the hostile section. As president of the Confederacy, Davis had an obligation to shape and to guide expectations among Southerners. Widespread false or inflated hopes would lead to moral disaster if the election failed to fulfill aspirations. Davis also needed to channel the peace zealots in a direction that would threaten neither his approach to the election nor the ultimate goal of Confederate independence.

The focus of this book is on the policies of Jefferson Davis in responding to the external and internal challenges which the Northern presidential contest posed for the Confederacy. The thesis is that, although Davis's evaluation of the potential of the election was reasonable, the tactics employed for influencing the contest were unimaginative and contradictory, and his response to aroused Confederate expectations was haphazard and inconsistent. Coping successfully with the dual challenge of the election proved beyond Davis's capabilities.

Bullets, Ballots, and Rhetoric

CHAPTER 1

Emergence of a Dual Challenge:
"It is the crisis with our oppressors."

Interest among Confederates in the Northern presidential contest dated at least from the year previous to the election. The New York *Herald* endorsed Abraham Lincoln for a second term in June 1863, and an editor at Richmond, bristling with defiance, seconded the nomination with the comment that reelection of the incumbent would be the finishing blow to the United States because his administration was ruining the finance and commerce of the nation while bungling the conduct of the war.[1] Whether the journalist really hoped Lincoln would be reelected seems doubtful, but he was expressing an early Southern interest in the course of Northern presidential politics.

As the year of the election opened, Northern politicians scrambled for position, and Confederates from Virginia to Texas watched and commented on developments. Evidence of apparent intensification of tension in the enemy section encouraged expectations among Southerners that peace through a favorable outcome of the election was a genuine possibility. Northern distress also invited Confederate intrigue in Federal politics, and Southerners privately and publicly speculated on means to influence the canvass. The external and internal challenges of the Northern presidential election for the government of Jefferson Davis emerged during the first months of 1864: Meaningful manipulation of Northern politics seemed possible, and Southern expectations of peace through the election were aroused.

The Northern troubles that Confederates found most promising involved finances, conscription, and unrest in the Northwest. Early in the war, Southern observers learned that the value of greenbacks in the Northern money market fluctuated with the ebb and flow of public confidence in Lincoln's war policy. Many Confederates also concluded that the financial strain of the simultaneous loss of revenue from Southern exports and the cost of waging the war would eventually bankrupt the enemy section. The Northern financial situation in early 1864 prompted a Southern editor to remark: "With gold at the North nearly two for one; the commercial collapse so long talked of cannot be much longer postponed. With financial derangement, the overthrow of the party who will be held responsible for all the mischief will be inevitable." The journalist added that financial chaos would prevent the North from prosecuting the war even if Lincoln's successor should desire to continue the conflict.[2]

Resistance in the North to conscription was another subject commonly discussed among Confederates. On February 1, 1864, Lincoln ordered another draft, which increased the number called within the past six months to five hundred thousand men, and the Confederate press reported criticism and resistance in the North.[3] A bureaucrat in Richmond, impressed by this apparently widespread opposition to conscription, concluded that the majority of resisters were "peace men at heart" only awaiting an opportunity to immobilize the Lincoln administration.[4]

Southerners carefully observed the Northwest, where events in the past had seemed propitious for Southern hopes and where prospects for the future were bright. When describing a dispute in the Federal Congress between representatives of the Northwest and the Northeast over fishing bounties, an editor in South Carolina remarked: "Nothing gives our readers more unfeigned pleasure than the evidences that are daily multiplying, of the existence of a feeling of jealousy and discord between the sections North and West, into which the United States are divided."[5] The development of secret, and allegedly disruptive, societies in the Northwest was particularly promising. When the Chicago *Tribune* published an exposé on one of these groups, the Knights of the Golden Circle, the Augusta *Constitutionalist* eagerly relayed the report to its readers: "This organization has a double object in view, first, the election of a Copperhead like McClellan or Vallandigham to the Presidency, by which the independence of the rebels may be secured, with slavery restored to them; or, failing in that, the kindling of the flames of civil war in the North, which shall compass the same object, and to this end these clubs are being extended all over Illinois, and will rapidly spread through the other States."[6]

Confederates had long predicted that tensions in the North would eventually erupt in violence, and reports of scattered outbursts seemed like prophecy on the verge of fulfillment. After a Copperhead newspaper in the Northwest warned Democrats to arm and prepare for interference from abolitionist mobs, an editor in Georgia commented: "We trust the little speck of trouble which has now appeared in the Northern political sky will prove to be the forerunner of a tempest of blood and ruin which will sweep over that section of the old Union."[7] When a mob destroyed a Copperhead press in Illinois, Southern newspapers gleefully carried the story.[8] Speculating on the election and the condition of Northern sentiment, I. B. Cohen, an attorney in Columbia, South Carolina, noted: "The germ of revolution seems to be budding in the North and I hope it will break forth, whether in blood or in violent opposition to the continuance of a fruitless war I care not."[9]

Southerners also listened to the comments of Northern peace advocates in hopes of discerning some indication of their conduct in the campaign and election.[10] The *Consti-*

tutionalist, for example, dutifully copied the following advice given by the New York *News* to the peace Democracy: "We mean peace—let us talk it and act up to our words. Let us look about for a true Peace man to bear the standard, and then, its folds to the breeze, we will advance in the name of Peace, State Sovereignty, and self-government."[11] In analyzing the composition of the peace party, the Northern editor concluded that it was an amalgam of persons who accepted the validity of secession or acknowledged that the South was exercising a legitimate right to revolution, opposed the conflict because of the high cost in blood and treasure, and believed that continued war was futile. At any rate, "The peace party has increased and is increasing rapidly."[12]

Southerners took particular interest in the activities of peace leaders in the Federal Congress, of whom some were exceedingly vociferous. An editor in Georgia described the Congress that met during the first half of 1864 as "mainly a hustings for the next presidency."[13] Southerners read of peace resolutions introduced into the Federal House of Representatives, analyzed the congressional votes that indicated the nature and depth of peace sentiment, and studied statements from the caucus of congressional Democrats.[14] An editor in Texas surveyed such evidence and concluded that "the peace party in the Federal Congress is gradually on the increase."[15]

Without question the most exciting revelations of feeling among Northern opponents of the war came from speeches delivered on the floor of the House of Representatives by peace Democrats. An address by William J. Allen, Copperhead from Illinois, that attacked Lincoln for his conduct of the war, his favorable attitude toward blacks, and the astronomical cost of the war, caught the attention of the Confederate press.[16] A speech by Alexander H. Long, Copperhead from Ohio, precipitated a bitter row in the North and created a sensation in the South. The representative charged that Lincoln deliberately sought war against the South and was subverting civil liberties in the North. After three years of war, Long contended, the Confederacy was still strong and vigorous despite the administration's predictions of a short war and statements that the rebellion was almost exhausted. He alleged that harsh and vindictive policies of the Lincoln administration, such as emancipation and confiscation, prolonged the war by inspiriting Southerners to resist subjugation. Without qualification, he pronounced the war unconstitutional and destined to destroy the Union forever.

The portion of the speech of most interest to Southerners and Northerners alike was Long's expression of willingness to recognize Confederate independence: "I am reluctantly and despondingly forced to the conclusion that the Union is lost never to be restored. I regard all dreams of the restoration of the Union . . . as worse than idle. I see, neither North nor South, any sentiment on which it is possible to build a Union." In remarks that must have set Confederate hearts to palpitating, Long expressed his opinion on the position the Democratic party should take in the forthcoming presidential election:

> Nothing could be more fatal for the Democratic party than to seek to come into power pledged to a continuance of the war policy. Such a policy would be a libel upon its creed in the past and the ideas that lay at the basis of all free government, and would lead to its complete demoralization and ruin. I believe that the masses of the Democratic party are for peace, that they would be placed in a false position if they should nominate a war candidate for the Presidency and seek to make the issue upon the narrow basis of how the war should be prosecuted.[17]

The unabashed call for peace and recognition of the Confederacy incited four days of vitriolic debate in the Federal House of Representatives in which supporters and opponents of Long hurled verbal brickbats at each other. Republicans sought to expel him, but his Democratic colleagues sprang to his defense although they did not necessarily share his sentiments. One who did agree with Long was Benjamin Harris, peace Democrat from Maryland, who had owned slaves and was dedicated to the cause of peace. Insisting that peace might reunite the nation but that war never could, he said: "I am a peace man, a radical peace man; and I am for peace by the recognition of the South, for the recognition of the southern confederacy; and I am for acquiescence in the doctrine of secession."[18] In the end, the Republicans were unable to muster the votes to oust Long and had to settle for a resolution of censure.[19]

Southerners watched and marveled at the fight in the Federal House of Representatives. Some Confederate newspapers published the speeches of Long and Harris and the subsequent proceedings in Congress and also reproduced comments from the Northern press and public favorable to these representatives.[20] From abroad Henry Hotze reported that Europeans were studying the speech of Representative Long and related materials and were interpreting the events as a symptom "of a revulsion of feeling in the North" against the war.[21] As might be expected, Southern newspapers lauded the controversial addresses as evidence that "honest men at the North are coming to their senses, and Abolition scoundrels are coming to justice."[22] In Shreveport, Louisiana, a regular correspondent of the Galveston *News* was particularly impressed with the significance of Long's address and described it as "the most important speech in the United States since the commencement of the war, and by far the most honest and able."[23] The Augusta *Chronicle & Sentinel* reported that the speech would furnish the "platform upon which the Democratic party of the North will make the issue in the coming Presidential election."[24]

Southern editors provided liberal excerpts from Northern newspapers and the statements of politicians that gave Confederates some understanding of the maneuvering among the various presidential contenders. The newspaper accounts sometimes garbled details and made inaccurate predictions, but Confederates who read one of the major journals of their section knew that serious intraparty and interparty strife racked the Northern political structure. With reference to "caucuses, conventions, resolutions, and platforms" in the rival section, one Southern editor commented, "The political cauldron is beginning to bubble, and expectation is aroused to see what will emerge from its agitated depths."[25]

Among the likely possibilities for the Republican nomination were Nathaniel P. Banks, who had led Union forces at Port Hudson; Benjamin Butler, "Beast Butler"; John C. Frémont, former commander in Missouri; Salmon P. Chase, secretary of the treasury; and, of course, Abraham Lincoln.[26] The latter three proved the strongest contenders, and Southern newspapers chronicled the evolution of their candidacies. As early as January, the Confederate press reported Frémont's determination to run as an independent, if necessary, and Southern readers caught a glimpse of his position on the issues when a meeting of his friends in New York informally nominated him and wrote a platform. This declaration of sentiments attacked Lincoln, called for civil rights for blacks, and pledged to subdue the rebellion.[27]

Confederates could study the rivalry between Chase and Lincoln through reports of public meetings endorsing Chase and excerpts from Northern newspapers discussing the struggle.[28] Commenting on the dispute generated by the Pomeroy Circular, one Southern editor said: "We are glad to notice that the discord so much talked about in Republican ranks is beginning to show itself openly. If the rascals get into a good jolly fight politically among themselves, and refuse to settle amicably, all the better for us."[29]

Among the Democrats, the persons suggested for the nomination were such disparate personalities as Ulysses S. Grant, who had won a shining reputation in the West; Franklin Pierce, former president of the United States, who was sympathetic to the South; and George B. McClellan, who had commanded the Army of the Potomac.[30] Identified with the war faction of the party, McClellan clearly emerged as the front-running Democrat.[31] Reports focused upon the peace and war divisions of the Democratic party of which Southerners had long been aware.[32] An editor in Georgia, for example, insisted that the Democrats would provide a strong opposition to Lincoln but was uncertain "whether a Democrat 'pledged to vigorous prosecution of the war,' or a conservative man willing to cease on some more equitable terms the desolating strife" would bear the Democratic standard.[33]

In addition to monitoring developments within the Democratic party, Southern editors provided their readers with generous excerpts and summaries from the endless flow of criticism against Lincoln generated by Democratic politicians and newspapers.[34] Confederates castigated the Republican champions, but not all comments were automatically in favor of the Democrats. Arguing that the principal benefit of the Northern election was the accompanying strife and dissension, the Charleston *Mercury* said, "For the South, as matters stand at present, there is small reason to desire the success of one candidate more than the other."[35] Declaring a similar disenchantment with the most likely candidates, the Richmond *Sentinel* expressed a preference for the incumbent: "Lincoln is likely to wear out sooner than a fresh man, and is, therefore to be preferred."[36] The North Carolina *Standard* described the Democrats as "the party at the North that is out in the cold and have not got the beef and shoddy contracts, and hence wish a change of administration, that they may carry on the war on their own account."[37]

The heightened tensions and open calls for peace at any price in the North encouraged Southerners to indulge in hopes that peace might come through Federal political developments. Some Confederates expected that the election might bring a beneficial change of administration at Washington or that the stress of the campaign might palsy the Northern war effort. Speaking of the election, the editor of the Richmond *Examiner* said: "Although it is difficult to penetrate the dark curtain of the future, and to discern exactly how our own welfare may be affected by the political complexion of the United States, yet it is evident that the whole solution of the mighty question which agitates the continent may hang upon it, and scarcely possible that it will not be essentially concerned by it."[38] In a similar vein, an editor in Georgia reviewed the situation and declared, "It is the crisis with our oppressors."[39] Such sentiments extended into the Confederate army, where a soldier wrote to his wife, "I don't think the war can last much longer unless Lincoln is reelected."[40]

Even if the candidates proved unacceptable to the South, many Confederates eagerly anticipated the campaign. One Confederate said: "It is in the contest itself, in the feuds and disintegration produced by the struggle for plunder that she [the South] may hope for relief from the attacks which have heretofore been concentrated upon her."[41] A commentator in Savannah, Georgia, expected to see "the North torn by intestine feuds, and utterly demoralized in the Presidential election."[42]

Speculation that Northern political developments would redound to the benefit of the Confederacy became so prevalent that some Southerners felt obliged to sound a note of caution. "It would be very unwise to make our calculations for the present year upon the assumption that the war is dying out," wrote an editor in Richmond. "The war interest is still strong enough to rule our enemy's country with absolute sway."[43] About the same time, newspapers in Georgia and Texas issued similar warnings to readers.[44]

Southerners did not have to rely upon their imaginations, however, to conjure visions of the North convulsed by the strain and excitement of the election. Reports from abroad and from the North itself also recognized such a possibility. The *Times* of London editorially wondered whether the Republican party had the strength and acumen to "carry on the war and maintain, at all hazards, its own political domination."[45] From Paris, John Slidell reported that Jules Vete de Treilhard, the late chargé d'affaires at Washington, had returned to France and "speaks in strong terms of the growing lassitude of the North and anticipates a general breaking up of the Lincoln Government before the end of the year."[46] The New York *Sunday Mercury* discussed the coming election with grave foreboding: "It is not to be disguised that the wisest men at Washington, as well as throughout the country, look with fear and dread upon the issues of the coming Presidential canvass. The temper of the people is so excited, the issues so vital, the disturbances—civil, social, and political—created by the war are so profound, that it is feared an excited Presidential canvass will plunge the nation into chaos."[47]

Not content as passive spectators, various Confederates speculated on steps that their government could take to influence the outcome of the election. Among Confederates there was recognition that the coming military operations would exert a drastic, perhaps decisive, impact on developments in the North.[48] Believing that Confederate military success would bolster the Northern peace party and topple Lincoln and the Republicans, one editor said: "Every bullet we can send . . . is the best ballot that can be deposited against his [Lincoln's] election. The battle-fields of 1864 will hold the polls of this momentous decision. If the tyrant at Washington be defeated, his infamous policy will be defeated with him, and when his party sinks no other war party will rise in the United States."[49] Thinking along similar lines, another Confederate weighed the consequences for Northern politics of Southern defeat and made an unwittingly accurate prophecy: "A serious disaster to our armies in Georgia and Virginia would promptly revive the enemy. It would secure the re-election of the present incumbent, would silence the voices of our friends, and would stimulate new efforts to effect our subjugation."[50] In the harrowing days at the end of August and the beginning of September, the writer would learn the accuracy of his assessment.

In late spring, the *Constitutionalist* felt obliged to warn against the growing belief that defeat of Federal forces in Georgia or Virginia would destroy Northern war fervor and result in the election of a peace candidate and, ultimately, a peace favorable to the Confederacy. The editor observed that the utter rout of the large and well-disciplined Federal armies was highly unlikely: "We will have no second Manassas." The mighty blow required to destroy the invading forces would "benumb the arm that strikes" and leave no capability to exploit the victory with a pursuit of the retreating Federals.

Such a follow-up, the editor insisted, would be necessary "to overbalance all the patronage, bribery, negro votes, army votes, *bogus* State votes, etc. that Lincoln can command."[51]

Recognition that the election might well be determined on the battlefield also extended to the North. "First in order and importance is the grand struggle of the war upon which we are about to enter," declared the New York *Herald,* "for upon its results the Presidential contest will be shaped and determined."[52] Southerners listened to such comments and speculated that Lincoln was conducting the war with political consequences uppermost in his mind. General Robert E. Lee said, "The importance of this campaign to the administration of Mr. Lincoln and to General Grant leaves no doubt that every effort will be made to secure its success," and other Southerners expressed similar sentiments.[53]

Some Confederates charged that Lincoln's plan of reconstruction was little more than a scheme to steal the election. During the spring of 1864, presidential reconstruction, which authorized formation of a new state government when 10 percent of the voters in a state would swear allegiance to the Federal Constitution, was proceeding apace in Louisiana, Arkansas, and Tennessee. Southern editors insisted that the true purpose of the process was to gain electoral votes for Lincoln because states reconstructed under his tutelage would be loyal to him.[54] The Galveston *News* suggested that the Northern army would attempt to occupy as many Southern states as possible to erect a government under the 10 percent plan and deliver the electoral votes of those states to the president.[55] Denouncing presidential reconstruction as "one of the vilest cheats of the war" designed to "answer the lowest and vilest party purpose," the Richmond *Examiner* described the plan as the Republican "method of stumping the South."[56]

In addition to military action, Southerners hatched schemes for direct political intrigue in the North. A letter from Lieutenant Colonel Frank Ruffin to Secretary of War James A. Seddon provided an example of a Confederate plan to influence the election based upon a recognition of alleged Northern instability and the plight of the Confederacy. He proposed clandestine intrigue "with one or more of the factions or parties in the United States with a view to give us an influence upon their affairs." Noting that the Confederacy had made secret contracts in the past with disloyal Northerners to obtain commissary supplies for the Confederate armies, Ruffin suggested that this procedure be continued and expanded as a tool for secret diplomacy in the North. He speculated that the South might win support among Northern dissidents through an appeal to reason by showing the consequences of the war for the North, and, if this failed, he advocated an appeal to Yankee avarice through liberal bribes paid in cotton. He suggested that the Confederacy capitalize on the Northern political situation by subsidizing the peace Democrats, who could then marshal the "large majority" of peace men, who "only want a proper organization to range themselves openly in a peace party of such extent and power as will demoralize the Army and paralyze Mr. Lincoln."

Ruffin not only argued that the North was ripe for intrigue but insisted, "Our own condition would seem to require the effort." He emphasized the disaffection and desire for peace among some politicians and in some regions of the Confederacy and pointed to the brutal facts of insufficient supplies of food to provide full rations for the army and citizens. Suspecting that the secretary might be reluctant to recommend nefarious dealings, Ruffin argued: "The character which the war has long since assumed justifies, in my judgement, a resort to much more questionable measures than I have suggested, which are in fact among the commonest expedients of hostilities."⁵⁷

Benjamin H. Hill, Confederate States senator from Georgia, took an early and continuing interest in the Northern election and described a policy for responding to Northern politics in a speech at LaGrange, Georgia. Hill contended: "The presidential election in the United States, in 1864, then, is the event which must determine the issue of peace or war, and with it, the destinies of both countries." The reelection of Lincoln would mean the ratification of his principles and war policy by the North and continuation of the war for at least four more years, but the defeat of Lincoln would be a repudiation of his position and an unmistakable signal that the North stood ready to negotiate. Arguing that Lincoln would not accept a peace short of Southern submission, Hill commented, "Proposals of negotiation from us, as matters now stand, are inconsistent with honor and futile for good."

Recognizing the importance of the election for the Confederacy, the Georgian insisted that the South make an effort to influence the situation, and he concluded, "I say we can control that election." The first step was "to defeat Mr. Lincoln's armies in the fast approaching campaigns. Without this nothing else, we can do will, or can, avail." In addition, the senator proposed a direct appeal to Lincoln's opponents in the North who "declare their willingness to discuss, to negotiate, whenever they" win power in the United States:

> I think that we of the Confederate States, both government and people, ought to declare that, if the people of the United States will, at that election, withdraw authority from those who will not themselves honorably propose, and will not permit us, in honor, to propose negotiations for peace; and will confer authority on those who are willing either to make, or respond, to such honorable

proposal, that we are then ready and willing to make, or to receive, such proposal, and to agree to terms consistent with the honor of both peoples, and conducive to the interests of all parties.

Through defeating the Federal armies and openly endorsing the peace Democracy, Hill believed that the Confederacy could establish the central issue of the campaign: "Whether the people of the United States will elect Mr. Lincoln and continue the war, or whether they will defeat him and accept an honorable peace."

Warming to the subject, Hill went on to discuss the means for negotiation and terms of acceptable peace. He suggested that the national governments of the belligerent powers or the state governments could appoint representatives to meet for peace talks, but he favored the latter mode. Under the terms of peace he envisioned, "the most liberal relations of unity and commerce should exist" between the sections without political union.[58]

An Alabamian, William A. Samford, had also been giving extended thought to Northern politics, and on the first day of 1864 he wrote a letter to Alexander Stephens proposing a Confederate response to the election. Operating from the assumption that the people in both of the contending sections desired peace although the respective central governments were committed to a policy of war, Samford suggested that the people, acting through the state governments, intervene to bring about peace. As a theoretical justification for this approach, he wrote: "The people are *Sovereign*. The *States* are independent. The *State Governments* represent the Sovereign people. The states in *Convention are Sovereign* because they are the people." To secure peace, Samford was willing to accept close relations between the sections through treaties of commerce, offensive and defensive coordination in time of war, and guarantees for the preservation and extension of slavery.

To implement his plan, Samford proposed that General
Robert E. Lee be appointed military dictator with complete authority to command the resources and armies of
the South while each of the seceded states met in individual conventions "to consider the state of public affairs
and propose to the Northern people some proper terms of
peace." As an alternative, Samford suggested that the
existing Confederate government be preserved while
delegates from the Southern states gathered with representatives of the Northern states during the period of an
armistice to discuss peace. In either event, he said the
South should energize its military organization and hold
a strong defensive position while treating for peace.

The plan, Samford argued, would have a drastic impact
upon Northern politics favorable to the South:

> I submit it to the Statesmen and Patriots of the Confed-
> eracy if this policy would not enable us to *divide our
> enemies* by presenting *material issues* on the eve of their
> Presidential Election in which rational and Christian
> men would be constrained to concur with us, and in the
> interest of humanity and justice and true liberty—over-
> throw the Despotism of blood and [illegible] which pre-
> vails in Washington City? Would not such a movement
> towards peace on our part inevitably drive the abolition-
> ists from power, and enable the peace party to consolidate
> a resistless organization? *I think so!*[59]

Although Samford's proposals for appointment of a dictator must have offended the vice-president's constitutional sensitivities, certain features of the plan were in
general harmony with ideas entertained by Stephens. He
was developing thoughts on the election which he intended to express directly to the president.

During the first months of 1864, the twofold challenge
of the Northern election for Confederate policy emerged.
The external aspect of the challenge required the Davis

government to evaluate the potential of the election and to devise a scheme that would derive the maximum benefit to the Confederacy from the political disarray in the North. The internal facet of the challenge was of equal, if not greater, import. The prospect of the election aroused considerable interest among Confederates in the possibility that Northern presidential politics might bring peace. Davis thus needed to guard against unrealistic expectations in the general public and to guide Southern peace advocates along a path that, at least, would prevent interference with the administration's electoral strategy. Dealing with the complexities of the challenge presented major problems for Davis throughout 1864.

CHAPTER 2

The President's Strategy for Influencing the Election:

"... the peace party was quite encouraging."

Within the context of mounting expectations, Jefferson Davis recognized the external challenge the election presented. After the events, he wrote: "Political developments at the North [in 1864] . . . favored the adoption of some action that might influence popular sentiment in the hostile section. The aspect of the peace party was quite encouraging, and it seemed that the real issue to be decided in the Presidential election of that year was the continuance or cessation of the war."[1] Amid the ongoing problems of the Confederacy, Davis, in consultation with various advisers, devised a scheme during the winter and early spring of 1864 for influencing the course of the Northern political contest.

Davis had long known of dissension and disaffection in the North, and the prospect of fishing in troubled Northern political waters was not new to him. He had made an overt effort to intensify debate on the peace issue in the Federal congressional elections of 1862, appealing directly to dissident elements in the North through a proclamation which he prepared for release that fall by Braxton Bragg during his invasion of Kentucky and by Robert E. Lee during his drive into Maryland. Davis told his Northern audience that the Confederacy was fighting "solely for self-defense." He placed the onus for the war on Abraham Lincoln, who had rebuffed the Southern commissioners sent to Washington to effect "a peaceful adjustment of all differences" in the months before the firing on Fort Sumter. Promising attractive terms, Davis encouraged the Northern electorate "to prevail on the Government of the United States to conclude a general peace" or to act through individual state governments to effect separate treaties of peace.[2]

The results of the effort were difficult to measure precisely, but Davis was not discouraged about the prospects of benefit to the Confederate cause from Northern political developments. The election had gone against the Republicans, and the Copperheads of the Northwest had been particularly vociferous. They agitated Northwestern resentment of the Northeast and condemned Lincoln's handling of the war, his emancipation plans, suspension of the writ of habeas corpus, arbitrary arrests, and suppression of the press. With such developments in mind, Davis said, during a speech in late 1862, that he was looking to the Northwest "for the first gleam of peace."[3]

In devising an approach to Northern politics in 1864, Davis did not rely entirely upon his own experience and observations. He received both voluntary and solicited suggestions from various sources in the Confederacy. In the first months of 1864, the Confederate government received fresh reports of seething discontent in the Northwest. One such report came from Captain Thomas H. Hines, who had served with John Hunt Morgan on his cavalry raid into Ohio during July 1863. Hines came to Richmond to discuss a scheme for releasing Confederate soldiers held in Northern prisons for the purpose of fomenting a rebellion among the discontented in the states of the Northwest.[4] Colonel R. A. Alston, also of Morgan's command, reported to the War Department that he had learned of "a perfect organization all over the North, for the purpose of revolution and the expulsion or death of the abolitionists and free negroes."[5]

General Leonidas Polk, commanding a Confederate force in northern Mississippi, sent a report of Northern disaffection to Richmond by the hand of Minor Major, a citizen of Missouri whose credentials, said Polk, had been "properly authenticated." The general explained that Major "has been employed in the work of destroying the property of the enemy on the rivers, and is a member of an organization of a formidable character extending through the North." Urging Davis to listen to the messenger, Polk asserted that the group with which Major was associated "could be of great value to our cause."[6]

J. W. Tucker, who had direct contact with Northern dissidents and was apparently serving as a Confederate agent operating behind Union lines in the South to destroy supplies and disrupt transportation, provided the president with a glowing description of rampant discontent in the North. Tucker told of a secret political organization existing throughout the North with a membership of 490,000 men which, he insisted, was "the most perfect and most secret the world has known." The organization was well disciplined and espoused objectives favorable to the Confederacy. The group championed state rights; opposed the Republican party; proposed the formation of a Northwestern Confederacy with friendly relations toward the South; favored recognition of Confederate independence and the right of Kentucky, Missouri, and Maryland to join with their sister slave states; and avowed a willingness to take up arms against the government at Washington, if necessary, to achieve these objectives. Tucker suggested that Davis place $100,000 in the hands of General Polk to finance continued activity by and cooperation from this group.[7]

Such reports undoubtedly had reference to organizations in the North known variously as Knights of the Golden Circle, Sons of Liberty, and Knights of America. The descriptions of extensive membership and effective organization were gross exaggerations, and Davis was apparently not overly impressed with the reports. He was not as enthusiastic about the possibility of utilizing the Northern peace movement as were some of his advisers, but he was inclined to send secret agents to Canada with instructions to stir the Northern political caldron.[8]

Davis discussed the matter with various leading politicians of the Confederacy. He most likely consulted the entire cabinet, and he definitely talked with Judah P. Benjamin, who worked closely with the president in the steps that were eventually taken. Davis confided in Robert M. T. Hunter, who had served in the cabinet, was serving in the Confederate Senate, and was still an advocate of the administration.[9] The president did not limit his conversations on the subject to the circle of dependable supporters. He talked freely with Herschel V. Johnson, senator from Georgia, who did not always vote with the administration.[10] Because he had been Stephen A. Douglas's running mate in the election of 1860, Johnson was well acquainted with the leadership of the Democratic party and probably able to provide Davis with worthwhile insights. The president also discussed the issue in a secret session of Congress where funds for a mission to Canada were authorized.[11]

While considering the appointment of agents to assume overall supervision of the operation, Davis appointed Hines to undertake a secret mission. The specific object was to secure the escape of Confederate prisoners of war in the North and to arrange for their return to the Confederacy. The instructions to Hines also authorized him to work directly with Confederate sympathizers and peace advocates: "In passing through the United States you will confer with the leading persons friendly or attached to the cause of the Confederacy, or who may be advocates of peace, and do all in your power to induce our friends to organize and prepare themselves to render

such aid as circumstances may allow; and to encourage
and animate those favorable to a peaceful adjustment to
the employment of all agencies calculated to effect such
consummation on terms consistent always with the independence of the Confederate States."[12]

In the search for agents to direct the secret mission,
Davis considered various individuals before finding men
he deemed competent who would accept the assignment.
Herschel Johnson said that Davis considered sending
Alexander Stephens, but this seems unlikely because of
the rancor and distrust between the two men.[13] Given
Johnson's own qualifications and the fact that Davis
carefully discussed the matter with him, Johnson may
have been offered the assignment. Among the persons
approached was James L. Orr of South Carolina.[14] He
was well known among Democrats because of his ten
years as a Democratic congressman (including one term
as Speaker of the House) and because of his prominent
support of Stephen Douglas at the national Democratic
convention of 1856. When approached about the mission,
Orr was serving in the Confederate Senate, and he decided to remain in Richmond.

The appointment was also offered to Alexander H. H.
Stuart. His credentials were not as strong as those of
some of the other men who were considered. A Whig,
rather than a Democrat, Stuart had spent much of his
public career in Virginia politics. At the national level,
he served one term (1841–43) in the House of Representatives and had been secretary of interior under Millard
Fillmore. Although a reluctant secessionist, Stuart was
an outspoken defender of slavery. Secretary Benjamin
invited him to Richmond in March 1864 and sketched a
proposal.

Stuart later recounted the interview: "The plan was
that I should sail to Nassau and thence to Canada.
Arrived there, I should have a sort of diplomatic family

or court, the mission of which, by means of a secret service, would be to foster and give direct aid to a peace sentiment which it was understood was then active along the Border States, and particularly to give aid to a peace organization known as the 'Knights of the Golden Circle,' which flourished in the Northwestern States." The Virginian politely listened to Benjamin, but "soon found that he was laboring under a remarkable delusion as to the peace sentiment at the north, as well as about the probable efficiency of such a Commission as he proposed." Excusing himself because of family responsibilities, Stuart declined the appointment.[15]

The president's search ended in April 1864, when he obtained the services of Jacob Thompson of Mississippi and Clement C. Clay of Alabama. Davis was personally acquainted with both men, and the background of each seemed suited for the task. Davis knew Thompson from the old days of Democratic politics in Mississippi where they were leaders and sometimes rivals. Thompson had served six terms as a congressman and was secretary of interior under James Buchanan. Widely known among Democrats, he had played a prominent role in the national conventions of 1852 and 1856. A secessionist, Thompson served in the Confederate army and was involved in Mississippi politics when summoned to Richmond.

Clay became well acquainted among Democrats during his eight years (1853–61) in Washington as a Democratic senator. Davis served with Clay in the Senate and came to respect him. When organizing the cabinet in 1861, Davis offered Clay the post of secretary of war, but the Alabamian preferred service in the Confederate Senate, where he warmly supported the programs of the administration. Close identification with Davis was probably one of the reasons that Clay lost a bid for reelection in 1863. He was casting about for a position in either private or

public life when the offer of a diplomatic assignment
came.

The agents received only verbal instructions. L. Quinton Washington, an assistant secretary of state who was
present when the commissioners received their instructions, reported that the authorization was "suggestive
and informal."[16] In Davis's memoirs, he recorded that he
dispatched the agents "with a view to negotiation with
such persons in the North as might be relied upon to aid
the attainment of peace. The commission was designed to
facilitate such preliminary conditions as might lead to
formal negotiations between the two Governments, and
they were expected to make judicious use of any political
opportunity that might be presented."[17] In a confidential
dispatch to John Slidell in Paris, Judah Benjamin commented that the agents were sent "to Canada on secret
service in the hope of aiding the disruption between the
Eastern and Western States in the approaching election
at the North. It is supposed that much good can be done
by the purchase of some of the principal presses in the
Northwest."[18] The mission outlined for Thompson and
Clay was not unlike that described to Alexander Stuart a
few weeks earlier. The agents interpreted their instructions to authorize support and encouragement to peace
groups and disaffected elements, direct meddling in
Northern politics, an attack on the Northern monetary
system, efforts to release Confederate prisoners of war,
and schemes otherwise to wreck havoc and destruction
behind enemy lines.

After final preparations, Thompson and Clay traveled
to Wilmington, North Carolina, where they slipped
through the Federal blockade. Following a voyage via St.
George in Bermuda, the agents arrived in Canada. They
joined forces with James P. Holcombe, a former professor
of law at the University of Virginia, who was already in
Canada on other business for the Confederacy.

While the president was making preparations for the mission to Canada, he was also receiving suggestions for military action specifically designed to influence the election. General John Morgan proposed a raid into Kentucky as a show of strength to counter Northern reports of waning Confederate energy and capacity.[19] Perhaps the general who was most enthusiastic about the consequences of military operations for the Northern election was James Longstreet, who was with a Confederate force in eastern Tennessee. Discussing the importance of a vigorous effort, the general said: "An effective campaign, early in the season, will have greater effect upon our people and upon our cause than anything that may happen at a latter day. If we can break up the enemy's arrangements early, and throw him back, he will not be able to recover his position nor his morale until the Presidential election is over, and we shall then have a new President to treat with. If Lincoln has any success early he will be able to get more men and may be able to secure his own re-election."[20]

To discredit the war policy of Lincoln and thereby strengthen his political enemies at home, Longstreet evolved a scheme for invading Kentucky and holding a large portion of the state. Proposing to mount his infantry on horses or to secure ample reinforcements from General P. G. T. Beauregard in South Carolina, Longstreet submitted his plan to General Lee, who passed it to Davis as a possible alternative. Although sympathetic to an invasion of middle Tennessee and Kentucky, if possible, the president recognized the stratagem as impractical and rejected it.

Davis expected that events on the battlefield would have an impact on Northern sentiment, but he was steadfastly unwilling to conduct military operations for purely political reasons. Indeed, he did not feel that the prospect of the Federal election warranted any alteration in his basic military policy of the offensive-defensive. The best way to bring the United States to the peace table on acceptable terms, thought the president, was to demonstrate Confederate military strength. Davis wrote to a Southern governor in January 1864: "To obtain the sole terms to which you or I would listen, this struggle must continue until the enemy is beaten out of his vain confidence in our subjugation. Then and not till then, will it be possible to treat for peace."[21] There would be no massive invasions of Northern territory as there had been during the elections of 1862 because the South lacked such capacity in 1864, but the president still believed that offensive action would promote a disposition for peace in the North.

An illustration of the president's confidence in the coincidence of objectives for the Northern election and existing Confederate military policy came early in the spring of 1864, when he unsuccessfully urged General Joseph E. Johnston to mount an invasion of Tennessee. The president had valid military reasons for wanting the invasion, but he was also concerned about the consequences for public sentiment in both sections. Brigadier General William N. Pendleton, whom Davis sent to Dalton, Georgia, to confer with Johnston, reiterated the president's military reasons for the offensive and explained that Davis wanted the operation "to inspirit it [Army of Tennessee], and the country, and to depress the enemy, involving greatest consequences."[22]

Consistent with the policy of taking the war to the enemy when possible, Davis favored offensive action by the Confederate navy.[23] In laying plans for naval operations in 1864, Stephen R. Mallory, secretary of the navy, subscribed to this general philosophy. Mallory stressed to Commander James D. Bulloch: "The simultaneous appearance of efficient cruisers on the New England coast and fishing banks, in the West Indies and South Atlantic, in the Pacific among the whalemen, and in the East Indies, would have a decided tendency to turn the trading mind of New England to thoughts of peace. I am exceedingly anxious to do this."[24]

Proposals for action that would influence Northern politics also came from Alexander H. Stephens. In a letter to Davis, the vice-president expressed his belief that defeat of the Republican party in the approaching election was of utmost importance. He proposed to strengthen the peace faction of the Democratic party by a direct assurance from the Confederate president that the Confederacy would agree to settlement of the war on the basis of state sovereignty. This would be sufficient assurance, insisted Stephens, because the "ablest champions of the Peace Party at the North now stand upon the grounds of the Ky. & Va. Resolutions of 1798–99 and deny the power of the Federal government to coerce a State."

The possibility that Northern concessions might bring an end to the war through restoration of the Southern states to the Union had long haunted ardent Southern nationalists, and Stephens believed Davis was in that camp. In the letter, Stephens sought to allay fears that "the election of a so called conservative Northern President" would bring reconstruction on the basis of Northern concessions. Stephens argued: "Should the peace party then *once* be put in power a suspension of arms would immediately issue—negotiation some way would commence and the war would certainly after a while end upon the principles of a full perfect & final separation. Of this I feel confident. The Union or Reconstruction would be found to be out of the question and would ultimately be abandoned by the most ardent advocates of it on that side of the line."[25] The vice-president's arguments were not persuasive, and he was correct in his suspicion that

Davis was apprehensive about the possibility that the election of a Northern peace candidate might bring disintegration of the Confederacy.

With the letter to Davis, Stephens included a note sent to him by David F. Cable, who was a Federal prisoner held at Andersonville. Declaring that he was from Ohio and an intimate of Clement L. Vallandigham and other peace leaders, Cable requested a meeting with Stephens to discuss the best means for the South to aid in the election of a peace candidate.[26] Stephens asked Davis to have Cable investigated and, if his claims proved genuine, to send him north with a message of support for the peace party.

The vice-president's suggestions and underlying assumptions ran contrary to Davis's thinking. The guiding principle of the president's plan was his unconditional commitment to complete and unencumbered nationhood for the South. Confederate independence, not state sovereignty, was the issue for Davis. Although recognizing that some Northern peace advocates were motivated by a philosophical conviction that the war violated constitutional principles, Davis believed that the most powerful sentiment motivating Northerners toward peace was despair of ever forcing the South back into the Union. He expected to continue his policy of fostering this despair by carrying the war to the enemy when possible and by hurling defiance at the enemy section.

Davis should have recognized that his response to Stephens's letter was a serious matter. Relations between the two men were notoriously poor, and Davis needed at least benign passivity from Stephens with regard to the administration's policy for the election. Although distrusting Stephens and unable to take him into his complete confidence, Davis at least could have offered assurance that he was aware of the import of the election. Instead, his reply was terse, and he rejected Stephens's proposals in the worst possible way. He offered no explanation of his own thinking on the election and simply ignored Stephens's suggestions. This action laid groundwork for a future argument with Stephens and also offended his sensitive ego, results Davis could ill afford.

The president did, however, promise that a staff officer would examine Cable's claims. If the prisoner's pretensions proved valid, he would be sent to Stephens and finally exchanged to the North.[27] As the year unfolded, the seemingly innocuous case of David F. Cable would become incredibly complicated, and Stephens's yeasty suspicion that Davis did not favor the election "of a so called conservative Northern President" would continue to grow until these two issues burst into a bitter controversy.

By April, the president's plan for influencing the course of the election was fairly under way. Guided by his own insights, suggestions from other Southerners, and consultation with the Congress, he dispatched agents to Canada. Their mission was to work directly with Northerners sympathetic to the Confederacy or the cause of peace, to exploit every opportunity for agitating enemy politics, and otherwise to foster the growth of war weariness and disaffection. The president also determined to continue the military strategy of the offensive-defensive. Davis expected that carrying the battle to the enemy whenever possible would demonstrate Southern determination to resist and thereby stimulate Northern distaste for the war and increase willingness to conclude peace on terms of Confederate independence.

Much depended upon military operations in Virginia and Georgia and upon the effectiveness of the mission to Canada. Of particular importance was the balance of emphasis between the military and the diplomatic components of the plan. Military operations would demand an inordinate amount of presidential time and energy, but Davis could not neglect the diplomatic opportunity to weaken the enemy at home. Another crucial nexus of Davis's strategy was the degree of coordination and cooperation between the commissioners and the president. The declarations and actions at Richmond should complement the covert remarks and activities in Canada.

CHAPTER 3

Dealing with Aroused Public Expectations:
"Every avenue of negotiation is closed . . ."

Although alert to the external challenge of Northern politics, Davis was slow to respond to the challenge presented on the home front. Events within and without the Confederacy during the spring of 1864 reinforced Southern expectations for the election. The Confederate Congress released statements implying confidence that the course of Federal politics was favorable to the Confederacy. Some of the president's bitterest enemies in Georgia stirred controversy by launching their own scheme for influencing the election. Public interest was further whetted when the legislature of North Carolina showed interest in the election. In the North, the Republican party opened the campaign in a seriously divided condition, and Southerners warmly applauded. As Confederate chief executive, Davis had a responsibility to assert leadership in the formation of public opinion and in the development of foreign policy, yet his responses to public expectations for the election and to direct challenges to his control of foreign affairs were erratic.

Statements and actions of the Confederate government promoted public interest and speculation regarding the Northern election. At first, Davis himself encouraged belief that Northern politics would somehow benefit the Southern cause. In a widely circulated address to the soldiers of the Confederacy, he cited conditions in the North as reason to be hopeful. He told the battle-weary veterans that "dissensions occasioned by the strife for power, by the pursuit of the spoils of office, [and] by the thirst for plunder of the public treasury" would sap the strength and resolve of the enemy.[1]

An even greater stimulus to public interest and discussion came from the Confederate Congress. The Fourth Session of the First Congress, which met from December 7, 1863, to February 18, 1864, took a position on Northern political developments. This session was involved in the evolution of Davis's strategy through the appropriation of money for secret service in Canada and the participation of some members in conferences with the president regarding his plan and selection of personnel, but the Congress also took more direct action.

Near the end of the session, Representative Augustus R. Wright of Georgia introduced a resolution that had a bearing on Northern politics. Wright's purpose, according to the resolution, was to justify the position of the Confederacy with respect to the war "in the sight of Conservative men of the North of all parties" and to place the burden for continuation of the conflict on Lincoln. Responding directly to Lincoln's contention in a recent statement that the South had made no propositions of peace to the United States government, the proposed declaration briefly explained that the Northern president had avoided Southern peace overtures. The Georgian proposed that representatives of the two governments meet in a peace conference, and he suggested guidelines for that meeting. If the negotiators agreed upon recognition of Confederate independence, they should immediately consider "formation of a new government, founded upon the equality and sovereignty of the States." In the event that the conferees could not reach agreement on the creation of a common government, they should consider "treaties, offensive, defensive, and commercial." Wright's immediate goal, apparently, was to strengthen the opponents of Lincoln by inspiring them with the belief that the South would accept reunion on the basis of Northern concessions, which was a position that the peace Democrats had long held.[2]

The proposal by the representative from Georgia brought varied responses in the Confederacy. Describing the resolution as a maneuver for the benefit of the Northern Democrats, John B. Jones, from his vantage point in the War Department, expressed hope that the proposal would "give the Abolitionists trouble in the rear while we assail them from the front." Recognizing that the resolution was a two-edged sword, Jones also hoped that nothing further would be done to promote it among Confederates.[3] The North Carolina *Standard* enthusiastically endorsed Wright's resolution, and the Selma (Alabama) *Daily Reporter* also supported the proposal, commenting, "It should be our business and pride to hold aloft the olive branch to our implacable foe, and thus put ourselves in sympathy with the antiwar party at the North, thereby facilitating the overthrow of the Black Republican party."[4] Some observers, such as the Augusta *Constitutionalist,* attacked Wright's resolution without qualification. Insisting that "absolute independence" was the only acceptable condition of peace, the newspaper expressed "astonishment and regret" that a congressman from Georgia had introduced the proposals, and it denounced them as "submission resolutions."[5]

The Congress did not adopt Wright's resolution, but chose instead to release a statement to the people of the Confederacy that promised continued war for independence but also directed some comments to Lincoln's opponents in the North. The document rehearsed the Southern interpretation of events from the secession crisis of 1860 to the winter of 1864 and urged the Southern people to renewed efforts and continued sacrifices. Describing Lincoln as totally committed to subjugation of the South and unwilling to listen to any other terms, the statement opposed efforts to negotiate unless "some evidence is given of a change of policy on the part of the [United States] Government, and some assurance received that efforts at negotiation will not be spurned." Until that change, the Congress was of the opinion "that any direct overtures for peace would compromise our self-respect, be fruitless of good, and interpreted by the enemy as an indication of weakness." Recognizing a "powerful political party" in the North opposed to Lincoln's measures, the legislators urged its members to resist his tyranny. The Congress described this group:

> Many sagacious persons at the North discover in the usurpations of their Government the certain overthrow of their liberties. A large number revolt from the unjust war waged upon the South and would gladly bring it to an end. Others look with alarm upon the complete subversion of constitutional freedom by Abraham Lincoln, and feel in their own persons the bitterness of the slavery which three years of war have failed to inflict on the South. Brave and earnest men at the North have spoken out against the usurpations and cruelties daily practiced. The success of these men over the radical and despotic faction which now rules the North may open the way to peaceful negotiation and a cessation of this bloody and unnecessary war.[6]

With these words, the Congress pandered to the concerns often expressed by the peace Democrats and held out the possibility of negotiations which they so ardently desired.

On the day before the session ended, concluding the labors of the first permanent Congress, the members ordered publication of forty thousand copies of the address.[7] The message brought praise from the Augusta

Chronicle & Sentinel, which fervently wanted a Democratic political victory and negotiated peace, although some who favored vigorous prosecution of the war until achieving Confederate independence were less satisfied.[8] Colonel Lawrence M. Keitt, who had been instrumental in taking South Carolina out of the Union, wrote: "I do not like the Address of Congress. . . . It looks to reconstruction—that is unless it is meant to deceive the North, and aid the democrats in the coming elections." Although Keitt wanted "to see the democrats succeed," he opposed any inducements that might alter or weaken the Confederate resolve for independence.[9] When the Congress disbanded in February 1864, it had taken a position on the election, but a new Congress would assemble within three months, and it, too, would have ideas and issue statements regarding the Northern election.

The resolution introduced by Augustus Wright, although unacceptable to the Congress, was indicative of the thinking among three of Georgia's most influential politicians: Alexander Stephens; Linton Stephens, brother of the vice-president; and Joseph E. Brown, governor of Georgia. Davis had clashed with these men over such questions as conscription, suspension of habeas corpus, and military policy. The Georgians shared a genuine animosity for the president and suspected him of all manner of skullduggery. Seeking to make strategy for the election a central feature of Confederate policy for 1864, they decided to launch an initiative of their own. However unwittingly, Davis had contributed to the emergence of a rival electoral scheme by his abrupt dismissal of Stephens's letter regarding the election.

Stephens and his associates were particularly enamored of the Copperhead movement, and, indeed, their thinking was strikingly similar to that of Northern peace leaders. Like their Northern counterparts, they denounced their president as a tyrant and a usurper; opposed the centralization of power in the national government through such measures as conscription, suspension of habeas corpus, and impressment; and believed that the war must be stopped to preserve constitutional liberty. In a very real sense, Stephens and politicians like him were Confederate Copperheads. In their zeal for state sovereignty, however, they exceeded the devotion of most of the peace Democrats of the North, who were generally unwilling to accept the logical extreme of the state rights dogma, dissolution of the Union.[10] But in 1864, Brown and the Stephens brothers believed that the theory of state sovereignty was the key to ending the war. These Southern conservatives were in the tradition of Thomas Jefferson as transmitted through John Taylor of Caroline and the later John C. Calhoun; the Northern Copperheads were inheritors of the Jeffersonian legacy as interpreted by Andrew Jackson.

Because Alexander Stephens was the vice-president of the Confederacy, his participation in any program enhanced its prestige, and he was a prime mover in the strategy initiated in Georgia.[11] A crucial factor in Stephens's conduct was his conception of Southern war aims. The vice-president commented on this matter in mid-1863 to Jefferson Davis: "Of course, I entertain but one idea of the basis of a final settlement or adjustment; that is, the recognition of the sovereignty of the States and the right of each in its sovereign capacity to determine its own destiny. . . . The full recognition of this principle covers all that is really involved in the present issue." [12] Stephens made a similar remark in early 1864: "I fight Lincoln because he was against the Sovereignty of the States and almost every personal right secured in the Constitution."[13] Stephens's thoroughgoing commitment to state sovereignty was demonstrated in his attitude toward developments among peace advocates in North Carolina: "If he [William W. Holden] believes it is for the best interests of North Carolina to go out of the Confederacy it is his constitutional right to say so. It is no treason. And if the people of N. C. in sovereign convention should be of the same opinion it is their right so to declare."[14]

Stephens also saw military developments as a key to Northern politics. Recognizing that Federal military success encouraged Northern war fervor, he favored strong defensive efforts by the Confederacy, but he opposed a Confederate invasion of the North in the belief that such action would force the peace element there to support the war for self-defense. The foundation of this conviction was Stephens's experience with his abortive peace mission of mid-1863 which he believed was doomed, in large measure, by the revival of Northern war sentiment that accompanied the fall of Vicksburg and the invasions of the North by Lee and Morgan.[15] The Georgian also believed that the North was approaching a crisis and would soon need a significant victory to sustain its war fervor. "If they gain no victory before mid-summer," he wrote, "there will be with them a tremendous collapse—a fearful and disastrous crash—from the stunning effects of which they can not rally soon. Then the election if [illegible] conducted with them will effect results which without doubt will end after a while in peace without any further effusion of blood on great fields of battle."[16]

Alexander Stephens exchanged letters virtually every day with his brother Linton, and their thinking became thoroughly intertwined. Linton served as leader of the Brown faction in the General Assembly of Georgia, and his ideas on peace were in general agreement with those of his brother and the governor. Relating an informal conversation with a group of gentlemen in Atlanta, Linton wrote: "I told them that permanent peace involved a great constitutional problem of which the only solution was the recognition, North and South, of *State Sovereignty* the perfect right of each State on this continent to choose and to change her political associations according to her own will, regulated and limited by nothing but the necessity of finding other States willing to associate with her."[17]

While the Stephens brothers and Brown were privately conferring, the Augusta *Chronicle & Sentinel,* which they controlled, was preparing for presentation of the plan.[18] The newspaper, which claimed the largest circulation of any journal in the state, took the position as early as January 1864 that the war "must be settled by compromise" because neither side possessed the military capability to impose a settlement.[19] Insisting that the political defeat of the Republicans would bring an end to hostilities, the *Chronicle & Sentinel* proposed that the Confederacy recognize and support the Northern peace movement.[20] Despite calling for strong defensive measures and demanding an armistice for the period of negotiations, the editor urged that the South continually indicate a willingness to confer with the North.[21] By March, the newspaper offered a fairly coherent plan for securing peace through manipulating Northern political developments:

> It is unquestionably our policy to do everything in our power to increase the number of unconditional peace men at the North. We believe that this can be done by carrying the sword in one hand and the olive branch in the other. Let us strengthen our armies to the utmost limit of our capacity. . . . At the same time let us steadily remonstrate on the injustice of the war, and hold up our earnest desire to be relieved of the necessity of periling our own lives and of shedding the blood of the invader. To

strengthen the Northern peace party, is at the same time
to undermine the influence of the bloody dynasty who
wields power in the Federal states.

With the fall of the Republican party, the *Chronicle &
Sentinel* promised, an armistice would ensue and peace
would follow "at no distant day."[22]

Alexander Stephens and his colleagues were ready to
launch their plan by early spring, and Governor Brown
summoned a special session of the state legislature for
March 10, 1864. The governor laid a plan for obtaining
peace before the legislature. Hoping to be heard in the
North, Brown rehearsed the state rights justification for
secession and exonerated the Democrats from any culpa-
bility in initiating hostilities against the South. He accused Lincoln of seeking war to free the Negro and to
subjugate the South while subverting constitutional liberty throughout the land. Brown warned, "There must be
a change of administration, and more moderate councils
prevail in the Northern States before we can ever have
peace." The governor then explained how peace should be
sought. Insisting that continued war would not bring a
settlement, he said, "The pen of the statesman, more
potent than the sword of the warrior, must do what the
latter has failed to do. . . . It is our duty to keep it always
before the Northern people, . . . that we are ready to
negotiate for peace whenever the people and Government
of the Northern States are prepared to recognize the
great fundamental principles of the Declaration of Independence, maintained by our common ancestry—the
right of all [to] *self-government and the sovereignty of the
States.*"

Brown proposed that the South publicly offer to negotiate, after each military success, on the basis of state
sovereignty. Under the terms of the settlement he envi-

sioned, each of the border states and Southern states would be free to determine its future allegiance through the ballot box. He recognized that such a plan would allow states to leave the Confederacy, but he denied that any state would ever be so inclined. On the other hand, Brown explained that his approach would provide for the addition of Maryland and Kentucky to the Confederacy. He had no doubt that such terms would be wholly unacceptable to the Northern president, but by frequently proposing peace talks the South could hold Lincoln in the embarrassing position of rejecting negotiation and thereby agitate Northern politics.[23]

Pursuant to the plan for peace described by Governor Brown, the legislature adopted a peace resolution which Linton Stephens had prepared and sponsored after full consultation with his brother, the vice-president.[24] Although not as consistently committed to dogma as was Brown's message, the measure accepted by the legislature called for state action and peace on the basis of state sovereignty. The document presented the Southern contentions that the Declaration of Independence was a statement of the doctrine of state rights, that the Northern states had violated the Constitution, which justified secession, and that Lincoln was waging an unconstitutional and an unholy war. "The people acting through their State organizations and popular assemblies, and our Government through its appropriate departments," declared the legislators, should "use their earnest efforts to put an end to this unnatural, unchristian and savage work of carnage and havoc." The legislature recommended: "Our Government, immediately after signal success of our arms and on other occasions when none can impute its action to alarm instead of a sincere desire for peace, shall make to the Government of our enemy an official offer of peace on the basis of the great principle declared by our common fathers in 1776." The resolution was silent on the question of a popular referendum in the states of the Confederacy but expressed a willingness "that any Border State whose preference for our association may be doubted (doubts having been expressed as to the wishes of the Border States) shall settle the question for herself by a convention to be elected for that purpose after the withdrawal of all military forces of both sides from her limits."

The legislators insisted that the course they proposed would have a beneficial impact for the Confederate cause in both of the rival sections. Such a policy "would constantly weaken and sooner or later break down the war power of the enemy by showing to his people the justice of our cause, our willingness to make peace on the principles of 1776 and the shoulders on which rests the responsibility for the continuance of the unnatural strife."[25] Frequent offers of negotiation would bolster Southern morale by assuring Confederates "that peace will not be unnecessarily delayed nor their sufferings unnecessarily prolonged." Perhaps in an effort to make the resolution more palatable to diehard Confederates, the legislators concluded with a pledge to prosecute a defensive war "until peace is obtained upon just and honorable terms and until the independence and nationality of the Confederate States is established upon a permanent basis." Privately writing of the resolution, Alexander Stephens said, "If any one is responsible for it, no one is more so than myself."[26]

Governor Brown made provision for publication and distribution of his address and the resolutions to every accessible regiment of Georgia troops and officers of every accessible county in the Confederacy.[27] Some Southern newspapers also published all or part of these documents.[28] Many Confederates saw in the Georgia

peace plan the haunting implication that Southern
states, exercising their sovereignty, were free to secure
peace separate from the rest of the Confederacy. When
Brown's address reached Virginia, the *Examiner* attacked "the absurd project for peace" and hopefully contended that the governor was not seriously suggesting
that any Southern state would leave the Confederacy.[29]
When the editor read the resolution of the legislature, he
became more emphatic: "A more serious matter is the
heresy of a separate peace, and if this project is meant to
apply to any of the undoubted members of the Confederacy, it is a monstrous treason."[30] With reference to the
contention that frequent offers of negotiation would
weaken Northern resolve, the editor insisted, "The Yankees would regard any propositions for peace by the
Confederacy as a simple cry of weakness, and redouble
their exertions." He suggested that the agitation in Georgia might encourage the Federal army to make a particularly determined effort to invade the state in the belief
that Georgians were willing to make a separate peace.[31]
The Savannah *Republican* complained that the conduct
of the governor and the legislature gave comfort to the
enemy and reported that newspapers in New York were
publishing the peace resolution and related documents as
evidence that the South was nearing exhaustion.[32] The
brigade commanded by General George T. Anderson near
Zollicoffer, Tennessee, passed a resolution "almost
unanimously," condemning the message of the governor
and the resolutions passed by the legislators.[33] Admit-
tedly bowing to public pressure, the *Chronicle & Sentinel*
published a letter that attacked the peace resolutions.[34]

The *Chronicle & Sentinel*, as might be expected, also
published the governor's message and the legislative
resolutions in full and praised them in glowing terms.[35]
Governor Brown publicly charged that opposition in the

army to the peace plan and related matters came only from officers seeking to curry favor with the Davis government and that the rank and file "will be unable to discover any dishonor in the resolutions of the General Assembly of their State upon the subject of peace."[36] Vowing to accept no terms that did not secure "the independence of all the States," Brown vigorously denied allegations that he intended "to ignore the Confederacy or to open negotiations as a separate State."[37] Endorsement of the peace plan came from such newspapers as the North Carolina *Democrat*, which was a fervent advocate of peace.[38] Joseph C. Bradley, a member of the Alabama legislature who represented a district of strong Unionist sentiment, privately wrote to Linton Stephens and endorsed the peace plan: "I can see no hopes for the election of a Democratic or Conservative Candidate but at the same time it is our duty—as it seems to me to give the conservative element in the North all the aid & encouragement we possibly can."[39] Herschel Johnson, who had opposed secession, said that he had long favored a plan similar to that proposed in the peace resolution and would gladly have voted for it had he been a member of the General Assembly.[40] Henry C. Cleveland, a newspaperman in Augusta and confidant of Alexander Stephens, wrote the vice-president expressing the conviction that the peace plan did not go "far enough to have the slightest effect upon the North." He believed that the resolution should have explicitly called for an armistice to be followed by a convention in any Southern state wishing to give immediate consideration to its future allegiance.[41]

Alexander Stephens probably suspected that the Confederate government would not accept the plan for exploiting Northern politics embodied in the speech of Governor Brown and the action of the General Assembly of Georgia. Nevertheless, Stephens had used the state

legislature as a forum in which to offer encouragement to
Northern Democrats who were looking for indications of
Southern willingness to negotiate, and Stephens would
seize other opportunities to express similar convictions
as the year progressed.

The initiative taken by Georgia was a direct challenge
to Davis's role as chief architect and spokesman in matters of Confederate foreign policy. He favored a covert
and indirect approach to Northern public opinion
through agents operating from Canada, vigorous prosecution of the war, and proclaiming defiance and invincibility. His object was complete independence for the
Confederacy. The Georgians favored overt and direct
assurances to the Northern Democrats and believed that
strong defensive measures to prevent Federal military
success and frequent appeals for peace talks would
strengthen the Democratic party while weakening the
Republicans. The goal of the Georgia plan was election of
a Northern president who was willing to acknowledge
the doctrine of state sovereignty, which neither prescribed nor proscribed the territorial integrity and independence of the Confederacy. Despite these significant
differences, Davis made no firm public response.

The meeting of a new Congress at Richmond on May 2,
1864, gave Davis a platform from which to counter the
action taken by his opponents in Georgia through a
statement of his position on the Northern election. In his
message to the Congress, Davis did not make the most of
the opportunity. His comments were vague and indirect
and made no specific references to Northern politics. As
he had done before in other contexts, he argued that only
through dispelling Northern hope of subjugating the
South could the Confederacy win independence, and he
urged united effort among Southerners for continued
prosecution of the war. He made no mention of the

Georgia initiative, although he said: "It may be that foreign governments, like our enemies, have mistaken our desire for peace, unreservedly expressed, for evidence of exhaustion. . . . In the meantime it is enough to know that every avenue of negotiation is closed against us."[42] The president had addressed some of the issues, but the intensity of public interest and the seriousness of the challenge from Georgia demanded a much stronger assertion of presidential leadership.

The president was also overlooking a possible instrument for influencing the election. The suggestion that the Confederate government propose negotiations after every Southern military success was overdone, but not entirely without merit. Carefully crafted diplomatic initiatives from Richmond at crucial moments might effectively aggravate tensions in the North, but Davis rejected this option. Believing that his forte was directing military affairs, not foreign intrigue, he emphasized military operations rather than imaginative manipulation of sentiment in the enemy section.

Through the efforts of Governor Zebulon Vance of North Carolina, another statement of the president's position came to public attention. Vance was in the midst of a bitter campaign against William W. Holden for the governorship. Holden, editor of the North Carolina *Standard*, was calling for a state convention. He explained the reasons for his demand: "We are, therefore, for a convention, and for a cooperation with our sister States of the South in obtaining an armistice so that negotiations may be commenced." Although the editor denied that his purpose was to obtain a separate peace for his state, many of his friends as well as foes thought otherwise.[43] For political reasons, Vance sought permission to publish certain of the letters that had passed between himself and Davis during the first month of

1864.[44] On that occasion, Vance had urged Davis to make
an attempt to negotiate as a concession to peace advocates in North Carolina.[45] The president responded with
a lengthy letter that recounted the failure of various
efforts to initiate negotiations. Although not written
with reference to Northern politics, the letter set forth
the president's views on the general subject of peace
talks: "All tender of terms to the enemy will be received
as proof that we are ready for submission, and will
encourage him in the atrocious warfare he is waging."
With regard to the situation in North Carolina, Davis
recommended that Governor Vance take steps to suppress dissenters.[46] In response to Vance's request to publish the letter, Davis gave his consent with the comment
that he had intended it as a public document.[47] Given the
link the Georgia politicians had forged between proposals for negotiations and hopes for the election, Davis
should have been working to get the letter published
himself, but the initiative came from Vance.

Davis's statement was spread across the Confederacy,
reprinted in various newspapers. The Richmond *Sentinel*
declared: "The subject [of peace negotiations] is treated
with great point and clearness in the President's letter,
and we think, is shown to leave no room for two opinions
as to our proper course."[48] The *Examiner*, which was
certainly no admirer of the president, endorsed his remarks and commented, "If there were anything honest in
the whole outcry about 'Negotiations for Peace,' this
letter would silence it for the remainder of the war."[49]

The president's remarks were not pleasing to all Confederates, of course, and his letter sent Alexander
Stephens into a paroxysm of rage. With his pen dipped in
gall, Stephens expressed himself in a protracted letter to
his brother Linton, who was in Atlanta. "This whole
letter of the President," wrote Stephens, "is in bad tone

and temper and shows his utter want of statesmanship."
In Stephens's view, Davis's opposition to offering negotiations and his insistence upon conquering peace on the
battlefield revealed either a misunderstanding of the
Copperhead movement and an ignorance of diplomacy as
a tool for dividing the enemy or a desire to prolong the
war to enhance the opportunity of becoming a dictator
through usurpation. As the vice-president wrote, he became more enraged, and near the end of his disjointed
tirade he concluded that Davis was "quite as much knave
as fool" and seeking "absolute power 'a la mode' Louis
Napoleon." Upon rereading the letter, even Stephens
recognized that it was intemperate, and, afraid to trust it
to the vicissitudes of the mail, he laid it aside for Linton
to read when he returned.[50]

While Confederate politicians were maneuvering, the
Republicans were nominating their favorites for the
presidency, and Southerners scrutinized the political, as
well as military, proceedings. A group of abolitionists,
Republicans, and Democrats who shared a dislike for
Lincoln and his policies met at Cleveland, Ohio, on May
31, 1864, and officially opened the presidential campaign. The convention organized the Radical Democratic
party, constructed a bold platform, and nominated John
C. Frémont for president and John Cochrane of New
York for vice-president.[51] The pertinent planks of the
platform declared:

> That the Federal Union shall be preserved. . . . That the
> rebellion must be suppressed by force of arms, and with-
> out compromise. . . . That the rebellion has destroyed
> slavery, and the Federal Constitution should be amended
> to prohibit its reestablishment, and to secure to all men
> absolute equality before the law. . . . That the national
> policy known as the "Monroe Doctrine" has become a
> recognized principle, and that the establishment of an

anti-republican government on this continent by any
foreign power cannot be tolerated. . . . That the confiscation of the lands of the rebels, and their distribution
among the soldiers and actual settlers, is a measure of
justice.[52]

In a lengthy letter, Frémont, whose antislavery position was well established, accepted the nomination. He
explicitly rejected the provision calling for confiscation of
rebel property but accepted the basic principles underlying the platform with "unqualified and cordial approba-
tion." He unleashed a tirade against Lincoln's alleged
dictatorial policies and offered to withdraw from the race
if the convention soon to convene at Baltimore would
refuse to nominate the incumbent.[53]

The Cleveland gathering came as no surprise in the
Confederacy because Southern newspapers carried advance notices of the gathering and speculation concern-
ing its significance from the Northern press. As the
convention proceedings and related documents became
available to Northern newspapers, Confederate journals
presented the material as a matter of interest to their
readers.[54] Drawing upon past knowledge and current
information, Southerners publicly and privately evalu-
ated the nominees and the platform. Describing Frémont
as an "unprincipled adventurer" and his supporters as a
"mongrel herd of Northern fanatics," the *Chronicle &
Sentinel* argued: "Fremont will rally to his standard the
atheistical German, and radical Abolition elements, with
other malcontents of the old Republican party."[55] The
Examiner published a lengthy editorial analyzing and
attacking the planks in the platform of the radical Democrats.[56] Alexander Stephens recorded his estimation of
Frémont in a private letter: "Any change except Fremont
would be beneficial to us. . . . Fremont is a very bad

corrupt unprincipled man. Lincoln has principles even if they are bad ones but Fremont is as unprincipled as Cicero represented Catiline to be. He is a very bad man."[57]

The vice-presidential nominee of the radical party received special abuse in the Southern press because of his past activity. When Virginia was considering secession, Cochrane had come from New York in an effort to keep Virginia in the Union and to preserve the peace. One editor reminded his readers: "This Cochrane will be remembered in Richmond as the New York politician who from the steps of the Exchange Hotel declared and vowed, with solemn appeals to the Almighty, that if the Federal Government should attempt to coerce the South, he, Cochrane, would be found sword in hand on the side of Old Virginia." With satirical understatement the writer added, "Some circumstances with which we are unacquainted, have changed his mind materially."[58] Reporting that Cochrane had raised a regiment and served as a colonel in the Union army, the Richmond *Dispatch* declared that he hated the South "with all the bitterness of an apostate."[59]

Shortly after the Cleveland convention, the Union party, a coalition of the great majority of Republicans and some war Democrats, gathered at Baltimore to draft a platform and to select candidates.[60] The delegates constructed a platform that supported the "Government in quelling by force of arms the Rebellion now raging"; admonished the "Government . . . not to compromise with Rebels, or to offer them any terms of peace, except such as may be based upon an unconditional surrender of their hostility and a return to their just allegiance to the Constitution and laws of the United States"; called for "such an amendment to the Constitution . . . as shall terminate and forever prohibit the existence of Slavery

within the limits of the jurisdiction of the United States";
and approved (with reference to Napoleon III's Mexican
adventure) "the position taken by the Government that
the people of the United States can never regard with
indifference the attempt of any European power to overthrow by force or to supplant by fraud the institutions of
any republican government on the Western Continent."[61]
The convention nominated Abraham Lincoln for president and Andrew Johnson, a war Democrat from Tennessee, for vice-president. In a brief letter, Lincoln
"gratefully accepted the nomination" and "heartily approved" the platform. He did, however, qualify his endorsement of the plank on the Monroe Doctrine with the
comment that future developments might dictate a modi-
fication of the existing policy of opposition to French
designs in Mexico.[62]

Confederates watched for reports of the Baltimore convention, and some editors charged that Grant was tele-
graphing false accounts of military success to the North
in an effort to enhance Lincoln's prospects for renomina-
tion.[63] When the proceedings of the convention and the
campaign documents appeared in Northern newspapers,
Southern editors republished the material.[64] The nomination of Lincoln could not have been unexpected in the
South, and some Confederate newspapers had carried
predictions that Johnson would be the vice-presidential
nominee.[65] For nearly four years Southerners had been
heaping opprobrium upon Lincoln, and their evaluation
of his candidacy was consistent with past practice. The
Richmond *Dispatch* denounced the terse letter of acceptance as an example of Lincoln's irreverent attitude
toward government and the people and the complete
arbitrariness of his power and authority.[66] The *Examiner*
charged that the support for Lincoln came from office-
holders and army contractors who, for selfish reasons,

wanted "four years more in all respects like unto the last four years."[67] That Lincoln's reelection would mean continued war was a theme Southerners had long been discussing. As early as January 1864, the *Chronicle & Sentinel* declared: "It cannot be too earnestly impressed upon every man in the Confederacy, that the re-election of Lincoln means war, obstinate, sanguinary, relentless war."[68] Southern editors were quick, however, to observe, "Whether they [Lincoln and Johnson] shall ever be elected or not depends upon the Confederate army altogether."[69]

Although neither of the Republican candidates for the presidency was acceptable to the South, some Confederates saw distinct benefits in the nominations. A clerk in the War Department wrote: "We have heard to-day that Lincoln was nominated for re-election at Baltimore. . . . Fremont is now pledged to run also, thus dividing the Republican party, and giving an opportunity for the Democrats to elect a President. If we can only *subsist* till then, we may have peace, and must have independence at all events."[70] Describing the bolt of the radicals as "auspicious for the South," an editor concluded that the Republican victory of 1860 was predicated on an alliance with the extremists and that the current schism meant defeat for the Republican party in 1864.[71]

Confederates also seized upon the fact that the platforms of both parties pledged their candidates to enforcement of the Monroe Doctrine. The Richmond *Sentinel* suggested that Lincoln's equivocation on the issue might alienate some of his followers and generate further divisiveness within the Republican party.[72] Of greater importance was the prospect that the Republican pronouncements might hasten the fulfillment of the long-standing Confederate hope that Napoleon would aid the South in order to further his ambitions in Mexico. Secretary Benjamin recognized this potential and took steps to exploit the opportunity.[73] At the Navy Department, Secretary Mallory expressed hope that Northern political developments would induce Napoleon to cooperate in launching Confederate sea raiders from French ports.[74]

While the tempo of Northern politics increased, Southern disagreement over the best response to the situation continued through developments at both the national and state levels. In North Carolina, Governor Vance had no intention of relaxing his efforts to promote a Confederate offer to negotiate with the enemy. Seeking to capture the votes of peace advocates and still keep North Carolina in the Confederacy and thus in the war, Vance portrayed Holden's ambiguous peace plans as treasonable and potentially catastrophic for the state while contending that continued allegiance to the Confederacy was honorable and destined to bring peace.[75] His platform called for "an unbroken front to the common enemy; but timely and repeated negotiations for *peace* by the proper authorities."[76] Under the governor's direction, the state legislature passed a resolution recommending that the Confederate "government, after signal success of our arms, and on other occasions when none can impute its actions to alarm, instead of a sincere desire for peace, shall make to the government of our enemy an official offer of peace on the basis of independence and nationality, with the proposition that the doubtful border States shall settle the question for themselves by Conventions to be elected for that purpose, after the withdrawal of all military forces of both sides from their limits."[77]

The demands for peace diplomacy echoed in the new Confederate Congress, whose membership was significantly different from the previous Congress. During the congressional campaigns of 1863, voters had shown discontent with the course and conduct of the war, and appropriate means for obtaining peace had frequently been an issue. Although the influence in the Congress of ardent secessionists and former Democrats remained substantial, most of the newly elected congressmen were of Whig and Unionist antecedents, and their willingness to call forth grave sacrifices for the sake of Confederate independence was dubious. Peace advocates, particularly in the North Carolina delegation, were destined to play an important role in the new Congress.[78]

In an open session on May 23, 1864, James T. Leach, representative from North Carolina, presented a resolution "in favor of peace by negotiation" that appealed to the president "to appoint commissioners whose duty it shall be to propose an armistice of ninety days to the proper authorities of the Federal Government, preliminary to negotiation upon State sovereignty and independence."[79] The proposition, according to press reports, created "quite a sensation" among spectators and precipitated a "stormy and personal" debate on the floor.[80] Among the senators and representatives working in secret sessions for resolutions bearing on the matter of peace diplomacy were James L. Orr of South Carolina, William C. Rives of Virginia, and Henry S. Foote of Tennessee.[81]

The editor of the Charleston *Mercury*, who generally opposed Davis but favored a vigorous prosecution of the war, felt constrained to condemn the public demands for negotiations. He expressed regret that "any of our State legislatures, or any of our people *anywhere* have recommended that propositions for peace should be made *at any time*." The *Mercury* argued that the South was the invaded and the weaker of the warring parties, and, therefore, "all cries for peace, from us, will be considered very naturally by our foes, as indications of exhaustion or subjugation."

The editor treated at length the proposition that Confederate expressions of a desire for peace and willingness to negotiate would strengthen the peace faction in the rival section. He argued that "the peace party of the North is a party of despair" and the South should be careful to encourage rather than discourage that emotion. Of Northern despondency the editor said: "Signal victories on the part of the Confederate States deepen as they have created it. A resolute, confident and unflinching front helps to produce it." On the other hand, "A failure of our arms, or any indications of weariness and weakness, or of a too great eagerness to end the strife, blunts the edge of their despair" by encouraging them "to fight on, under the hope that there may be some internal discontent which they may not see, or some turn in our affairs which they cannot now discern favorable to their success." The editor concluded that the Southern movement for negotiations was "unseasonable and unwise (although we do not suppose it to be treasonable), and calculated to defeat the very object in view by prolonging the war."[82]

Despite counsel from the press and the president, peace advocates in the Congress secured passage of a manifesto that reversed the position taken by the previous Congress and bore striking resemblance to the Georgia plan for influencing the election. Although the declaration made no reference to the political situation in the North, the Congress did submit its statement "to the sober reflections of our adversaries themselves." The document reminded Northerners of the Copperhead arguments that subjugation of the vast Southern territory and population was impossible, that the cost in blood and treasure was spreading "a pall of mourning" and threatening "financial exhaustion and bankruptcy" in the North, and that continued war meant "destruction of constitutional freedom by the lawlessness of usurped power." The manifesto reiterated the contention that violation of the Federal Constitution by the Northern states had justified the Southern exercise of the right of secession which the Declaration of Independence vouchsafed to each of the states. After disavowing any intentions of interfering with the internal affairs of Northern states, the legislators declared: "All we ask is a like immunity for ourselves, and to be left in the undisturbed enjoyment of those inalienable rights of 'life, liberty, and the pursuit of happiness' which our common ancestors declared to be the equal heritage of all parties to the social compact." In conclusion, the Congress expressed a willingness to negotiate: "Let them [the Northern states] forebear aggressions upon us, and the war is at an end. If there be questions which require adjustment by negotiations, we have ever been willing, and are still willing, to enter into communication with our adversaries in a spirit of peace, of equity, and manly frankness." The Congress requested the president to transmit copies of the declaration to Confederate agents abroad for official presentation to foreign powers, and Southern newspapers also published the document.[83]

Nowhere in the manifesto did the legislators demand or even mention Confederate independence, and they explicitly stated that their expression of a desire for peace and offer to negotiate was a follow-up to the series of Confederate military successes "on almost every point of our invaded borders since the opening of the present campaign." Because the manifesto contravened Davis's opposition to initiating negotiations and omitted a demand for Confederate independence, he could not have been pleased with it. Alexander Stephens, however, was satisfied and believed that Congress was following Georgia's lead.[84]

By the end of spring, the challenge of coping with aroused public expectations had become serious. Confederates found increased hope in the fact that the Republican party, the archenemy, had begun the campaign in a badly fragmented condition. Agitation of the issue in North Carolina, Congress, Georgia, and the press had only quickened public interest. The initiative taken by Alexander Stephens and his colleagues posed a particularly grave problem for Davis because their objectives and tactics were in conflict with his own. For Davis the objective was Confederate independence, but for the Georgians the goal was Northern acknowledgment of state sovereignty that neither prescribed nor proscribed the territorial integrity and independence of the Confederacy. Whereas the president preferred to approach Northern public opinion through covert agents operating from Canada, through vigorous prosecution of the war, and through proclamations of defiance, the Georgians favored overt expressions of Southern support for the peace Democrats, only defensive measures by the military, and frequent proposals for negotiation.

In the midst of these developments, Davis provided weak and inconsistent leadership in the formation of public opinion. On the one hand, Davis's message to the army had encouraged the belief that the Northern political contest might benefit the Confederacy. On the other hand, he had chided his opponents in Georgia for initiating their scheme to influence the election. Davis may not have been able to prevent Stephens and his friends from launching a rival plan, but by largely ignoring Stephens's private letter on the subject of the election and by being publicly indecisive, Davis only aggravated the problem. He could not, of course, reveal details of the secret mission to Canada, but presentation of a coherent statement of his administration's position would have at least placated the public interest in some government action to exploit the Northern political situation and might have attracted support. As the matter stood in the spring of 1864, most Confederates had no way of knowing that their government had even adopted a strategy for the election.

CHAPTER 4

Public Concern and Government Policies:

"I do not entertain your apprehension . . ."

Discussion of public affairs was common among Confederates, but the general interest in Northern politics added a new dimension to public discussion in 1864. Southerners watched military and diplomatic developments during June and July and debated the probable impact on Northern politics. Of particular interest were the raid led by Jubal Early, activity of the Confederate agents operating from Canada, a visit by two unofficial peace commissioners from the North, and the status of military affairs in Georgia. As public and private criticism mounted, President Davis responded with an unsystematic defense of some of his policies. Even though the basis for much of the criticism was public interest in the consequences of government policies on Northern politics, the president offered no general statement of his views on the election or of his position on the appropriate Confederate response. The events of early summer also produced a fundamental disparity between Davis's approach to Northern peace sentiment and that of his agents in Canada.

The decision to send Jubal Early raiding into the North was made for purely military reasons. While Grant maintained pressure of overwhelming numbers on Lee's front, Federal troops had invaded the Shenandoah Valley, and a force under General David Hunter threatened Lynchburg. To counter this menace and to throw Grant off balance, Lee decided to send Early with part of the Second Corps, which Stonewall Jackson had commanded, down the Valley. The instructions to Early were broad, leaving him much discretion. He was to defeat Hunter and, if the situation allowed, cross the Potomac and threaten Baltimore and Washington. Such a movement might force Grant to weaken his army by sending reinforcements to the Federal capital or to attack Lee in the trenches in hopes of forcing him to recall Early, and, in either case, Lee expected to benefit from the maneuver.

After moving down the Valley and defeating Hunter at Lynchburg on June 18, 1864, Early crossed the Potomac and menaced Baltimore. He reached Silver Spring, Maryland, on July 11 and began reconnoitering for an assault. The Confederate general finally decided that the reinforcements pouring into Washington made an attack inadvisable, but Confederate sharpshooters, nevertheless, had an unexpected opportunity to exert a drastic influence on the election. Abraham Lincoln visited the scene of battle to survey the situation personally, and while standing on the parapets of Fort Stevens, he was exposed to Confederate marksmen, who wounded a member of the president's party. Lincoln escaped unscathed. The Southerners pulled back from the Federal capital during the night of July 12 and recrossed the Potomac within two days. Like Hannibal before the walls of Rome, Early had thrown his defiant spear.

Although undertaken entirely for military purposes, the raid had political repercussions. The Confederate offensive belied the Republican contention that the South was extremely weak and incapable of sustaining the war effort much longer.[1] The *Examiner* gleefully declared: "Maryland and Pennsylvania are wild with excitement. The consternation and alarm are greater than ever before."[2] Among the Confederates watching the Northern expressions of terror and confusion was General Lee, who reported to Davis the favorable military consequences of the incursion and commented: "It seems also to have put them in bad temper as well as bad humor. Gold you will see has gone as high as 271 & closed at 266¾."³ Southerners also noted, however, a Northern reaction of quite a different variety. The *Dispatch*, for example, summarized an editorial from the New York *Herald* which stated that the rebel invasion of the North simplified Federal politics by forcing Lincoln's enemies to drop their opposition and to stand with the administration in defense of the country.⁴

Although Early's offensive was commensurate with Davis's electoral strategy of carrying the war to the enemy when possible, it contravened the philosophy of military operations expressed by those who favored the Georgia plan for influencing the election, and a controversy ensued. The Richmond *Examiner* praised the raiders for bringing the destruction and deprivation of war to the enemy and insisted that such operations would intensify the Northern desire for peace. The editor exuberantly declared, "General Early, it is said, has gone over to stump the States of Maryland and Pennsylvania for the Peace party."⁵ The Augusta *Constitutionalist* reprinted this editorial and added that Early's operations "have not increased the armies of Abraham Lincoln a man or made him a vote; but have given the peace party in the North another argument against the war—our strength and audacity."⁶

Opponents of the invasion generally centered their arguments on two contentions: that the raid weakened the Northern peace party and that Early's troops should have been sent to Georgia for duty with Johnston's army. Referring to the raid's impact on Northern dissension, a press correspondent in Richmond said: "An invasion of their country, marked by fire and sword, would, as is the case with all common perils from without, cause these intestine quarrels to be laid aside and to this extent strengthen the hands of the government now bent on our destruction."[7] Alexander Stephens's friend, Henry Cleveland, wrote: "The Maryland campaign is the climax of a long series of blunders. Lincoln's election is now beyond all doubt, and the Northern armies will get a flood of reinforcements."[8] Although the Charleston *Mercury* favored vigorous prosecution of the war, the editor condemned the raid as "foolish" and insisted that the troops should have been sent to Georgia. "If this policy had been pursued," argued the angry newspaperman, "there would not have been at *this moment* the *least* anxiety as to our future in any part of the Confederacy."[9]

In Georgia, Governor Brown and Alexander Stephens disapproved of the invasion,[10] and Herschel V. Johnson wrote a letter to Davis in protest. Johnson complained that Early's raid would strengthen Northern war fervor and contended that the soldiers could have been better used as an addition to the army in Georgia. Davis replied, "I do not entertain your apprehension." He argued that the offensive had made Northerners "feel the evils of war at their own door," which would cause them to "much more numerously sustain the policy of stopping the war." He explained that the threat posed by Hunter's army necessitated the assignment of Early's troops to the Shenandoah Valley and that Early's success against Hunter "gave us an opportunity to assume the offensive with not unreasonable hope of capturing" Washington instead of losing Richmond. The president added that the raid compelled Grant to weaken his army by sending reinforcements to his threatened capital. If, on the other hand, Early had been ordered to Georgia, said Davis, the Federal army would have been successful in the Valley and might have secured the fall of Richmond and the withdrawal of Lee's army from northern Virginia.[11]

While the struggle continued on Southern battlefields, the commissioners in Canada were busy. Soon after their arrival in Canada, their presence became known in the North, and "politicians of more or less fame and representing all parties in the United States" visited the agents "either through curiosity or some better or worse motive."[12] Hoping to gain a working knowledge of sentiment in the enemy section, Jacob Thompson, Clement Clay, and James Holcombe eagerly sought interviews with representatives of the various factions.[13] At one point, Clay communicated to Thompson, "I see people from the United States here daily who come to see me."[14]

Through discussions with several Northerners, the commissioners gained insights into the complexities of thinking among peace advocates in the United States. The Confederates learned that although war weariness and dissatisfaction with the Lincoln administration were widespread, the desire to preserve the Union was also pervasive—even among the Sons of Liberty. In conversations with the Southern agents, Northern votaries of peace frequently asked whether the South would consent to reunion on the basis of broad concessions from the North to remedy Southern grievances. If the Confederates replied that separation was inevitable, the questioner often proposed a peace that recognized Confederate independence but established close ties of commerce and foreign policy. Clement Clay privately said, "The [peace] Demos will yield a great deal, almost anything, for reunion."[15]

Despite the complexities of Northern peace philosophy, the commissioners still hoped to employ it in the cause of the Confederacy. They knew that Davis demanded complete and unencumbered independence, and they were not authorized to discuss any other terms. Concluding, however, that forthright statements of the Confederate demand would alienate Northern peace leaders and pre-

clude cooperation, the agents devised a strategy of skillful diplomacy and careful manipulation. In discussions
with friendly Northerners, the Confederates emphasized
the need for an immediate end to the carnage of the
battlefield and the policies of Lincoln, and they left
unchallenged, if possible, the belief that peace would
somehow bring a restoration of the Union.

The agents chose their words with care in conversations with Northerners. Because Jacob Thompson's head-
quarters at Toronto proved less accessible to Northerners
than was the residence of Clement Clay and James
Holcombe at St. Catherines, the latter two received a
greater number of the visitors from the United States.
Clay and Holcombe generally stressed the mutual suffering and injury of the war and predicted that as soon as
the belligerents were exhausted foreign powers would
intervene and impose a peace unfavorable to the interests of both the North and the South. They suggested
that the warring sections should agree to an armistice of
sufficient duration to allow passions to subside.[16]

When obliged to respond directly to the question from a
Northerner, "Will the Southern states consent to reunion," Clay typically commented:

> Not now. You have shed so much of their best blood, have
> desolated so many homes, inflicted so much injury, caused
> so much mental and physical agony, and have threatened
> and attempted such irreparable wrongs, without justifi-
> cation or excuse, as they believe, that they would now
> prefer extermination to your embraces as friends and
> fellow-citizens of the same government. You must wait
> till the blood of our slaughtered people has exhaled from
> the soil, till the homes which you have destroyed have
> been rebuilt, till our badges of mourning have been laid
> aside, and the memorials of our wrongs are no longer
> visible on every hand, before you propose to rebuild a

common government. But I think the South will agree to an armistice of six or more months and to a treaty of amity and commerce, securing peculiar and exclusive privileges to both sections, and possibly to an alliance defensive, or even, for some purposes, both defensive and offensive.[17]

Clay did not seek to discourage the proposition of peace with close ties between an independent Confederacy and the United States because he believed the South desperately needed to end the war and this compromise seemed the shortest route to peace, albeit minimally acceptable.[18]

About the time that Early was withdrawing across the Potomac, Clay and Holcombe made a public bid to influence the election. They had become associated in Canada with William C. Jewett of Colorado and George S. Sanders of Kentucky. Jewett was an eccentric who had logged three trips to Europe seeking mediation for peace on the basis of Union with slavery preserved and had been in Canada on two previous occasions communicating with Northern peace leaders. Clay described Jewett as "a man of fervid and fruitful imagination and very credulous of what he wishes to be true." Sanders was a minor political figure who had once served as United States consul in London, and he cast his lot with the Confederacy when the Civil War began. Sanders was probably in Canada with hopes of somehow securing the release of his father, who was a prisoner of war in the North. Clay viewed Sanders's services as valuable despite his public reputation as a crank. Both Sanders and Jewett busied themselves in arranging meetings on the Canadian side of the border for the agents from Richmond with various Northern peace advocates.[19]

Among Jewett's acquaintances was Horace Greeley, editor of the influential New York *Tribune*, who was exceedingly weary of the war and longing for peace. Jewett sent a brief note informing the editor that "two ambassadors of Davis & Co. are now in Canada, with full powers of peace" and inviting Greeley to a private meeting.[20] Although Clay and Holcombe learned that Greeley had been invited for a visit, they were completely unaware that Jewett had misrepresented their credentials as authorizing them to negotiate for peace.[21] After studying the invitation, Greeley determined to make an effort to persuade the president to grant an interview to the Confederate commissioners. He included Jewett's note with a letter in which he passionately pleaded with Lincoln to meet the Confederate agents. Greeley reminded the president of the profound desire for peace in "our bleeding, bankrupt, and dying country" and the conviction among some Northerners that "the government and its prominent supporters are not anxious for peace." By authorizing safe-conduct to the rebel envoys for an interview in Washington, said Greeley, Lincoln could demonstrate his willingness "to grant liberal terms" and thereby promote his presidential candidacy in the North and influence "the momentous election soon to occur in North Carolina."[22]

Lincoln doubted that Confederate peace commissioners actually were in Canada, but he decided to take advantage of the situation presented by Greeley's letter to counter allegations that he was unwilling to negotiate with the rebels.[23] He authorized Greeley to serve as his agent and to grant safe passage to "any persons any where professing to have any proposition of Jefferson Davis in writing, for peace, embracing restoration of the Union and abandonment of slavery, whatever else it embraces."[24] After a further exchange of letters between Greeley and the president, the editor reluctantly accepted the assignment and traveled to Niagara Falls,

New York, just across the border from St. Catherines, Canada West, where the Confederate agents were residing at the Clifton House. Greeley notified Clay and Holcombe that if they were "duly accredited from Richmond as the bearers of propositions looking to the establishment of peace," he had a guarantee of safe-conduct to Washington for them.[25] Greeley did not mention Lincoln's preconditions that the peace proposals must include restoration of the Union and an end to slavery.

The note put the Southerners in a particularly difficult position. Clay and Holcombe did not know how Greeley had come to believe they were authorized to treat for peace, but they suspected "Dame Rumor" or the "ignorance, folly, or knavery of Colorado Jewett."[26] Taken at face value, Greeley's note was an expression of willingness on the part of Lincoln to begin negotiations without preconditions and to settle the points at issue through diplomacy. If the Confederates terminated the correspondence at this juncture by simply informing Greeley of his misapprehensions regarding their credentials, Lincoln would have been placed in a strong moral position. He could cite the offer of safe-conduct to silence Northern critics who accused him of demanding subjugation and abolition in the South and of unwillingness to accept reunion on more generous terms. The repercussions in the Confederacy would have been equally disastrous because Southern peace advocates could have used Greeley's letter to refute Davis's contention that Lincoln would negotiate only upon completely unacceptable preconditions. The consequence would have been an even greater demand in the South for initiation of formal peace diplomacy.[27]

Because rapid communication with Richmond for instructions was impossible and because Jacob Thompson declined to come from Toronto for consultations, Clay and Holcombe wrestled with the quandary alone.[28] In a carefully crafted reply to Greeley, they informed him that they had no authority to enter formal peace talks. The envoys added, however, that they were "in the confidential employment" of the Confederate government and "entirely familiar with its wishes and opinions" on the matter of negotiations, and they felt "authorized to declare" that the Confederacy would be willing to appoint accredited negotiators when informed of the invitation. Implying that they would carry Lincoln's terms to Davis, the agents asked for a guarantee of safe passage, despite their unofficial capacity, to Washington and thence to Richmond for themselves and Sanders, who had asked to be included.[29] The purpose of this note, Clay and Holcombe privately said, was "to throw upon the Federal Government the odium of putting an end to all hope of negotiation, or of assuming a position which would enable our Government to approach it without compromising its own dignity."[30]

With this turn of affairs, Greeley telegraphed to Washington for further instructions, and Lincoln sent his secretary, Major John Hay, to Niagara Falls with a reply. Upon Hay's arrival, he and Greeley crossed into Canada and personally delivered Lincoln's message to the Confederates.[31] Addressed "To Whom It May Concern," Lincoln's response was a conditional offer of safe-conduct that prescribed terms of peace: "Any proposition which embraces the restoration of peace, the integrity of the whole Union, and the abandonment of slavery, and which comes by and with an authority that can control the armies now at war against the United States, will be received and considered by the Executive Government of the United States, and will be met by liberal terms on other substantial and collateral points, and the bearer or bearers thereof shall have safe-conduct both ways."[32]

After studying Lincoln's laconic dictum, Clay and Holcombe concluded that it was admirably suited for the Confederate propaganda mill. They doubted that a majority of Northerners would sustain the demand for abolition as a condition of peace, and the sequence of notes provided by Greeley placed the president in a pattern of deceitful inconsistency. All of the correspondence had heretofore been confidential, but now the Southerners sent a reply to Greeley which they also released to the Associated Press.

The agents began their letter by quoting Lincoln's terse statement, and then they sought to shift the onus for continuation of the war to him by skillfully accusing him of a breach of faith in the unofficial diplomacy conducted through Greeley. According to the Confederates, when Greeley's first note offered safe passage on the single condition that the envoys be properly accredited, they concluded that Lincoln had changed his previous stand against negotiation with the Confederacy, and they responded with a plan to secure adequate credentials. In the next note, "To Whom It May Concern," Lincoln increased the demands for a guarantee of safeconduct, they said, to include the requirement that the emissaries bear proposals accepting abolition and Union. In effect, the agents claimed, the president misled them by giving them to understand that he was willing to engage in unconditional negotiations, and, when they responded favorably, he abruptly shifted his ground and imposed preconditions that precluded meaningful negotiation by prescribing the terms of peace in advance.

Breathing defiance, Clay and Holcombe stated that if peace could be restored only after submission to such "terms of conquest, the generation is yet unborn which will witness its restoration." Now the war must continue, they said, in all its unrestrained brutality, whereas negotiations might have brought peace or at least put the struggle on a more humane footing. With the latter comment, the Confederates were implying that formal diplomacy could at least renew the exchange of prisoners that had almost completely stopped.

Clay and his companion warned in their statement that Lincoln's intemperate and unyielding demands would inspire fresh resistance in those Southerners who might have believed that honorable peace with Lincoln was possible or who had grown weary of the agony and hardships of war. Speaking to Northerners "who shrink from the illimitable vista of private misery and public calamity which stretches before them," the Confederates urged, "Recall the abused authority and vindicate the outraged civilization of the country."[33] The agents were careful not to elucidate on Confederate peace demands because they did not want to dispel the hopes of those Northern peace votaries who believed that cessation of hostilities would eventually bring reunion.[34]

Greeley published in the New York *Tribune* additional materials related to the Niagara conversations in an effort to refute charges that he had been meddling as a private citizen in national diplomacy. The documents he released began with a note from Sanders saying that he, Clay, and Holcombe were prepared to proceed to Washington upon assurance of safe-conduct; then followed Greeley's offer of protected travel to Washington, the Confederate disclaimer of adequate credentials, Lincoln's "To Whom It May Concern," and the propaganda letter sent by Clay and Holcombe to Greeley. The editor published nothing that contradicted the portrayal of Lincoln by Clay and Holcombe in their public letter. In an editorial, Greeley insisted that he was functioning only as an authorized intermediary to bring the antagonists together for talks and was not giving or receiving terms of peace.[35] The materials assembled by Greeley were widely disseminated through republication in various newspapers.

News of the affair at Niagara Falls came as a great surprise in the Confederacy. The Confederate government and the Southern public alike first learned of the matter through the Northern press, and a mixed reaction developed in the South as Confederate editors presented the documents originally published by Greeley.[36] Southern observers in various parts of the Confederacy who opposed the peace movements seemed to agree that the affair on the Canadian border would have a beneficial impact in the South. Secretary Mallory privately wrote: "Our weak brothers in N. C. & Geo. who have clamored so loudly that peace propositions should be made by us cannot fail to see that at present peace with Lincoln means degradation."[37] The *Sentinel* declared that the Niagara documents would convince "the miserable faction existing in a neighboring State" that peace with Lincoln meant "the most abject submission with the loss of honor, property, and liberty."[38]

When evaluating the consequences of the Niagara affair for the Northern political situation, however, Confederates were far from agreement. Because the correspondence assembled by Greeley began with a Confederate expression of willingness to travel to Washington and did not reveal that a conference with Lincoln was Greeley's idea, some Southern editors concluded that Clay and Holcombe had initiated events by requesting to meet with the Northern president to discuss terms of peace. Astonished and outraged, the *Examiner* declared: "To exhibit an ex-Senator and member of Congress of the Confederate States thus timidly crawling by a roundabout way to the footstool of the Emperor of the Yahoos, whining and sniveling about peace and 'liberal negotia-

tions,' and haughtily refused even admittance to the
sovereign presence will serve not the peace, but the war
party; because it will be used to create the impression
that the Confederacy must be in the agonies of death
when two distinguished legislators make so pitiful an
attempt to reach the ear of offended majesty."[39]

The editor of the Charleston *Mercury* agreed with the
interpretation by the *Examiner*, and the *Dispatch* discovered yet another reason why the correspondence with
Greeley would have a debilitating effect upon the Northern peace faction.[40] In order for the peace men to achieve
their goals, argued the editor of the *Dispatch*, they must
be free from all suspicion of association with any party in
the South. The editor suggested that because the statements of Clay and Holcombe were designed to aid the
peace party, Lincoln's partisans could logically infer that
Northern peace advocates were involved in its prepara-
tion, thus making them liable to charges of collusion
with the enemy. "In that view of the case," concluded the
editor, "we cannot see that the interference of Mr. George
N. Sanders and his colleagues is calculated to produce
anything short of unalloyed evil."[41]

Some Southerners also took offense at the personnel
involved in the communications. Describing Greeley as a
"bloody fanatic," an editor in South Carolina told his
patrons that the New York *Tribune* had once calculated
the number of Confederate soldiers who should be slain
as the best way for the North to achieve victory.[42] The
fact that the Confederate agents entered the exchange
entirely without authorization outraged some Southerners, such as the editor of the *Dispatch*, who expressed
dismay that "self-constituted diplomatists" had pros-
trated "their country at the footstool of Abraham Lincoln" and demanded that they be "properly rebuked."[43]
The participation of Sanders in the affair was another

source of controversy because of his reputation, and one
Southerner attributed the whole affair to "the meddling
officiousness of that restless Filibuster, Geo. N. Sanders."[44] The publication of the Niagara correspondence
caused embarrassment for the Confederacy in Europe,
where Henry Hotze did his best "to disconnect the Government and its trusted agents from the eccentricities of
persons whose notoriety in Europe is much greater than
the esteem in which they are held."[45]

Not all Confederates, however, were displeased with
the diplomacy at the Canadian border, and some took to
the rostrum in defense of Clay and his colleagues. Among
those seeking to counter the various charges raised by
critics was the Richmond *Sentinel*, arguing that because
of the Niagara documents, "The peace men of the U.
States will be satisfied that no peace can be obtained as
long as Lincoln presides over the destinies of the United
States."[46] The editor insisted that although Clay and
Holcombe were not authorized to speak for the Confederacy, they were "well acquainted with the views and
wishes of the [Southern] people," and their efforts to
initiate negotiations were "eminently proper." The *Sentinel* defended communication with Greeley by describing
him as willing to accept secession and as being one of the
most influential newspapermen of the North and "the
leader of the Republican party."[47] An editor in Georgia
watched the Northern response to Lincoln's demand for
abolition in his communication to the Niagara commissioners and happily reported that it was "having a dam-
aging effect upon his prospects for re-election."[48] Seeking
to assure Mrs. Virginia C. Clay that the diplomatic
efforts of her husband were beneficial to the Confederacy,
Stephen R. Mallory privately wrote: "The parties, frag-
ments, cliques & individuals in the U. S. who desire

peace, but differ only on the means operandi of getting it, will now learn that, with Lincoln at the head of affairs, no peace is possible."[49]

From Canada, Clay and Holcombe watched the debate in the Confederacy and were greatly distressed because they believed that their activities were both proper and efficacious. After observing the reaction in the Northern press and talking with Democratic politicians, Clay privately commented:

> Our correspondence with Mr. Greeley has been promotive of our wishes. . . . It has impressed all but fanatical Abolitionists with the opinion that there can be no peace while Mr. Lincoln presides at the head of the Government of the United States. All concede that we will not accept his terms, and scarcely any Democrat and not all Republicans will insist on them. They are not willing to pay the price his terms exact of the North. . . . All the Democratic presses denounce Mr. Lincoln's manifesto in strong terms, and many Republican presses (and among them the New York Tribune) admit it was a blunder. . . . From all that I can see or hear, I am satisfied that the correspondence has tended strongly toward consolidating the Democracy and dividing the Republicans and encouraging the desire for peace.

Clay also believed that the publication of Lincoln's ukase would have beneficial consequences in the Confederacy: "We have developed what we desired in the eyes of our people—that the war, with all its horrors, is less terrible and hateful than the alternative offered by Mr. Lincoln." Clay expressed hope that the peace forces in North Carolina and elsewhere in the South would now lay aside their demands for negotiation and renew their energy and dedication to continue the war.[50] James Holcombe shared these opinions, and he made similar comments in private correspondence with the Confederate government.[51]

Clay and Holcombe sent letters defending their conduct to Jefferson Davis and Judah Benjamin but offered no public defense. The agents explained how the exchange of communications with Greeley came about and emphasized that they had not sought an interview with Lincoln and had never intimated that the Confederacy would accept terms of peace that did not include independence. After outlining the reasons for making the correspondence public, Clay and Holcombe described the beneficial consequences they expected. Although they decried the attacks by some Confederate editors upon the exchange with Greeley, the agents believed that the cause was best served by their remaining publicly silent.[52]

Through a measure of good fortune and shrewd management, Clay and Holcombe had, in fact, scored a noteworthy blow against Lincoln's hopes for reelection. By arguing that the South would never accept Lincoln's stringent demands and by portraying him as unreasonable and capricious, the Southern agents undermined hopes and exacerbated fears in the North. The demand for abolition in "To Whom It May Concern" triggered an avalanche of criticism as moderates within the Republican party wavered and peace Democrats vociferously condemned the president. The Columbus *Crisis*, a Copperhead newspaper in Ohio, declared: "Tens of thousands of white men must yet bite the dust to allay the negro mania of the President. . . . A half million more are called for and millions in debts are yet to be saddled upon the people to carry out this single negro idea, while the negroes themselves will be literally exterminated in the effort to make them equals with the white man."[53] Perhaps the president hoped to attract radical support by linking abolition to peace, but the alienation of moderates seriously impaired his prospects for reelection. Of the Confederate declaration, two of Lincoln's close associates grudgingly admitted later, "It formed a not ineffective document in a heated political campaign."[54]

While Davis's agents were still involved with Greeley at Niagara Falls, the sponsors of an informal peace initiative from the North reached Richmond. Although not officially commissioned by Lincoln, James R. Gilmore and Colonel James Jaquess arrived in the Confederate capital on July 16, 1864, hoping to discuss possible peace terms with Jefferson Davis. Gilmore, who had frequently traveled in the South before the war, was an author of some repute who wrote under the pseudonym "Edmund Kirke." He was the leader of the mission and later recorded its events. Jaquess, formerly president of a small Methodist college in Illinois, was an officer in the Seventy-Third Illinois Infantry, and his "skill and personal courage" at Chickamauga won commendation from Major Philip Sheridan.[55] With a conviction akin to religious fervor, Jaquess believed that he could restore peace and Union to his war-ravaged country.[56]

Although Lincoln advised Gilmore that the Federal government demanded Union and abolition while offering amnesty, restoration of the Southern states with their rights unimpaired, and compensation for emancipated slaves, the envoys were not authorized to transmit proposals or to speak for the president. He was formally involved in their trip only to the extent of helping to arrange for their passage through military lines to their destination. Lincoln apparently hoped to show critics of his war policy that the Confederacy would not voluntarily accept reunion.[57] In Richmond, Gilmore and Jaquess sent a polite note to Judah Benjamin explaining that they bore no official credentials but asking for an inter-

view with President Davis in the hope of paving the way
"to such *official* negotiations as will result in restoring
PEACE to the two sections of our distracted country."[58]

The message did not catch Benjamin off guard because
he and Davis had ascertained the nature of the mission
through officials at the front before authorizing the
agents to enter Confederate lines and travel to Richmond
in the custody of Confederate authorities.[59] Benjamin
received the visitors briefly to confirm their purpose and
recommended to the president that he hold a conference
with them. Although Davis agreed to the meeting, he did
not relish the idea of discussing terms of peace with
unaccredited Northerners, but, on the other hand, he did
not want to be placed in the position of spurning preliminary overtures that might lead to full-scale peace talks.
Davis and Benjamin met with Gilmore and Jaquess in
the offices of the Department of State on the evening of
July 17.

For two hours the conferees discussed the broad range
of issues related to establishing peace. The Northerners
took the position that the South should seek terms because the armies of Grant and Sherman posed a great
and irresistible threat to the Confederacy. Generous concessions were available, they said, but the North would
become more radical and vindictive if the South insisted
on postponing the inevitable by prolonging the war.
Davis replied that the condition of the Confederacy was
not as precarious as the Northerners had contended. Lee
had repeatedly defeated Grant in the continuing campaign, and Southern forces were strong enough to defend
their own capital while threatening the safety of Washington. In Georgia, said the president, Sherman was
moving farther from his base, thus rendering his supply
lines tenuous and ultimate disaster inevitable. Davis
suggested that the Northern financial structure was un-
stable and that a substantial number of Northerners

opposed Lincoln and the war policy. Gilmore and Jaquess apparently did not respond to the issue of finances, but they insisted that Northern sentiment generally supported the war and that a candidate pledged to continue the struggle would win election in November.

The envoys asked Davis to state his position on the matter of peace terms. The president's answer was straightforward and forceful: the war must continue until Federal forces withdrew from Confederate soil and the United States recognized Confederate independence. He frequently affirmed that the South was fighting for independence and not slavery, and at one point in the conversation he said: "We will govern ourselves. We *will* do it, if we have to see every Southern plantation sacked, and every Southern city in flames."[60] Gilmore and his companion proposed an armistice to be followed by a plebiscite in each of the states with the will of the majority binding on all parties. The electorate would vote on the issue of peace with disunion or peace with Union, emancipation, amnesty, but no confiscation. The naiveté of this proposal was immediately apparent to Davis, who observed that such a procedure would subject the South to the will of the North, which was the majority section. Benjamin asked if the terms stated by the commissioners were Lincoln's, and they responded that they did not speak for the president but felt certain he would accept such propositions to end the war.[61] After reiterating that independence was the only acceptable condition of peace, Davis "terminated the interview" because he had "no disposition to discuss questions of state with such persons, especially as they bore no credentials."[62]

Upon returning to the North, Gilmore met with Lincoln to report on the conference, and they planned to release an account to the press. The president and Gilmore decided to follow the suggestion of Senator Charles Sumner of Massachusetts, who was present at the meeting, that a brief statement of Davis's position be sent to one of the Boston newspapers and a full-length account be prepared for the *Atlantic Monthly*.[63] The Boston *Evening Transcript* published a sketch of the trip and the following quotation attributed to Davis: "This war must go on till the last of the generation falls in his tracks and his children seize his musket and fight our battle *unless you acknowledge our right to self-government.* We are not fighting for slavery. We are fighting for INDEPEND-ENCE, and that, or extermination, we shall have."[64] Gilmore also wrote an article of some twelve pages giving a fuller record of the interview, which appeared in the *Atlantic Monthly*.

Southern newspapers copied Gilmore's account from Northern sources, and Judah Benjamin prepared a Confederate version of the affair which also appeared in the Southern press.[65] The secretary's statement did not take issue with the substance of Gilmore's account but emphasized that Davis met with the agents in the belief that they were prepared to lay groundwork for peace negotiated on the basis of Confederate independence. Benjamin stressed that Davis had vigorously rejected terms "of reconstruction of the Union, the abolition of slavery, and the grant of an amnesty to the people of the [Southern] States as repentant criminals."[66] Some of the Southern editors who took a hard line on negotiations charged that Davis should not have condescended to meet with unaccredited citizens of the United States to discuss peace, but there were many defenders who argued that Davis's action was necessary as a demonstration of his willingness to negotiate.[67]

Given the political climate in the South at the time, Davis probably avoided an avalanche of criticism from Southern peace advocates by at least meeting with the emissaries instead of responding with a terse declaration as Lincoln had done in the Niagara correspondence. Alexander Stephens was content to label the visit from the North a "curious affair," and the *Chronicle & Sentinel* published an editorial lauding the president's conduct.[68] The Richmond *Sentinel* took the occasion to praise Davis for waiving "questions of etiquette" by meeting with the Northerners and argued that his deportment during the interview "will satisfy all that the honor of the country, no less than the interests of peace, are safely in his hands."[69]

Another point that stimulated some disagreement was Davis's remark that the South was not fighting to preserve slavery. The Charleston *Mercury* agreed with the general tenor of the president's conversation but took exception to the comment on slavery.[70] The Richmond *Examiner*, on the other hand, condoned Davis's statement but argued that it should have been made in a state paper rather than to Northern travelers.[71] Among the president's defenders was the Augusta *Constitutionalist*, which mounted a striking and subtle argument. The editor declared that a Northern attempt to wrest the right to own slaves from the Southern people was the immediate cause of the war, but he insisted that behind this lay the greater principles of state sovereignty and self-government which were the true aims of the Confederate war effort. Davis's comment put the North on notice that the South would not accept preservation of slavery as a concession for ending the war and reconstructing the Union. The editor concluded: "It is not for slavery we are fighting, but for the power of saying, if we so desire, that it shall exist here or shall not exist here."[72]

Although the interview at Richmond generated some controversy, many Southern editors agreed that the Northern political situation prompted Lincoln to cooperate in the mission of Gilmore and Jaquess. The rising

pressure for peace was threatening Lincoln's prospects
for reelection, so the Southern argument ran, and he sent
the agents as a concession to Northern peace men while
hoping to extract proof that the South would neither
negotiate nor accede to terms of peace. An editor in
Georgia declared: "Lincoln was the prime mover of the
whole affair, and engineered it with no other object than
to promote his chances for re-election."[73] Had Davis
spurned the negotiators, said the *Dispatch*, "this would
have been repeated through five hundred newspapers,
and its consequences would have been fatal to the Peace
party of the North."[74] By meeting with the envoys and
prompting them to elaborate on Lincoln's terms of peace,
said the *Sentinel*, Davis had established the opportunity
to reiterate Confederate rejection of conditions similar to
those outlined in Lincoln's "To Whom It May Concern."
Characterizing the Northern proposals as a "deliberate
and wanton insult to a people who have repelled every
effort directed to their subjugation," the newspaper declared that the outcome of the mission of Gilmore and
Jaquess "will satisfy the people of the North who wish for
peace that the real obstacle to this desirable consummation does not exist in the views of Mr. Davis . . . but in
the sanguinary temper of the men at Washington."[75]

The president's stern demands for recognition of Confederate independence had, in fact, played into the hands
of Lincoln, who hoped to strengthen his political position
at home by demonstrating that no compromise with the
Southern leadership was possible. The Confederate
agents in Canada were dismayed when they read the
newspaper accounts of Davis's conversation with Gilmore and Jaquess and the official statement by Secretary
Benjamin. In a letter to the president, which could not
have reached him before the visit by the Northerners,
Clay and Holcombe had explained that many friends of

peace in the North "hug the idea that reunion would follow peace at no distant period." The agents had carefully avoided disturbing this conviction and asked that no formal statements of the uncompromising Confederate demand for independence be made at Richmond.[76] Whether Davis would have adopted this advice in dealing with the Northern emissaries, had he been apprised of it, seems doubtful because his categorical declaration was entirely consistent with his overall policy of defiance toward the enemy.

Acting at cross-purposes with the agents in Canada, Davis had undone much of their work with his defiant and unqualified demand for independence, which was published across the North. In another letter to Richmond, Clay sought for a second time to persuade the president to soften his statements. He explained in detail the necessity of leaving undisturbed the notion among peace Democrats that peace would somehow, someday bring restoration of the Union. He even included a sample of the scenario he employed in discussions with Northern peace leaders.[77] Clay's advice would go unheeded.

At the time that Gilmore and Jaquess were in Richmond, the Confederacy was experiencing its most critical crisis of military leadership since the battle of Chickamauga, and again the problem involved the Army of Tennessee. From the beginning of the spring campaign, Johnston had been gradually retreating, and with every mile of the Federal advance alarm increased at Richmond and in the country generally. The military and moral significance of the territory that Johnston was relinquishing was of vast consequence to the Confederacy, and Atlanta became a military, political, and moral symbol. Even before the military campaign began, an editor in Georgia reviewed the importance of the city and declared: "Atlanta is, then, the great strategic point. A crushing, decisive victory in Northwest Georgia will irretrievably crush the power of the enemy, and break down the war party of the North. A substantial victory now will lead to peace. If on the contrary, we meet with a reverse of a serious character in Georgia, the war will be hopelessly prolonged." The editor added: "The approaches to the Gate City—every one of them—must be made a second Thermopylae."[78]

Senator Benjamin Hill, who was keenly interested in the potential of the Northern election, visited Johnston at his camp in Marietta. In conversation with the general, Hill stressed his views on the critical nature of the campaign against Sherman. Speaking of the military consequences, Hill stressed that failure would ultimately mean not only the loss of Atlanta and Georgia but also the collapse of Lee in Virginia and the fall of Richmond, whereas success against the invader would bring relief to Georgia, recovery of Tennessee and Kentucky, and the defeat of Grant in Virginia. Emphasizing the political significance of the campaign, Hill argued that victory by Sherman would mean "that Lincoln's power at the North would be absolute, his re-election certain, and the war for independence must be prolonged for years, and under the most disastrous circumstances." On the other hand, if Sherman met decisive defeat, "Lincoln's power will be broken, and we shall speedily end the war on our own terms." Hill also contended that the issue of foreign recognition would be settled on the battlefields of Georgia.[79] General Johnston apparently agreed with Hill's assessment of the importance of the situation and emphasized that only through acquiring additional cavalry for duty in the enemy's rear could he hope to drive Sherman from the state.[80]

Hill left for Richmond with the impression that

Johnston would hold Sherman north of the Chattahoochee River, approximately seven miles from Atlanta, for
at least a month. Upon reaching the capital after a delay
of some eight or nine days, the senator met with Davis
and reported the conversation with Johnston. The president listened to the presentation, gave his view that
Johnston had sufficient cavalry, and read aloud a dispatch that announced that Johnston was retreating
south of the Chattahoochee.[81] Greatly alarmed and agitated, Hill telegraphed Johnston: "You must do the work
with your present force. For God's sake do it."[82]

The president and his cabinet were also gravely concerned, and pressure had begun to mount for the removal
of Johnston. Secretary Seddon was among the president's
advisers who recommended a change of commanders, and
Seddon asked Hill for a written summary of his conversation with Johnston for use in compiling a report for
Davis. The Georgian took this opportunity to recount the
events and to stress again the consequences for the
Northern election of developments on the field of battle
in his home state.[83] Undoubtedly, the Federal election
was among the welter of considerations that led to the
removal of Johnston and the appointment of John Bell
Hood to command the army.

Because Johnston served as a focal point in the Confederacy for the opposition to Davis, the removal brought
severe criticism upon the president. Some Confederates
literally wept, but others felt relieved at the news of a
change of leadership at Atlanta. The controversy raged
in the newspapers. The Richmond *Whig* bitterly assailed
the president's decision: "Our authorities are diseased in
mind, and the craziest of their crazes is the fancied
possession of an intuitive knowledge of men, especially
military men."[84] The *Chronicle & Sentinel* charged that
the uncooperative and spiteful conduct of the authorities

at Richmond doomed Johnston's campaign from the beginning.[85] Among the president's defenders were the *Dispatch* and *Enquirer*, and the *Sentinel* declared: "The people have seen enough of Johnston's retreats to satisfy them that, if let alone by the Government, he had no idea of making a stand this side [of] the Gulf of Mexico."[86] The controversy gradually and temporarily abated as Confederates awaited the outcome of the decision to place John Bell Hood at the head of the army in Atlanta. Confederates could not have known, although some guessed, that the future of their election hopes was bound to the fate of Atlanta.

The military and diplomatic events of midsummer were storm centers of public controversy in the turbulent atmosphere of the Confederacy, and interest in the presidential campaign at the North was a factor in each of the swirling debates. At the heart of the disagreements over the raid on Washington and the diplomacy at the Canadian border was Southern uncertainty about the consequences of these events for the Northern election. Preoccupation with the canvass also affected Confederate thinking on the nature of the diplomatic mission from the North and the significance of Atlanta. In the midst of public and private expressions of concern, Davis continued to neglect the internal challenge of dealing with the aspirations the election aroused. With regard to the external challenge, he was working at cross-purposes with the agents in Canada.

CHAPTER 5

Escalating Peace Hopes and a Missed Opportunity:

"Independence or fight"

In addition to debating the consequences for the Northern election of diplomatic and military events, Southerners spent the summer of 1864 in hopeful anticipation as the pace of Northern presidential politics increased. Behind the scenes, Confederate agents in Europe and Canada labored to exploit Northern political unrest to the best advantage of the Confederacy. The Southern public watched with satisfaction as factional strife within the Republican party continued and the agitation for peace among the Democrats persisted. Confederate hopes for an immediate and favorable consummation of the war escalated to dizzy heights in August, but Davis still made no major effort to shape public opinion. He also overlooked an opportunity to complement the work of his representatives in Canada while making a gesture to his critics at home.

Political developments in the United States attracted attention in Europe as well as in the Confederacy, and Lord Palmerston invited James Mason to London for an interview regarding conditions in America. The Southerner argued that the North was unable to replenish its armies and was disintegrating in a morass of factionalism and financial ruin. He predicted that "the war would terminate with the present campaign" and contended that the Northern masses were so weary of war that they would welcome foreign intervention to bring peace regardless of the official attitude of the Lincoln administration. When Palmerston asked specifically about the probable outcome of the Federal election, Mason was candidly cautious. He said that if both Grant and Sherman failed, anarchy would result in the North, making Lincoln's defeat certain, if an election could be held at all. The diplomat admitted the important qualification, however, that he was unsure of decisive Confederate successes in both Georgia and northern Virginia.[1]

The Confederate commissioners operating in Canada had no formal interviews with chiefs of state, but they were having private conversations with influential persons from the United States. Jacob Thompson traveled to Windsor, where Clement Vallandigham was residing in exile from the United States. He had been arrested in 1863 for agitation against the policies of the Lincoln administration and deported to the Confederacy, where he spent less than a month before traveling to Canada. Vallandigham was the supreme commander of the Sons of Liberty, and he gave Thompson exaggerated notions of the capacity and strength of the society. Thompson hoped that the clandestine group would eventually establish a Northwestern Confederacy, and he offered Vallandigham money to help finance the operation. The Ohioan refused the funds but introduced Thompson to another leader who subsequently accepted money for distribution to local units of the order.[2]

According to Thomas Hines, the Confederates "very soon discovered" contradictory sentiments among the Sons of Liberty. Hines later wrote:

> The leaders of this association were not Southern sympathizers, in any such sense as the term is generally understood. They had no personal sympathy with the Confederates at all. They desired that the war should cease; they did not believe in the constitutional right of coercion, and thought it unwise and harsh as well. But they deprecated, if they did not condemn secession. They

had no wish to see the South successful by armed superiority; and while they wanted the Federal armies withdrawn from Southern territory, and many of them, unquestionably, were willing to adopt active measures at home, in aid of a policy calculated to produce such a result, and so embarrass the conduct of the war as to render its continuance impossible, there were few of them who would have contributed in any way to a Confederate victory, or wished disaster to the Union arms in the field.[3]

Given the reluctance of most members of the society to accept direct financial aid and leadership from the Confederates, the commissioners at first decided to play a largely supportive role. They discreetly provided money and moral encouragement. They anticipated that an insurrection would lead to the release of Confederate prisoners held in various camps throughout the Northwest and thus provide an able force of Southern veterans to bolster the ranks of the Sons of Liberty, who would most probably accept direct Confederate aid after incurring the wrath of the Federal government.[4]

Thompson and his colleagues expected a spontaneous uprising in the Northwest, triggered perhaps by the arrest of some prominent Northern peace advocate. Vallandigham told Thompson that he planned to return to the United States and expected to be arrested. The arrest, Vallandigham confidently predicted, would precipitate an insurrection by the Sons of Liberty. The Southern agents watched anxiously as the exile made his public appearance in Ohio, but no arrest followed, and the anticipated uprising failed to materialize.[5] Rumors circulated to the effect that the Republicans planned to interfere with the Democratic national convention, which was originally scheduled for July 4, 1864. The Southern agents hoped that disruption of the meeting would lead to violence by the Sons of Liberty, but the Democrats postponed their gathering until August 29, 1864.[6]

Dissatisfied with inaction, the leadership of the secret society in Illinois planned an outbreak for July 20, 1864, with the hope that the membership in other states would rise once the struggle began. The agents in Canada learned of the plan and aided the preparations, but the Northern leadership meeting at Chicago decided to postpone the revolt. Thompson and Clay had a direct influence on the planning when leaders of the Sons of Liberty from various states met at St. Catherines on July 22, 1864, to discuss a new date for the uprising. The Confederates strongly urged August 16, 1864, but the Northerners were reluctant to make a firm commitment. In another meeting of the conspirators at St. Catherines some two weeks later, the Southerners again insisted on August 16 as the most appropriate date. The Confederates were becoming alarmed at the continued postponements because they believed that delay increased the chances of detection by Federal authorities without enhancing the preparedness or capacity of the Sons of Liberty.

The Northerners declared that they could not be ready to act on August 16 and proposed August 29 at Chicago as the time and place for the uprising. The plotters expected to use the activity and immense crowds associated with the Democratic convention as a cover for assembling sufficient numbers of the Sons of Liberty to stage a successful outbreak. The Southern commissioners had no alternative but to acquiesce, but they stressed the necessity of executing the plan as scheduled and stated that a small nucleus of Confederate soldiers would be in Chicago to aid the Northwesterners to carry out the plan if the Sons of Liberty faltered.[7] If all went according to the wishes of the Southern agents, the meeting of the

Democratic convention would mark the beginning of a revolution in the Northwest.

Despite the disappointment of repeated delays, Jacob Thompson became convinced that with judicious encouragement and aid the Sons of Liberty could inaugurate a successful revolution that would culminate in a Northwestern Confederacy composed of Illinois, Indiana, Ohio, Kentucky, and Missouri. Speaking of the prospects for such a confederacy, Thompson privately wrote, "I am addressing every energy that is practicable and reasonable to assist the Northwestern people, and everything justifies the belief that success will ultimately attend the undertaking."[8] The commissioner hoped that a Confederate force could invade Kentucky and Missouri to engage Federal forces and thereby encourage and abet the Northwesterners to rise in rebellion. Thompson sent a request to Richmond for such an operation.[9]

In addition to cooperation with the Sons of Liberty, the commissioners sought to take advantage of other opportunities presented by the internal condition of the North. With the liberal use of funds channeled through intermediaries, the agents sought to induce influential newspapers to support and encourage a cessation of hostilities. The commissioners did not realistically expect that this activity would bring a rapid end to the war, but they did hope to increase Northern peace sentiment and to cause further resentment toward Lincoln should he disregard the intensified demands for peace. The agents also made discreet financial contributions to the campaigns of the most acceptable candidates for public office in some of the Northern states.[10]

Following a suggestion from Richmond, Jacob Thompson participated in schemes to aggravate Federal fiscal instability. He encouraged sympathetic persons in the North to convert their paper currency to gold and hoard the metal in an effort to encourage inflation. John Porterfield, a former banker of Nashville, Tennessee, who was residing in Montreal, conceived one of the most ambitious assaults on Northern finances. Porterfield's plan was to purchase large quantities of Federal gold and ship it abroad, where he would convert the yellow metal to sterling bills of exchange with which to purchase more gold for shipment out of the United States. The only cost in perpetuating this drain of gold from the North was the expense of shipment, and Thompson provided $100,000 to finance the scheme. Porterfield traveled to New York, where he managed to export some $2,000,000 in gold before becoming fearful of discovery by Federal agents and scurrying back to Canada.[11]

Thompson and his companions, as well as their countrymen in the South, found encouragement and hope in the evidence of intensifying tensions within the North. After the Baltimore nominations, Lincoln's bandwagon got off to a languid start, and Southern newspapers reported the uneven development of the president's campaign. Although Confederates hardly needed a reaffirmation of Lincoln's stand on the war, some Southern journals carried portions of a speech he delivered at Philadelphia. Among other comments, the president declared: "The war has now lasted three years, and as we accepted it to establish national authority over the whole national domain, we are to go through with it if it takes three years more."[12] Southerners, apparently, did not doubt Lincoln's personal resolve to destroy the Confederacy, but some of them openly suggested that a massive swell of peace sentiment among Northerners would force him to make peace in order to retain office.

The Confederate press reported the widening breach between Lincoln and the radicals of his party as the bitter wrangling that produced two Republican presidential nominees continued. Confederates who followed the course of public events understood that the resignation of Salmon Chase from his post as secretary of the treasury resulted from animosity between the president and extremists of his party.[13] Southerners noted with interest that Lincoln further antagonized the radicals with a pocket veto of the Wade-Davis bill regarding reconstruction and that the offended sponsors of the measure responded with a manifesto denouncing the president.[14] Reports and rumors also reached the Southern public of proposals among Republicans to unhorse both Lincoln and Frémont to clear the way for another nominating convention.[15]

While hoping that the Republicans would not amicably settle their differences and unite, Southerners studied the intriguing progress of Frémont's candidacy. Confederate editors gleaned commentaries on Frémont from the Northern press, including the New York *New Nation*, which was the organ of the Radical Democratic party.[16] Southerners read accounts of speeches and meetings held in the North to promote the candidacy of Lincoln's Republican rival.[17] As the campaign developed, some Southerners considered the possibility that peace Democrats might join with the radical Republican supporters of Frémont for the sole purpose of defeating Lincoln.[18]

Many Southerners considered the family quarrels among the Republicans providential, but some saw the Frémont candidacy as an untoward circumstance. Northern politicians, from the vantage point of some observers in the Confederacy, were divided into only two categories: supporters of Lincoln and the opposition. Examined in this context, Frémont's nomination represented another split in the already badly factionalized camp of Lincoln's opponents. Some feared that Frémont and the Democratic nominee would divide the anti-Lincoln vote and thereby throw the election to the incumbent.[19]

In addition to developments among the Republicans, the activities of the Democrats continued to be matters of prime interest for Southerners. When the National Executive Committee of the party changed the date of the national nominating convention from July 4 to August 29, the message to the Confederacy was loud and clear: the Democrats were awaiting the course of events on the battlefield before establishing the issues of the campaign and selecting appropriate nominees.[20] An editor in Georgia, speculating on the consequences of the Democratic decision, labeled the postponement "a judicious movement" because the delay not only provided a vantage point from which to respond to military affairs but also eliminated the inhibiting effect that an attack from a common rival might have on the Republican schism.[21]

To gain some indication of the course the Democratic national convention might take, Southerners studied the selection of delegates at the local level in Democratic meetings from the Midwest to New England.[22] An editor in Georgia applauded when Democrats in Connecticut called for the nomination of a candidate "possessing the patriotism, the honesty and courage to stop the war," who would "have no guide but the Constitution as interpreted by the Virginia and Kentucky resolutions."[23] When Democrats in Ohio, Illinois, and Kentucky adopted peace resolutions, the same editor saw "the first glimmer of the right kind of light" from the North.[24]

Southerners also gave attention to the speeches, messages, and activities of leading peace Democrats. When James C. Robinson, congressman from Illinois, released a public letter on the war to his constituency, some Southern editors published the document in full.[25] Contending that the Confederacy was still strong and resilient, that

Lincoln was subverting the Constitution, and that the nation faced bankruptcy, Robinson argued that only a drastic change of national administration and policy could save the Union. The *Sentinel* decried the notion of preserving the Union, but cited the letter as "another of those signs of returning reason among our enemies."[26] George Pendleton, representative from Ohio, attracted some attention in the South when he denounced a reconstruction measure before the Federal House of Representatives as subversive of state rights and said, "If this be the alternative of secession, I should prefer that secession should succeed."[27] The Richmond *Examiner* had lavish words of praise when Marshall Anderson of Ohio rejected the nomination for Democratic State Elector because the nominating convention endorsed the constitutionality and necessity of the war.[28]

Southern editors found space in their crowded columns to report the events when Congressman Alexander H. Long, who had been censured in the Federal House of Representatives for speaking in favor of recognizing the Confederacy, returned to Ohio. His constituency greeted him with a warm and enthusiastic welcome, and the congressman responded with a speech that reaffirmed his unqualified commitment to peace and opposition to the Lincoln administration.[29] Contending that the United States was becoming a centralized despotism like Austria or Russia, Long argued that persons opposed to the war faced mobs and risked illegal detention by the government. He alleged that Lincoln was subverting state and individual rights and seeking to place Negroes on a basis of equality with whites. Regarding the Confederacy, he told his listeners: "Though everything else falls, let us have no other Union than that based upon the consent of each and every State comprising it, and let us spurn with infinite disgust and abhorrence the idea of a

Confederacy 'pinned together by bayonets' and only sustained and upheld by arbitrary coercion and despotic powers."[30] He counseled against violence but urged his audience to use the ballot on election day to remove Lincoln and his minions from office and to restore peace. The meeting adopted a series of resolutions including one that declared, "We are in favor of immediate peace and against further prosecution of the war."[31]

Long's constituents, residents of Ohio's Second Congressional District, had ratified his extreme peace stand taken in the Congress, and Southerners were pleased. The *Sentinel* believed Long's address in Ohio was an indication that "the current in favor of suspending hostilities is rapidly swelling [in the North], and will, in November, overwhelm the infamous administration now ruling at Washington."[32] Another editor argued that Long was typical of the leadership among peace Democrats and that his speech was "an authoritative exposition of the views, the policy, and determination" of the peace faction.[33] Some Southerners insisted that Lincoln would not have tolerated such open expressions of unqualified peace sentiments as recently as 1863, and the failure of Federal authorities to take steps against Long was indicative of a growing Northern desire for peace and of the declining power of Lincoln.[34]

When Southerners spoke of previous action by Lincoln to suppress dissenters, they often had in mind the banishment of Clement Vallandigham from the United States. When the exile returned to Ohio in the summer of 1864, observers in the South carefully watched the reception he received. Vallandigham made his first public appearance at a Democratic convention in Hamilton, Ohio, and the crowd went wild with enthusiasm. After they designated him as a delegate to the national convention in Chicago, he delivered a rousing speech reiterating his position on the issues.[35] Southern editors republished Vallandigham's address in their journals and speculated that his triumphal return was yet another sign of Northern war weariness and of determination by peace Democrats to secure the nomination of a peace candidate at Chicago.[36]

Although other names appeared in Northern newspapers as possible Democratic nominees for the presidency, General George B. McClellan remained the foremost contender.[37] The South was not comfortable with the prospect of his nomination because he was identified with the war faction of the Democracy. Southerners gained an additional glimpse of McClellan's position when their newspapers published portions of a speech he delivered at West Point.[38] In this address, he argued that the North should continue the effort to preserve the Union and contended that Southern secession was unjustified because peaceful means of adjustment existed under the Constitution. A confederate soldier serving at Lewisville, Arkansas, may have expressed the feelings of many Southerners when he said of McClellan's prospects for the Democratic nomination, "I don't want such an intensely Union man, as he seems to be, to be their nominee."[39]

Recognizing that the intensity of peace sentiment among the Northern electorate was a decisive factor in the success or failure of the peace Democracy, Confederates continued to watch for signs of weakness, fatigue, and despair in the North. Southerners observed as the fluctuating price of gold reached new heights in the summer of 1864, and Northern editors expressed fear that the nation was on the brink of financial disaster.[40] Pressed by the urgent need for additional manpower, Lincoln issued a proclamation on July 18, 1864, ordering a draft of five hundred thousand men to begin immediately after September 5, 1864.[41] The draft continued to be unpopular in the North, and the Confederates, of course, applauded the opposition to conscription.[42]

In addition to such barometers of Northern resolve as currency prices and draft resistance, Confederate editors printed Northern cries of anguish and expressions of sympathy for the Confederacy.[43] Southerners read with satisfaction accounts of a meeting of a state rights association in New York where toasts of peace and recognition were drunk and statements such as the following were released: "It [the war] ought at once to stop; and if recognition for the purposes of negotiation, or even ultimate recognition of Southern independence, be necessary to arrest bloodshed, then there should be recognition."[44] Northern confessions of despair gladdened Southern hearts, and a Richmond newspaper copied the following comment from the Wilkes, New York, *Spirit of the Times*: "Never before have we felt a depression equal to that which assails us at this moment. . . . The elastic hope which buoyed the earlier stages of the struggle has largely faded out, while, so far as the Confederates are concerned, they are better off today to sustain three years' more contest than at any previous time."[45]

The enduring Southern hope that internal tensions would convulse the North continued as Confederates watched for the least hint of civil disturbances. Southerners speculated that the excitement of the presidential contest was polarizing the North into camps of potentially violent rivals.[46] Economic and political rivalry between the Northwest and the East persisted, and Southern editors published evidences of unrest and declared that the long-anticipated secession of the Northwest from the Union was imminent.[47] The editors at Richmond found a statement of Northwestern resentment from Marshall Anderson, Democrat of Ohio, particularly appealing: "Peasants and heroes of the West, you are but tenant vassals of the nabobs of the East. . . . I am tired of working for Yankee taskmasters; I hate their selfish meanness; and therefore I am in favor of a Western Confederacy. I have paid tribute long enough to the looms and spindles of the East. I wish no longer to be the political pack mule of New England."[48]

Another factor that encouraged Southerners to believe that a revolt was brewing in the Northwest was the publication in the Northern press of an exposé alleging a widespread conspiracy. The author of the document was Colonel John P. Sanderson, provost marshal general for the Department of Missouri. The colonel became interested in the activities of reputedly subversive societies and employed undercover agents who made investigations in Missouri, Illinois, Kentucky, Michigan, Indiana, and Ohio. Hoping to impress his superiors and thereby enhance his opportunity for promotion, Sanderson composed a report based on hearsay, innuendo, and pure fabrication and charged that a secret society, the Organization of American Knights, was preparing to create a Northwestern Confederacy under the leadership of Clement Vallandigham and other well-known peace Democrats. When the authorities at Washington summarily rejected the allegations, the ambitious colonel prepared a press release that revealed his findings to the public. The report first appeared in the St. Louis, Missouri, *Democrat* and was reprinted in various newspapers across the North.[49] Southern editors quickly reprinted the material in their columns and thereby fostered the belief that the Northwest was extremely volatile.[50]

Fundamental to Northern despondency was the lack of obvious military success in the South. On the seas, the Federal navy had scored notable achievements during the summer of 1864 with the sinking of the CSS *Alabama*

and the capture of Fort Gaines and Fort Morgan at
Mobile, but the focus of attention was on the land opera-
tions. The list of casualties grew longer and the tax
burden grew heavier, but Grant seemed stalemated at
Petersburg and Sherman apparently was bogged down
before Atlanta. The price of gold soared to record levels in
August, and even the president felt that the mood of the
North would mean defeat for him at the polls.[51]

At this juncture, Jefferson Davis neglected what may
have been an opportunity to exploit Northern political
tensions and, at the same time, to assure Southerners
that he was attuned to interest in the election. He might
have publicly called for peace negotiations. Davis's statement would have had to have been skillful enough to
avoid expressing Confederate demands without compromising his position. Lincoln would have been extremely
reluctant to recognize the Confederacy for purposes of
negotiation, and hesitation would most likely have produced acrimonious debate, division, and confusion in the
North. Such a situation would have strengthened the
influence of the peace Democrats in drafting the platform
and selecting a presidential nominee at the forthcoming
convention in Chicago. A carefully drawn initiative from
Richmond would have complemented the work of the
agents in Canada and given them a specific opportunity
to encourage dissidents to apply pressure for peace. Davis
would also have been making a gesture to his critics in
the Confederacy who had been demanding that he take
such action. There is no evidence, however, that Davis
considered such a move, and he probably never did because his emphasis was on military policy to the neglect
of diplomacy. He was still thinking in the terms he had
expressed to Jaquess and Gilmore, "Independence or
fight."

While Northerners looked to the future with grave

misgiving, morale in the South reached its apex for 1864 in August. The mood among Southerners was not one of militant determination to prosecute the war but rather a feeling that their desperate prayers for a favorable peace were soon to be granted. Confederates fervently desired and needed an end to the slaughter and destruction of the long war, and they thought they saw indications on the Northern horizon that the enemy was faltering. Linton Stephens, for example, said of Southern morale, "It has been sustained, and the collapse prevented even up to this time, only by the hopes which our people had from the peace party in the North."[52]

Intelligence gathered by Federal officials in the South also revealed that hope for an end to the war through Northern political developments was a major factor sustaining Confederate morale. A brigadier general in the Union army at Devall's Bluff, Arkansas, found a "new and earnest and hopeful spirit amongst the rebel citizens" which he attributed, after investigation, to a belief among them that successful Confederate resistance would produce Lincoln's political defeat in the fall.[53] Two Federal soldiers who escaped from a Confederate prison and traveled through the South to Union lines reported: "The South is now waiting for the election, in hopes of a peace candidate being elected. Vallandigham or McClellan they wish for, so long as they can defeat Lincoln."[54] A deserter from the CSS *Chicora* at Charleston told Federal authorities, "They [Southerners] think if Lincoln is reelected there will be a revolution in the West; if McClellan is elected they think he will recognize the Confederacy and there will be peace; that is their only hope."[55]

At the height of Southern optimism, the Confederates publicly discussed the probability of peace, circulated rumors of an armistice, and openly debated the peace terms the South should accept. Not every Southerner, of course, expected a cessation of hostilities in the near future, but the belief was widespread that the end was fast approaching.[56] After surveying Northern sentiment through excerpts from several journals in that region, the editor of the *Examiner* concluded: "What we have to learn from these facts is, that our independence is already conquered and won; that even though we may yet suffer some reverses, yet the neck of this war is broken."[57] A journalist in Georgia commented, "Amidst all the confusion that prevails among our enemies, it is manifest that peace principles are constantly gaining ground."[58] The discussions of peace were not confined to the columns of newspapers, for an observer in Richmond testified, "The words Armistice and Peace are found in Northern papers and upon everyone's tongue here."[59] The Confederate chief of ordnance, Josiah Gorgas, recorded a similar comment: "Peace begins to be very openly talked about."[60]

Rumors abounded as war-weary Southerners eagerly grasped for indications of an end to the war. The story circulated that representatives from Ohio, Illinois, and Indiana were in Richmond to ascertain the willingness of the Confederacy to negotiate a favorable treaty in the event that Northwesterners created their own confederacy. Drawing upon the long record of Northwestern dissatisfaction with the East, Confederates found reason to believe the report. The editor of the *Dispatch* candidly stated that he would be not at all surprised if the story proved entirely accurate.[61] Shortly after the visit of Gilmore and Jaquess became public knowledge in late July and early August, the rumor spread in the South that the Federal government was preparing to offer an armistice.[62] A Richmond editor said: "There is now certainly a renewal of those vague whisperings of peace, which have several times before circulated through society. Many think that Peace is in the air. . . . And it may be so. Peace may be nearer to us than we think."[63] The editor of the *Chronicle & Sentinel* suspected profound significance in the fact that the Niagara conversations and the Gilmore-Jaquess mission occurred simultaneously, and the Richmond *Sentinel* stressed Horace Greeley's comment that "the pacification of our country is neither so difficult nor so distant as seems to be generally supposed."[64]

The rumors of an armistice were given fresh vigor when reports reached the South that representatives of the Lincoln administration were secretly meeting with the Confederate commissioners in Canada.[65] Dame Rumor held that Lincoln had offered or would soon offer an armistice "to last ninety days, and to exist on the basis of *uti possidetis, durante pace*—each to hold their own."[66] The editor of the Augusta *Constitutionalist,* who believed the report was true, gave an indication of how widespread he thought the rumor was. After reviewing some of the arguments and indications supporting the story, the journalist said: "It is no wonder that the current rumors of an armistice should have taken so strong a hold on the popular mind. The soldier is thinking of it to-night . . . on his outpost. The home folks are talking it over and praying that it may be so. The whole great heart of our people . . . is tingling now with a delicious hope that all this talk about an armistice may mean something."[67]

Some of the most influential editors in the South were so convinced of the possibility of an armistice and peace negotiations that they devoted lengthy editorials to the subject. Explicitly appealing to the Northern public, the *Sentinel* denounced Lincoln as the stumbling block to peace and called for commencement of peace negotiations. The journalist declared: "Are ye of the North too weak and feeble, too tame, submissive and downtrodden, to oppose the tyrant's will? He, with his ultimata, stands in the way of peace. . . . We hope, however, that he will soon be driven from his position or, if necessary, from his seat." The Southerner called for the appointment of commissioners from both sides to discuss peace terms on the sole precondition that their decisions be subject to ratification by the respective governments. Declaring that even Confederate independence was open to negotiation, the editor said that Northern concessions to restore the Union were "worthy of consideration." On the subject of the South's peculiar institution, the editor said: "As to the slavery question we would leave that to be settled last. The question of independence concerns us all. The subject of slavery but a part of us."[68]

In another editorial, the *Sentinel* urged commercial concessions to the North as the price of peace and independence. The newspaper reasoned that the South would gladly grant liberal terms of trade to a major European nation willing to intervene in the South's behalf; therefore, why not offer the same trade agreement to the North for an end to the war and recognition of the Confederacy? The editor advised that the North should seize this economic opportunity quickly because European powers would probably soon enter the war as Confederate allies because the profitable trade status would more than offset the cost of war against the now enfeebled North.[69]

The editorials in the *Sentinel* precipitated heated discussion in the Confederate press that split along the general lines of the conflicting approaches to the Northern election. Among the critics was the Charleston *Mercury*, which uncompromisingly demanded Confederate independence and favored Southern defiance and vigorous prosecution of the war as the best method to intensify

Northern despair and thereby influence the election. The *Mercury*'s editor found the *Sentinel*'s editorials particularly disconcerting because this Richmond newspaper was the reputed organ of the Davis administration. The editor of the *Mercury* denounced the call for unconditional negotiation as profligate and treacherous to the Southern cause and insisted that the Confederate government had no constitutional authority to negotiate on terms other than Confederate sovereignty and preservation of slavery.[70] He viewed the *Sentinel*'s proposal for trade concessions to the North as "a distinct advocacy of re-construction of our former commercial union with the United States." The *Mercury* contended that ties of commerce to the Federal union would eventually lead to another war because of Yankee avarice.[71]

The editor of the Augusta *Chronicle & Sentinel* took quite a different view of the call for unconditional negotiations and commercial concessions. This newspaper, an avid supporter of the Georgia plan for influencing the election, had long been demanding negotiations and compromise. The editor argued that President Davis should "ignore the Lincoln Administration" and open "negotiations directly with the people of the North. . . .We can make known to them our sentiments and views, in reference to the settlement of the quarrel between us. The Northern press, in the peace interest, is ready to communicate them. The peace party of the North will be glad to receive, and discuss them, in the approaching Presidential canvass. We can, thus, furnish them the very capital they want to enable them to carry the election."[72] The editor in Georgia heartily endorsed the *Sentinel*'s editorials and insisted that the material had a special significance because the *Sentinel* "is understood to be the organ of the President." The journalist believed that he could trace "the hand of Secretary Benjamin in these editorials."[73]

The *Sentinel*, which generally sought to avoid controversy, felt compelled to respond to the comments provoked by its editorials. The newspaper reaffirmed its
commitment to peace "on terms that shall not impair,
trammel, or jeopard[ize] the thorough independence, the
honor, the rights, interests and territorial integrity of the
slave holding South." The editor insisted that his proposal for open peace talks was simply designed to counter
Lincoln's demands in "To Whom It May Concern." Stipulation of terms beforehand by either side, declared the
Sentinel, precluded meaningful negotiation.[74] Little more
than a week later, this newspaper published an editorial
under the title, "Let Us Be Patient and Wary." The editor
warned his readers against rushing into a hasty agreement with the North because "at no time during the war
have we stood on such high vantage ground. At no time
have we had so good reason to insist on all we have ever
asked: untrammeled, unconditional independence." The
journalist stated that the South should ever be ready to
engage in unrestricted peace talks but advised against
concluding any agreements before the outcome of the
Chicago convention and the September draft when the
North would most likely be even weaker. The editor
declared, "We hold the enemy in a tight place, and
probably should rather press our advantage than relieve
him of his difficulties by consenting to an armistice."[75]

In addition to the debate spawned by the editorials of
the *Sentinel*, the Confederate press considered a broad
range of issues related to the prospect of peace. Generally
coupled with calls for an armistice was the insistence
that all acts of hostility should cease, including the
withdrawal of Federal land and naval forces from Confederate territory and waters.[76] Northern proposals for a
convention of states to settle the points at issue were at
least as old as the secession crisis, and some Southern

editors expected that the Democratic convention might propose such a gathering. The Charleston *Mercury* took the position that a meeting of the states to negotiate terms of peace would contravene the Confederate Constitution and published lengthy editorials explicating this contention.[77] True to the tenets of the plan outlined by Governor Brown in his address of March 1864 to the legislature of Georgia, the *Chronicle & Sentinel* argued that the Confederacy should not relinquish the slaveholding border states to the United States during negotiations for peace.[78] Believing that Confederate peace hopes were dangerously inflated, the editor of the Richmond *Dispatch* attacked the premise upon which the bouyant expectations rested. He argued that demands for peace in the South were counterproductive and degrading and that Northern politics was nothing more than a struggle between the "ins and outs."[79]

Aware that Southern editorials were often reprinted in Northern newspapers, Confederate editors generally yearned to strengthen the hands of the peace forces in the United States, yet they faced a dilemma. Overt endorsement might taint the peace party with the stigma of association with rebels, but journalistic silence seemed unproductive of good.[80] By announcing a willingness to negotiate while vowing determined resistance to Lincoln's war policy, some editors undoubtedly believed that they were helping Northern peace men. The newspaper editors used other devices such as warning, "There must be a change of Administration [at Washington] before the Richmond authorities will make any effort, except those made by the army, toward peace."[81] With a Northern audience in mind, Southern newspapers sometimes repeated the rhetoric of the peace Democrats by insisting that the reelection of Lincoln would only perpetuate the war until the inevitable collapse of the economic, political, and social structure of the United States.[82] Southern editors frequently appealed to the grievances of the Northwest by reciting the alleged abuses of New England.[83]

Among the Southerners who shared the euphoria of August was Alexander Stephens, although he was nursing a particular grievance against Jefferson Davis in a matter directly related to the election: the case of David F. Cable. After writing to the president in the early part of 1864 asking for an inquiry into Cable's claim that he was a special representative of the Northern peace party, Stephens heard nothing of the matter for some weeks except Davis's assurance that the pretensions of the prisoner at Andersonville would receive prompt investigation. Impatient for some report, Stephens wrote the commandant at Andersonville, who replied that there were no plans for the release of Cable, and Stephens concluded that the investigation had proved the prisoner's claims false.[84] Much to Stephens's surprise, he received a letter several weeks later from Cable asking why he had not been approached and complaining: "I have no hopes of surviving in my present position very long. . . . If my mission here should fail there is most important work for me to do in the North West during the present election. At all events do not allow me to perish here for my family's sake."[85]

Although Stephens was probably angered by the apparent neglect of his first request for an investigation of the prisoner, the vice-president sent a restrained letter to Richmond asking Davis to look into the matter.[86] Davis made inquiries and learned that the original order for an investigation had never reached Andersonville. Seeking to make amends for an embarrassing situation, the president ordered the secretary of war to send an officer to see Cable, but when the investigator reached the prison,

Cable was dead. Stephens responded bitterly to this news: "The conduct of the President in relation to this man Cable has really outraged my feelings. It has caused me to believe . . . that he does not want the war to end until he is absolute military ruler."[87]

Stephens had also been watching the agitation for peace in the North during the summer, and he was convinced that it resulted from the peace maneuvers in the legislature of Georgia during March 1864. Although not certain, Stephens believed that he could see signs that Davis had accepted the approach to the election that Georgia had espoused or at least that the president would not interfere with the plan. The vice-president told his brother: "I feel strong confidence & hope at last that if our officials civil & military make no blunders and only hold our own for ten weeks that Lincoln may be beaten— a Peace man elected in his stead at the North and with that result sooner or later Peace will come. . . . I am much more hopeful of the future than I have been since the war began."[88] Communication between Davis and his vice-president was so poor that Stephens was unaware that the president's approach to the election had not changed.

Optimism extended to the agents in Canada, who were encouraged not only by their observations of Northern events but also by a visit of Jeremiah Black from the United States. Black's visit was the substance behind the rumor in the South that diplomatic contacts were continuing along the Canadian border between representatives of the Federal government and the Confederate commissioners. Black, Thompson, and Edwin Stanton were old acquaintances because they had served earlier in the cabinet of President James Buchanan. The visitor told Thompson and his colleagues that he was in Canada at the behest of Stanton to determine whether the South

would consent to open negotiations without first demanding recognition of the Confederacy. Stanton believed,
according to Black, that Lincoln was doomed at the polls
and that Northern unrest might erupt in violence unless
the president could do something dramatic toward ending the war, such as commencing negotiations.[89]

Exactly what the Confederates told Black remains
unclear, but they were elated with the revelation of
despondency and apprehension at the highest levels of
the Lincoln administration. Thompson and Clay concluded that the trend of events justified the belief that
the Federal government would soon offer terms. Clay
told a correspondent: "You need not be surprised by the
announcement of L[incoln]'s proposal of an armistice, at
any time. It may enable him to ride into office on the
flood tide of Peace which is now sweeping over the
country and threatening to overwhelm all who resist it."
The agents expected that the North would first offer
concessions to restore the Union but, finding restoration
impossible, finally propose a settlement based on Confederate independence with close commercial ties and agreements for a cooperative foreign policy. Thompson and
Clay believed that although the Confederacy preferred
unconditional recognition, it would probably grant concessions to the North in the areas of trade and foreign
affairs to obtain peace and independence. They were so
thoroughly convinced that an end to the war was in the
offing that each of them prepared a letter to the Confederate agents in Europe advising them of the imminence
of peace and suggesting a course of diplomatic action.[90]

Pervading the Southern optimism was the oft-repeated
recognition that an early and acceptable conclusion to
the fighting depended upon the ability of the Confederate
army to prevent an outstanding Northern military success. If Confederate forces could continue to frustrate the

Northern invasion, so the Southern logic ran, the peace sentiment of the North would intensify, a peace candidate would be elected, and an end to the war would soon follow. In the event of a major success of Federal arms, however, Southerners believed that Northern war spirit would revive, Lincoln would win reelection, and the struggle would continue with renewed vigor. Relying upon such reasoning, the editor of the Richmond *Sentinel* published his conclusion that the conflict had reached a truly critical phase:

> Now is the time for us to exert every energy, to put forth every effort, to rally to the support of the Government and the army, and to press upon the enemy with all our vigor; thus shall their present despondency as to our subjugation be turned into despair, and their inclination for peace be stimulated into a passion. Let every officer be doubly vigilant and enterprising, and on the alert to guard against and to make surprises, and to get in a blow upon the enemy. Let our own soldiers remember that a success at this time will be exceeded in its military, by its political importance, and will do more to expedite peace than half a dozen military achievements last year or next. The scales of decision are hanging in uncertain balance at the North—let us, by brilliant exertions in war, throw what we can on the side of peace.[91]

Amid the surging optimism, speculation regarding the probable course of the Democratic national convention increased as the date for that meeting drew near. Some Southerners speculated that the Federal army would launch a major effort, possibly involving a desperate gamble, to achieve some semblance of a victory with a view to swaying the convention in favor of continuing the war.[92] Expecting a struggle in the convention between the war and peace factions of the Democracy, Southerners advanced various prophecies of the outcome. In a marked understatement, the editor of the Augusta *Constitutionalist* expressed the Confederate concern: "And to us it is a question of interest, will the nominee and the platform be a man and principles pledged to a cessation of the war."[93] Editors seemed to anticipate that the platform would embody the principles of the peace faction, perhaps even a call for an armistice and negotiations to restore the Union. Predictions of the probable nominee ranged across the spectrum from McClellan, favorite of the war Democrats, to a peace man, such as Alexander Long, or a compromise candidate.[94]

As the day of the long-awaited convention finally dawned, the excitement became intense for some Southerners. Alexander Stephens wrote: "This is Monday—the great day at Chicago. I feel a deep interest as well as anxiety to know what shall be done there. Very great events and results depend upon it."[95] Edmund Ruffin, the crusty fire-eater from Virginia, had been watching Northern political developments, and he, too, was anxious. The old Southerner noted in his diary: "This is the day for the meeting of the Democratic Convention at Chicago. I look for the report of its composition, disposition, & action with intense interest. According to the results of this meeting, we may soon be enabled to anticipate the probability of speedy peace—or otherwise have to acknowledge the vanishing of all hope of early peace."[96]

The Democrats gathered, as planned, in Chicago, and a band of determined Confederates from Canada also traveled to the city. Serving under the orders of Jacob Thompson, Captain Thomas H. Hines and Captain John B. Castleman, both of the Confederate States Army, brought a group of sixty Southern soldiers, who had managed to escape from Northern prisons, to cooperate with the Sons of Liberty in the uprising planned for

Chicago during the Democratic convention. Among the huge crowds in the city were members of the secret order and various of their leaders.

Hines and Castleman met in their rooms at the Richmond House on the night of August 28 with some of the leaders of the Sons of Liberty to ascertain their state of readiness for the proposed operation. To the utter dismay of the Southerners, they found that although many members of the clandestine society were in Chicago, they were indiscriminately scattered through the city with no effective organization or communication. The Confederate officers scheduled a similar meeting for the following night, where they learned that the situation among the Sons of Liberty had degenerated rather than improved. After pondering the alternatives, Hines and Castleman concluded that the available Confederate force was inadequate for the assigned mission, and they withdrew from the city. The Southern officers attributed the failure on the part of the Sons of Liberty to the overawing presence of reinforcements at the Federal garrison at Camp Douglas near Chicago, the pathetic lack of organization in the society, and the timidity and irresolution of some of its members.[97]

In the convention the Democrats went about the business of drafting a platform and selecting nominees for president and vice-president. After much wrangling, the politicians adopted a brief platform of only six resolutions that praised the concept of Union, recognized "the brave soldiers and sailors of the republic," and excoriated Lincoln for his conduct of Northern internal affairs and his war policy. The crucial plank on the war, which was largely the handiwork of Clement Vallandigham, stated: "That this convention does explicitly declare, as the sense of the American people, that after four years of failure to restore the Union by the experiment of war . . .

justice, humanity, liberty, and the public welfare demand that immediate efforts be made for a cessation of
hostilities, with a view of an ultimate convention of the
States, or other peaceable means, to the end that, at the
earliest practicable moment, peace may be restored on
the basis of the Federal Union."[98] The platform said
nothing about the Negro or slavery, but the comments of
speakers at the convention exuded racism. The overwhelming choice of the delegates for the presidential
nomination was General George B. McClellan, although
the peace faction did seek to muster support for Horatio
Seymour, governor of New York. As the vice-presidential
nominee, the convention selected George H. Pendleton of
Ohio, who was a scion of the Virginia aristocracy and an
outspoken Copperhead.[99]

Southerners were eager for any reports of the proceedings at Chicago, and Confederate editors published bits
of information as they became available.[100] At home in
Georgia, Vice-President Stephens, who was carefully
watching the newspapers, wrote to his brother: "I am
now very anxious to hear from the Chicago Convention.
When I see what has been done there I can form some
more rational conjecture as to the probable general prospect before us."[101] When a deserter from the Federal
army entered Confederate lines at Petersburg, his report
that the Democrats had nominated McClellan found its
way into a prominent Richmond newspaper.[102] War Department clerk John Jones recorded in his diary, "Our
people take a lively interest in the proceedings of the
Chicago Convention, hoping for a speedy termination of
the war."[103]

As soon as the platform and the identity of the nominees became known to Southerners, they made preliminary evaluations even though the candidates had not
publicly acknowledged their nominations. Jones studied
the resolutions of the convention and concluded that the

platform amounted "to a defiance of Lincoln" and predicted that the Democratic ratification meetings "will inaugurate [Northern] civil war."[104] Discussions generally focused on the resolution calling for an armistice and negotiations, and Confederates wondered whether the proposal of a cease-fire was dependent upon Southern willingness to accept reunion. The Richmond *Examiner* took the position that the resolutions "do not breathe the faintest hint of even an armistice except upon the terms of our coming into a convention . . . on the basis of the Union," while the Charleston *Mercury* drew the inference from the resolutions "that the election of Gen. McClellan upon such a declaration of wrongs and platform must lead to peace and our independence with one essential condition, however, that for the next two months *we hold our own and prevent military success by our foes.*"[105]

The whole idea of an armistice and a convention of states presented serious problems for the South. In an atmosphere of negotiation and concession, some war-weary Southern states might be willing to leave the Confederacy and return to the United States. Another consideration was the status of military affairs. Grant was threatening Richmond; Sherman was at the gates of Atlanta, and if the gray combatants hailed a cease-fire as a signal to disband while the soldiers in blue remained at their posts, Southern negotiating strength would be emasculated and the cause lost. Josiah Gorgas touched upon the military problem in a private letter: "We cannot stop the fighting until their [Federal] troops are withdrawn. Cessation of hostilities would be fatal. Our armies would dissolve like frost before the rising sun."[106]

Of greatest concern, perhaps, was the attitude of the presidential nominee because he probably would establish the policy of the administration, regardless of the platform, if the Democrats won the election. A newspaper

correspondent articulated the question regarding
McClellan that was in many Southern minds: "Are we to
take him for a peace candidate or a reconstruction war
Democrat [?]"[107] After reviewing the nominee's record on
the war, the *Dispatch* declared, "How, then, can he be
considered any better for our purposes than Lincoln
himself . . . we are unable to see."[108] Upon hearing of the
general's nomination, John A. Campbell, assistant secretary of war, shook his head in dismay and declared that
McClellan was "not the right man."[109] Josiah Gorgas
observed, "I don't think we have any reason to expect a
cessation of War from the election of McClellan if peace
or war depends on his volition."[110]

Other Southerners, such as the editor of the *Sentinel*,
diligently searched for evidence that McClellan had ex-
perienced a change of opinion toward the Confederacy.
The journalist informed his readers of reports that the
candidate had "greatly modified, if not, indeed, abandoned, his belligerent sentiments." To buttress this contention the editor cited the "support given him
[McClellan] by so many decided peace men" and the
evidence that Pendleton was "an ardent peace man."[111]
The *Sentinel* developed a rationale that McClellan could
employ to remain consistent with his past declarations
for war while negotiating for peace with an independent
Confederacy. From the beginning, said the editor,
McClellan had warned that Lincoln's policy of savage
warfare would generate fierce passions and sentiments
making reunion impossible. All that McClellan need do,
therefore, was to blame the failure of the war to restore
the Union on Lincoln, while garnering to himself the
plaudits for restoring peace.[112]

The outcome of the Democratic proceedings did not
meet the high expectations of Alexander Stephens, but
he did find reason for optimism. He had hoped that the
Democrats would nominate a peace man on an unconditional peace platform, and he believed that such would

have been the case had the Confederate authorities been supportive of the peace Democracy. The vice-president was convinced, however, that the platform committed the Democrats to a policy of peace even if negotiations failed to restore the Union. Operating on the assumption that the vast majority of the delegates at Chicago favored peace with Confederate independence if such were the only alternative to continued war, Stephens guessed at the strategy of the convention. In his view, the Democrats took a stand for negotiation because they sincerely wanted to restore the Union through concessions if feasible, hoped to attract as many voters as possible, and realized that diplomacy would at least bring an end to the war. The great imponderable in his calculations was the probable conduct of George B. McClellan. The Southerner had hoped that the general would not get the nomination and feared that he would not adhere to the platform if elected.

Despite apprehensions, Stephens privately voiced optimism for the future. In the second of two letters regarding the Democratic convention which the vice-president sent to his brother on September 4, 1864, Alexander Stephens wrote: "And my opinion now is if our side make no blunders . . . that McClellan will be elected. And with his election will come a suspension of hostilities and attempts at some sort of negociation [sic] that will end after a while[,] a long while it may be[,] in peace. This is not only my hope but my opinion."[113] After confiding his thoughts on Northern politics to Herschel V. Johnson, Stephens said of the Chicago convention: "It presents a ray of light, which if we make no mistakes, may under providence prove to be the dawn of day to this long & cheerless night. The first ray of real light I have seen since the war began."[114]

Since the Gilmore-Jaquess mission, Davis had not been particularly active in advancing government policy for the election. Various of his agents were busy, but

Davis did not seize, and probably did not recognize, an opportunity to exploit Northern political tensions through proposing negotiations during the period of low Northern morale in August. Likewise, the president still made no major effort to mold Southern opinion regarding the election. By the end of August, there was confusion in the mind of the vice-president, and probably in the minds of many other Southerners, as to exactly what the government's position on the election was. The exuberant optimism in the Confederacy at the end of summer set the stage for a serious morale problem, which Davis would be unable to ignore, in the event of a drastic reverse in the outlook for the election.

There were signs of potential trouble. Despite concentrated efforts, the Confederates in Canada had been unable to provoke the Sons of Liberty to action. McClellan had yet to announce his position with respect to the platform, and, even as Southerners basked in the glow of hope, disconcerting rumors of military disaster emanated from Atlanta.

CHAPTER 6

Politicians on the Hustings:

"Let fresh victories crown our arms . . ."

Following the Democratic convention, critical events moved rapidly. Atlanta fell on September 1, and within approximately one week McClellan announced his position on the Democratic platform, which was disheartening and confusing in the South. Belatedly recognizing the depth of Southern interest in the election, Davis made one of his rare speaking tours. He explained his stand on the election and labored to rally Confederates, but the president's action was proverbially too little, too late. The response of Southerners to his pleas clearly revealed that the internal challenge generated by the election was out of his control. The possibility of favorably influencing Northern sentiment was also very dim. Davis called for decisive victories, and the agents in Canada doggedly continued their efforts.

Confederates had long recognized that their hopes for influencing the election rested on the course of military events, especially on the battlefields in the vicinity of Richmond and Atlanta. The Richmond *Examiner* reminded its broad readership on August 31, 1864, "If Atlanta were to fall, or Petersburg, or if Sheridan should drive Early back to Lynchburg—or if any one of these events should befall, then all the Peace principles and peace Presidents of Chicago would be at the election next November where last year's snow is, and last night's moonshine." Unknown to most Confederates, the fate of Atlanta was sealed on the very day that the *Examiner* made this prophetic statement.

During the first few days of September 1864, rumors circulated in the Confederacy that dire events were occurring or had occurred near Atlanta. Mary Boykin Chesnut took time from her active social schedule to record in her diary, "The battle is raging at Atlanta, our fate hanging in the balance."[1] Alexander Stephens, writing from his home in Crawfordville, Georgia, confided to his brother: "We had news yesterday that a great fight was progressing near Atlanta. I need not say that I am exceedingly anxious to learn the result."[2] As Confederate readers eagerly scanned their newspapers for information, they encountered the telegraphic report of the press association which announced that communication with the beleaguered city was impossible, but rumors in Macon had it that Hood had abandoned Atlanta.[3]

In fact, vigorous fighting had developed on the last day of August when General William J. Hardee's corps tried unsuccessfully to dislodge the Federal troops at Jonesboro. Because the failure of this Confederate attack rendered Hood's position in Atlanta militarily untenable, he retired from the city on September 1, 1864, and the Union forces took possession of the former Confederate stronghold on the following day. Rain was falling in Richmond on the evening of September 3, 1864, when Hood's dispatch announcing the fall of Atlanta reached Confederate authorities.[4] Upon reading the message from Hood, Davis may have pondered in his heart whether Johnston might have held Atlanta, at least until after the election, if he had been left in command. The decision to change commanders was fateful and produced an unending debate. In the light of recent scholarship, it seems doubtful that Johnston, at the time he was relieved, had a definite plan to hold Atlanta, but Davis was wrong to make a drastic shake-up in the leadership of the army at such a crucial moment.[5]

A stifling gloom settled over the South as newspapers spread the official report of catastrophe in Georgia. A Southern nightmare had materialized. Confederate journalists, such as the editor of the Augusta *Constitutionalist*, regretfully reported, "Atlanta is in the possession of that scourge of God—the Yankee."[6] The Confederacy staggered under the news because the defeat meant that a position of great psychological and military significance was lost and that Southern hopes for the Northern presidential election had suffered a serious setback.

Confederates gave expression to their profound feelings of anguish and remorse in private and in public. A close observer of public affairs in North Carolina secretly wrote: "Never until now did I feel hopeless but since God seems to have forsaken us I despair. At present I see no hope but in Divine intervention—our enemies are mightier than we, and are full of hate and fury against us."[7] A Georgian described his feelings upon hearing news from Atlanta in a letter to his brother: "I shall never forget last Sunday. A load seemed to weigh down the spirits of the old and young. Friends passed and offered no words of greeting, while many shut themselves out from the world and tried to forget the gloom overhanging our late cheerful prospects."[8] The lamentation occasionally intruded into editorial columns of Southern newspapers as, for example, the Augusta *Chronicle & Sentinel*: "We have suffered a great disaster. We cannot conceal from ourselves the magnitude of the loss we have sustained in the fall of Atlanta."[9]

Confederate despondency was intensified by the recognition that the Federal victory would revive Northern war spirit and thereby enhance Lincoln's chances for reelection and diminish, if not destroy, prospects for an early and satisfactory peace. John W. Graham, one of the Confederate soldiers serving at Petersburg, wrote, "I am

afraid that the fall of Atlanta will secure Lincoln's re-
election and do much to prolong the war."[10] Speaking of
the consequences for the Northern election of the loss of
the Gate City, the Richmond *Examiner* commented, "It
will render incalculable assistance to the party of Lincoln, and obscures the prospect of peace, late so bright."[11]
On the following day, the editor added, "The Demo-
cratick [sic] party would have been forever obliged to
General Hood if he had managed to hold Atlanta for
another fortnight."[12]

Southerners watched sullenly as jubilation over the
victory burst forth in the North.[13] The Richmond *Sentinel*
reported, "All Yankeedoodledom is clapping hands, and
huzzaing and flinging up caps, as though there was no
longer a 'live rebel' in all America."[14] The editor of the
Augusta *Chronicle & Sentinel* commented on the Northern celebration: "The fickle and besotted multitude but
recently clamoring for peace, now elated by a single
success after a multitude of defeats, is shouting with mad
enthusiasm for the subjugation of the South."[15] Sherman's triumph did induce a dramatic change in the
climate of public opinion at the North, and victory cele-
brations often turned into Union party rallies favoring
the election of Lincoln and the continued prosecution of
the war. Within the weeks following the capture of Atlanta, General Philip Sheridan decisively defeated Jubal
Early and devastated the Shenandoah Valley as par-
oxysms of joy and enthusiasm continued to pass through
the North.

The Charleston *Courier* commented on the developments of early September: "The prospect of an early
termination of hostilities has suddenly become darkened.
The hope of receiving deliverance from our crushing woes
has been abandoned, and at the beginning of another
season we are admonished to prepare to pass through

more months of blood and tears and suffering."[16] But Southern morale simply was not prepared to endure an indefinite prolongation of the war. The prospect that the Northern election would bring peace had been a significant factor sustaining Confederate perseverance, and now, with that support seriously weakened, Southern resolve tottered dangerously. As the *Dispatch* observed: "The mind is never so deeply dejected as at the period which immediately follows an unusual elevation of the spirits. The people had been indulging the hope that peace was near. They were taught to believe it by those who should have known better; and believe it they did."[17] The buoyant editorials proclaiming the imminence of peace, which had been so characteristic in August, disappeared immediately as Southern editors put the best face possible on the recent calamities. Recognizing, perhaps, that the press bore a large measure of the responsibility for the escalation of Southern peace hopes during the weeks preceding the disaster at Atlanta, journalists worked to buttress sagging Confederate morale by minimizing the military significance of the defeat; by stressing the vulnerability of Sherman's supply lines; by dismissing Northern exuberance as artificial, unfounded, and temporary; by appealing for renewed commitment to the war; and by arguing that strenuous Confederate military efforts could still influence the outcome of the election.[18]

Another disappointment to the already stunned Confederacy came with George B. McClellan's letter accepting the nomination of the Democratic party for the presidency. As McClellan composed his letter of acceptance, he considered offering the South an unconditional armistice and unrestricted peace talks, but he decided to require Confederate agreement to the principle of Union as a precondition for a cessation of hostilities and negotiation.[19] After expressing "love and reverence for the Union, Constitution, laws and flag," the candidate expressed his position on the question of negotiations:

> The reestablishment of the Union in all its integrity, is, and must continue to be, the indispensable condition in any settlement. So soon as it is clear or even probable, that our present adversaries are ready for peace upon the basis of the Union, we should exhaust all the resources of statesmanship practiced by civilized nations, and taught by the traditions of the American people, consistent with the honor and interests of the country to secure such peace, reestablish the Union and guarantee for the future the constitutional rights of every state. The union is the one condition of peace—we ask no more.

The general tone of McClellan's remarks to the South were conciliatory, but his demand for reunion was unqualified. He specifically extended to any state willing to return to the Union a "full guarantee of all its constitutional rights." He made no mention of slavery, and the implication was clear that he would accept preservation of the institution as a concession for reunion. In defining the issues between himself and Lincoln, the Democratic nominee stated that the vindictive war measures of the Republican administration should stop and the war be prosecuted for the sole purpose of restoring the Union. McClellan stressed limitations on executive power, protection of individual and state rights, and a return "to a sound financial system." In conclusion, the Democrat pledged to do his "best to restore Union and peace to a suffering people, and to establish and guard their liberties and rights."[20]

Confederate editors watched for the appearance of McClellan's letter in the Northern press and reprinted the document when it became available.[21] Some Confederates interpreted the letter to mean literally what it said while others probed for double or hidden meanings. After reading the statement of acceptance, John Slidell observed, "It effectually destroys the hopes that we had begun to entertain of an early termination of the war and renders the success or failure of his [McClellan's] candidature a matter of comparative indifference."[22] The Richmond *Sentinel* argued that McClellan would run with all the odium of a peace candidate because of the platform but would not garner the votes of peace advocates because his warlike stance would rupture the Democratic party. The editor argued that the challenger had not left sufficient issues between himself and Lincoln to justify opposition and that the contest had been reduced to a mere struggle for the spoils of office between "the ins and the outs."[23] The editor of the Richmond *Examiner* advanced quite a different construction. He suggested that "the affair of Atlanta" had "dictated the tone" of McClellan's letter "and made it less conciliatory and more sanguinary than the platform. . . . When Atlanta is found to be no such valuable acquisition at all, . . . it may easily be made to appear that McClellan's letter meant Peace all the time."[24]

In addition to disappointment, the general's statement aroused a particular interest in the South because peace Democrats at first seemed ready to unhorse the nominee or to bolt the party. Citing excerpts from Northern peace journals and reports that Vallandigham, after reading the letter of acceptance, had refused to take the stump in McClellan's behalf, an editor in Richmond declared, "As we anticipated, the Peace men of the North are repudiating McClellan with as little ceremony as he observed in repudiating the Platform of the convention which nominated him."[25] Confederate newspapers carried the various reports of dissatisfaction among the peace Democrats and gave space to Democratic calls for a new convention. The *Chronicle & Sentinel*, for example, reprinted an article from the New York *News* that castigated McClellan for his stand and declared, "The Democracy must seek a candidate who will stand upon the platform for they cannot consistently support one who is in collision with a convention that tendered him the nomination."[26] When a group of dissatisfied Democrats met in the St. Nicholas Hotel in New York and demanded another convention, reports of their meeting, complete with resolutions, reached the South, and the *Sentinel* published a notice that McClellan was preparing to shift his ground in an effort to mollify the dissident wing of the party.[27]

Despite the early appearances, however, most Democrats finally decided to support the party's nominee. A group of ultra peace men did meet at Cincinnati to consider placing a new candidate in the field, but the meeting came to nothing when the delegates failed to find a nominee.[28] The Democratic vice-presidential choice, George Pendleton, who had been billed as a peace man, went on record in favor of preserving the Union and in support of McClellan's position.[29] Clement Vallandigham grudgingly endorsed the general but insisted that the letter of acceptance was only an expression of the candidate's opinion, whereas the Chicago platform contained "the law and the prophets of the Democratic party."[30] Fernando Wood, a peace leader in New York, spoke out in favor of McClellan in the belief that "he will entertain the view and execute the principles of the great party he will represent, without regard to those he may himself possess."[31] The press of the Confederacy reported developments and speculated on ulterior motives as one after another of the nationally prominent Democrats threw their support to McClellan.[32] An editor in South Carolina claimed to have no favorite hypothesis but described various theories to explain the growing support for McClellan among Democrats. According to the journalist, Northern peace men endorsed McClellan because they wished to share the spoils of office if he won election, because he was a lesser evil than Lincoln, because they would support anybody against the incumbent, because they had secret assurances that McClellan was not as belligerent as his public statements indicated, or because they expected to dominate his policy once he gained the White House.[33]

Hope that the Democrats could dash through the breach in Republican ranks and capture the presidency disappeared as Republicans began to settle their internecine quarrels, and Southerners watched in dismay. Rumors reached the South that Frémont and his running mate, John Cochrane, were preparing to drop from the presidential race, and the Richmond *Examiner* observed, "The Fremont party, however, which was likely to break up the 'Republican' strength, is now likely to be itself dissolved into its elements, and to merge into the general Abolitionist force."[34] The possibility of a new Republican convention faded as such radical leaders as Henry W. Davis took to the stump for Lincoln.[35] The Republicans, spurred by the revival of Northern war fervor and the threat of McClellan's candidacy, engineered Frémont's withdrawal from the contest and closed ranks behind Lincoln.[36] Various Southern newspapers reprinted Frémont's public letter announcing his retirement from the field in favor of the incumbent, and the Charleston *Mercury* commented, "Fremont's withdrawal from the canvass has healed the great breach in Republican ranks."[37]

During the campaign, the exact position of the Democratic party on the issue of peace remained shrouded in ambiguity. While the peace leaders were insisting that McClellan's letter of acceptance was only a statement of personal preference, the war faction of the party stressed

his war record and circulated a statement he had made in
July 1862 calling for preservation of the Union through
humane warfare and denouncing confiscation, emancipation, and arbitrary arrests. While the Democrats dissi-
pated their strength in confused squabbles, the
Republicans labored diligently to brand them as traitors
and to link them with various militant peace groups.
Seeking to soften Lincoln's stand on slavery in "To Whom
It May Concern," Secretary of State William H. Seward
suggested, in an important speech at Auburn, New York,
that Lincoln viewed emancipation as a war measure that
would terminate when the war ended. Most of all, the
Republicans played upon the revival of Northern morale
and stressed the importance of continuity of administration in prosecuting the war to a successful conclusion.
The Democrats counterattacked with charges that Lincoln was fighting a war for abolition with the goal of
elevating Negroes to a plane of social and civil equality
with whites. Although the Democrats did not exploit
Lincoln's vulnerable record on civil liberties as effectively as they might have, they charged that the president was systematically subverting state and individual
rights. Both sides exuded confidence, and the outcome
remained in doubt right down to the day of the election.[38]

Drawing upon press reports, among other sources,
Southerners labored to understand the conundrum of
Northern politics. One of the Confederates studying developments among the Democrats was Jefferson Davis,
who received a variety of information from various
sources. S. J. Anderson, a clerk in the Office of the Mayor
in New York City and apparently a peace Democrat,
wrote a letter to Davis describing McClellan's position.
Warning that the general had great political ambition,
Anderson declared, "I do not doubt his ability to accept
any platform, altho' I may doubt the ability of any

platform to bind him strictly." After describing the overwhelming desire of Northerners to preserve the Union,
the correspondent predicted that McClellan would, if
elected, offer concessions for reunion "which it would be
difficult to reject."[39] The president also received a some-
what contradictory letter from a Southerner who had
been at Chicago, where he became convinced that the
nominee was secretly pledged to accept Confederate independence if necessary to obtain peace.[40]

From the vantage point of Canada, Clement Clay sent
one of the more lengthy and informative letters to the
Confederate government regarding McClellan's political
predilections. The Confederate commissioner reported
that the Federal successes at Mobile and Atlanta had
produced a dramatic change of feeling in the North and
speculated that "those events caused McClellan to ignore
the platform or the construction given it by the unconditional peace men in his letter of acceptance." With regard
to the portent of the general's candidacy, Clay explained
that he had received conflicting ideas from the Democrats with whom he had conferred. One group argued
that the platform obligated the nominee "to cease hostilities and to try negotiations" and that once stopped the
war could never be revived regardless of the outcome of
the talks. Defenders of this logic contended that McClellan was pledged to peace on the basis of separation if
negotiation failed to restore the Union and that if successful in the election, he would be under the influence of
the ultra peace men of the party. These sources asked
that the Confederacy publicly show a preference for
McClellan on the theory that such an endorsement "will
aid him, increase the desire and disposition for peace in
the North, and will foster the revolutionary spirit in the
Northwest in case of Lincoln's election—which may be
effected by force or fraud."

Clay also presented the arguments of contacts who believed that the reelection of Lincoln would be better for the Confederacy. According to this thinking, the election of McClellan would "infuse new life, hopes and vigor into the war party," including Republicans and Democrats, which Lincoln could not do. These informants insisted that McClellan was committed to peace only on the condition of Union and that Vallandigham had been wooed to the support of the general by the promise of a cabinet seat. Adherents of this philosophy also argued that "Lincoln's election will produce revolution in the Northwest—McClellan's will not." After describing the arguments for and against supporting the Democratic candidate, Clay concluded: "Perhaps our true policy is to keep our own counsels, withhold any further declaration of purpose, and let the so-called peace party of the North have no excuse for laying its defeat at our door, if Lincoln should be elected."[41]

After studying the variety of information available from the public press and private sources, President Davis was not enthusiastic about the candidacy of McClellan. Expressions of sympathy for the doctrine of state rights and silence on the question of slavery did not appeal to Davis because the burning issue for him was neither state sovereignty nor Negro bondage but Confederate independence, and McClellan explicitly opposed recognition of the Confederacy. The possibility of a meeting of all the states to discuss peace, which the Chicago convention had proposed, ran contrary to Davis's belief that negotiation of a settlement was the sole responsibility of the national government, and especially the executive branch. He further believed that action for peace on the basis of individual states would be divisive and productive of great harm to the cause of Confederate independence.[42] The platform of the Democrats and the nomination of McClellan meant that neither of the candidates was acceptable. From Davis's point of view, the only benefit still to be derived was the stress that would accompany the campaign in the North.

Davis was most likely among the Confederates who recognized that McClellan as president of the United States would pose a new, and perhaps insurmountable, threat to the survival of the Confederacy. If the Democrats came to power in Washington and adopted conciliatory policies while offering constitutional guarantees for state rights and slavery, some of the Southern states might be induced to leave the Confederacy and return to the Union for the sake of peace. Regarding such an eventuality, a politician in North Carolina said, "You cannot restrain our people [North Carolinians] from accepting liberal terms of compromise, whenever such are offered by the North—as such will be if Lincoln is succeeded by a conservative."[43] In the opinion of a journalist in Georgia, the same situation obtained in his state: "I fear the people of Georgia would, today, go back into the Union, on the platform of McClellan's letter of acceptance. . . . I dread McClellan. We are indebted to the followers of Lincoln for all we are, and I prefer him."[44] Although not referring to the election or the presidential candidates, General E. Kirby Smith warned Jefferson Davis that a Federal policy of conciliation in Arkansas would cause "a formidable party for reconstruction to spring up on the basis of further disaster to our cause."[45] Robert G. H. Kean, head of the Bureau of War at Richmond, wrote in his diary that McClellan as president would be an incubus to the Confederacy "because he would constantly offer peace and reconstruction on the basis of the Constitution, which would rapidly develop a reconstruction party in the South."[46]

In the atmosphere of depressed morale and military crisis, Davis could not follow Clement Clay's advice to "withhold any further declaration of purpose." Public

interest in the election was simply too keen. Davis went
on a brief tour to bolster Southern spirits through public
appearances and speeches and to confer with the leadership of the army in Georgia.[47] In his addresses, the
president touched on several issues related to the Northern presidential contest. With "fierceness and determination" in his countenance, he argued that Confederates
need not despair for their cause and urged them to
greater efforts.[48] Declaring that Sherman's victory was
inconclusive and his military position precarious, Davis
told an audience in Georgia: "Our cause is not lost.
Sherman cannot keep his long lines of communication,
and retreat, sooner or later he must. . . . Our cavalry and
our people will harass and destroy his army as did the
Cossacks of Napoleon, and the Yankee General, like him,
will escape with only a bodyguard."[49] Davis called upon
malingerers and deserters to return to their posts and
told the women of the South: "Use your influence to send
all to the front, and form a public opinion that shall make
the skulker a marked man, and leave no house wherein
he can shelter."[50] Pleading eloquently for support, Davis
told his listeners in Columbia, South Carolina, "I only
ask you to have faith and confidence, and to believe that
every faculty of my head and my heart is devoted to your
cause, and to that I shall, if necessary, give my life."[51]

With enthusiasm and candor, Davis proclaimed his
uncompromising devotion to Confederate independence.
He compared the wishes of Southerners who would be
"willing to rush into a reconstruction of the Union" to the
desire of some of the ancient Israelites "to turn back to
the fleshpots" of Egypt.[52] Davis voiced a resounding rejection of reconstruction on any terms: "We are not engaged
in a Quixotic fight for the rights of man; our struggle is
for inherited rights; and who would surrender them? Let
every paper guarantee possible be given, and who would
submit. . . . There is but one thing to which we can

accede—separate State independence." To those Southerners who would accept reunion with the peculiar institution preserved, he declared: "Some there are who speak
of reconstruction with slavery maintained; but are there
any who would thus measure rights by property? God
forbid."[53] With these comments, Davis publicly rejected
the Democratic offer of concessions, including preservation of slavery, as a quid pro quo for Southern acceptance
of reunion.

The Confederate president was careful to assert his
willingness to negotiate, but he opposed the scheme of
negotiation by states and rejected negotiation on any
basis other than recognition of Confederate independence by the United States government. In Augusta, Georgia, he said: "Some have spoken of the executive, and
declared that executive hardness and pride of opinion
was opposed to any negotiations. Those who think so
must imagine me more or less than man."[54] In Columbia,
he sketched some of the previous peace diplomacy involving the Confederate commissioners who visited Washington before Sumter and Alexander Stephens's
unsuccessful effort to cross Union lines in 1863. Davis
then insisted that he had employed "every possible
means of settlement honorable to ourselves, based on a
recognition of our independence."[55] Denouncing the plan
for negotiation by states as traitorous and unconstitutional, he contended that even if such diplomacy were
possible, the Northern government would listen to no
other terms than emancipation and reconstruction.[56]
Davis had responded to the Democratic proposals for
negotiation by rejecting a convention of the states and
demanding recognition of the Confederacy as a precondition to peace talks.

The president proclaimed his conviction that negotiation of a settlement resting on Confederate independence
could come only after the North was convinced that

conquest of the South was impossible. In South Carolina
he said: "Does any one believe that Yankees are to be
conciliated by terms of concessions? Does any man imagine that we can conquer the Yankees by retreating before
them, or do you not all know that the only way to make
spaniels civil is to whip them?" Davis encouraged Southerners to win "those great victories, which will teach the
world that we can defend our rights, and the Yankee
nation that it is death to invade them."[57] The president
unflinchingly told the residents of Augusta, "We are
fighting for existence; and by fighting alone can
independence be gained."[58] With apparent reference to
the Federal election, which was then barely a month
away, Davis said:

> I believe it is in the power of the men of the Confederacy
> to plant our banners on the banks of the Ohio, where we
> shall say to the Yankee, "be quiet, or we shall teach you
> another lesson." Within the next thirty days much is to be
> done, for upon our success much depends. Within the next
> thirty days, therefore, let all who are absentees, or who
> ought to be in the army, go promptly to their ranks. Let
> fresh victories crown our arms, and the peace party, if
> there be such at the North, can elect its candidate. But
> whether a peace candidate is elected or not, Yankee
> instinct will teach him that it is better to end the war and
> leave us to the enjoyment of our own rights.[59]

The president was correct in his contention that now only
significant Southern military success could influence
Northern sentiment, but the magnitude of the required
victory was beyond the moral and material capacity of
the Confederacy.

The Confederate president was well aware that some of
his countrymen did not agree with his approach to the
Northern election. Anticipating criticism, Davis declared

at Montgomery, Alabama: "If there be those who hoped to outwit the Yankees, and by smooth words and fair speeches, by the appearance of a willingness to treat or to listen to reunion, hope to elect any candidate in the North, they deceive themselves. Victory in the field is the surest element of strength to a peace party. Let us win battles and we shall have overtures soon enough."[60]

The president's speeches, especially those at Macon, Augusta, Montgomery, and Columbia, were widely published in the Confederacy and elicited a varying response from Southerners. Some observers, such as H. L. Flash, who was a newspaperman in Georgia, believed that the addresses "tended to cheer the despondent and strengthen the weak."[61] After weighing the alternatives, Herschel V. Johnson concluded that the president's "defiant tone" with regard to the Northern election was probably the best policy.[62] Davis's opponents and some of his friends found much to criticize, however, in the speech delivered at Macon.

Without mentioning names, but with apparent reference to either Governor Joseph E. Brown or General Joseph E. Johnston, Davis had commented: "It has been said that I abandoned Georgia to her fate. . . . The man who uttered this was a scoundrel." During the same address, the Confederate leader made revealing remarks about the condition of the Southern army: "Two-thirds of our men are absent—some sick, some wounded, but most of them absent without leave." The president also admitted in this public assembly that the South did not have "many men between 18 and 45 left."[63] Given the president's objective of firing Confederate morale and jeering at ambiguous Northern proposals for negotiation, these remarks were indeed unfortunate. The speech provoked accusations that Davis had made an intemperate political attack and had revealed too much information to the

enemy about the manpower and morale of the Confederate army.[64] A Georgian, embittered by the speech, wrote
to Davis and suggested that his comments were the
product of "great fatigue and perhaps a little too much
wine."[65] In fact, General Sherman did find the address at
Macon particularly interesting, and the speech became a
topic for editorials in Republican newspapers.[66]

The president's tardy attempt to mold public opinion
regarding the election largely failed. The effort came too
late, after many opinions had become fixed. In the eyes of
many Southerners, his emphasis on military operations
to influence the election had already proved a failure. His
speeches neither quelled the opposition nor persuaded
Confederates to ignore the election and to concentrate on
the fighting. The internal challenge posed by the election
was out of hand.

Decidedly unwilling to follow presidential leadership
in the matter, some of the president's strongest opponents thought that the South should make an official and
public statement endorsing the plan for a convention of
the states as described in the Democratic platform. Pro-
ponents of this view believed that such a gathering was
entirely consistent with Southern war aims and that a
favorable response from the Confederacy to the proposal
of the Chicago convention would immeasurably
strengthen the hand of the peace Democrats, who could
point to the Southern endorsement as proof that their
plan would end the carnage of the battlefield and restore
peace. Supporters of this plan were generally of dubious
loyalty to the cause of Southern independence. Various
advocates of a convention prepared unofficial acknowl-
edgments of the Democratic proposal and put pressure on
Davis to release a formal and positive response.

Sentiment in favor of the gathering of the states was
not restricted to any single region of the Confederacy,

and a broad debate ensued regarding the propriety of the proposed convention. Newspapers such as the *Examiner, Sentinel,* and *Mercury,* which had favored vigorous war and adamantly demanded Confederate independence, aligned in opposition to the meeting while journals such as the *Chronicle & Sentinel,* North Carolina *Standard,* and Raleigh *Progress,* which supported negotiations and compromise, favored the assembly.[67] In a public letter, Representative Henry S. Foote of Tennessee declared that the Confederacy should respond favorably to the peaceful overtures of the Democratic party.[68] An editor in North Carolina contended that the Confederate Congress should have met in special session to endorse the proposal of the Chicago convention.[69] The legislature of Alabama considered a resolution declaring that if the Democratic party were successful in the coming elections, "We are willing and ready to open negotiations for peace on the basis indicated in the platform adopted by said [Democratic] convention—our sister States of the Confederacy being willing thereto."[70] The calls for a convention of the states that attracted the most attention, however, came from William W. Boyce and Alexander H. Stephens.

Boyce was a member of the congressional delegation from South Carolina and had been a leader of peace forces in his state since 1863.[71] He was thoroughly disenchanted with the leadership and policies of the Davis administration, and he wrote in a personal letter: "I don't see how we can come out without ruin if the matter is left entirely to Davis and Lincoln. I have always thought Davis should have brought every point of diplomacy into play to build up the opposition party North. Surely any change is for the better. . . . If the war goes on we are ruined."[72] The South Carolinian believed that the Confederacy should endorse the Democratic plan for a con-

vention of the states, and he would have introduced such
a proposal into the Congress at Richmond had it been in
session. Rather than remain silent, however, the congressman drafted a public letter to Jefferson Davis.

The letter Boyce released to the press rang with a
rhetoric and logic that was similar to the language and
philosophy of the Northern Copperheads. In his lengthy
statement, he presented a carefully constructed argument. War with a stronger neighbor, contended Boyce,
always forces a republic to abandon its republican institutions and adopt the forms of a central despotism because the latter is the best government system for
mobilizing a nation's resources in time of war. To prove
this contention, he cited various examples from European history and the contemporary condition of the Confederacy. Insisting that the exigencies of war had forced
the once republican South to accept a military dictator-
ship, he cited conscription, direct taxes, inflation caused
by paper currency, seizure of railroads by the national
government, strict regulation of exports and imports,
suspension of the writ of habeas corpus, and the system of
passports to control travel in and out of the country.
Boyce argued further that the advent of peace would not
bring an end to the structure of despotism unless the
peace rested on genuine harmony between the former
belligerents. An armed peace, said the congressman,
would demand constant vigilance and preparedness for
war that would require the continuance of military despotism. Boyce's suppositions and allegations against the
Confederate government were only a Southern version of
the Copperhead declarations and accusations aimed at
the Lincoln administration.

Boyce argued that the peace and harmony necessary
for the preservation of republican institutions could
never come as long as Lincoln occupied the White House.

He told the Confederate president:

> You and Mr. Lincoln can never make peace. You may
> traverse indefinitely the same bloody circles you have
> been moving in for the last four years, but you will never
> approach any nearer than you now are. Your only hope of
> peace is in the ascendancy of the conservative party
> North. Fortify that party if you can by victories, but do
> not neglect diplomacy. . . . I think our only hope of a
> satisfactory peace, one consistent with the preservation of
> free institutions, is in the supremacy of this party at some
> time or other. Our policy, therefore, is to give this party
> all the encouragement possible, by declaring your wil-
> lingness to an armistice, and a convocation of all the
> States in their sovereign capacity to enter upon the sub-
> ject of peace.

The congressman recognized that legal obstacles blocked
the path to a convention of the states, but he called for an
amendment to the Confederate Constitution that would
make such a meeting possible. Boyce concluded: "A Congress of the States in their sovereign capacity is the
highest acknowledgment of the principle of State Rights.
This imposing assemblage is, in my opinion, the best,
while it is the most august tribunal to which the great
question of peace could possibly be referred."[73]
If Boyce hoped that the North would find his remarks
reflective of the prevailing sentiment among his constituents or if he expected that his letter would serve as a
rallying point for Confederates to force Davis to endorse
the plan for a convention of the states, Boyce suffered a
rude shock indeed. Shortly after the letter became available to the public, a group of his constituents met on the
Court House Square in Columbia, South Carolina, to
express their views on his position. Several persons addressed the gathering, including Boyce himself, but in
the end the meeting ratified resolutions that denounced

the letter as "full of gloomy despondency" and tending "to instill feelings of submission and suggest the wish for reconstruction." The meeting condemned the course advocated by the letter and called for Boyce's resignation from his congressional seat.[74]

Confederate newspapers reprinted the controversial letter and the resolutions of condemnation, and editors commented on the situation.[75] The journalists who supported the president or at least favored continued commitment to war for Southern independence attacked the ideas in Boyce's statement as impractical at best or traitorous at worst.[76] The Charleston *Mercury* reasoned that the North would be satisfied only with a peace that included restoration of the Union, and, because the congressman called for an end to the war on terms acceptable to the North, "the conclusion is irresistible that Mr. Boyce is in favor of a reconstruction of the Union."[77] The congressman was not, however, without his defenders who sympathized with his comments regarding the growth of despotism in the South, pointed out that he had not specifically called for reconstruction, and insisted that his ideas for promoting the prospects of the Northern Democracy were both honorable and correct.[78] Constituents of Boyce serving in a unit of South Carolina cavalry with the Army of Northern Virginia adopted a resolution declaring, "We commend the policy and endorse the principles he has so ably elucidated."[79] Contending that "Boyce uttered no strange or injurious doctrine," the Augusta *Chronicle & Sentinel* leaped to the front ranks of his defenders and denounced the proceedings of the meeting at Columbia as "inflammatory and impudent."[80]

Among those who sympathized with Boyce and who were also enraptured by the rhetoric of state rights in the Chicago platform was Alexander Stephens.[81] Despite the reverse at Atlanta and McClellan's letter of acceptance, the vice-president still entertained hopes that the Northern election would rebound to the benefit of the South. He remained steadfast in his conviction that the Confederacy should openly endorse the peace efforts of the Democratic party, and he was disappointed by the defiant speeches of Davis during his tour.[82] The Georgian was not surprised, however, because he had already concluded that the policy of the Davis administration "seems to be to have Lincoln re-elected or at least to be indifferent as to the result of the election either way."[83]

The idea of a convention of the states fascinated Stephens. He viewed such an assembly as the ultimate acknowledgment of state sovereignty, and he fervently believed that this doctrine was the formula for peace. The gathering of the states was but a logical extension of the philosophy explicated in the message of Governor Brown and the peace resolution adopted by the General Assembly in the special session of March 1864, and Stephens had heartily supported both declarations.

Stephens felt that a convention, regardless of its outcome, would accrue to the benefit of the South. He expected that in a meeting of the states Southerners might be able to unite with Northern supporters of McClellan to pass resolutions denying the national government power to coerce a sovereign state and reaffirming the principles of the Virginia and Kentucky Resolutions. Such action, in Stephens's view, would virtually end the war and recognize Southern independence. On the other hand, Stephens recognized that if the convention failed to accomplish anything positive and the Southern states rejected concessions, including preservation of slavery, for reunion, McClellan might well resort to force, but Stephens believed that an abortive convention would badly divide the North and strip the Federal cause of its moral fervor. Abolitionists would not, he hoped, support a war simply to reconstitute the Union as it was, and genuine peace advocates might join with them to palsy the Northern war effort. In addition, if the North disavowed emancipation as a war aim, the moral barriers to foreign recognition of the Confederacy would drop, believed Stephens, and England might come to the aid of the South.[84]

Anticipating that the convention of states would be a first step toward peace but recognizing that a Federal proposal for a meeting of the states would not come unless McClellan won the election, Stephens was prepared to endorse the plan for a convention in the hope that acknowledgment and support from the Confederacy would enhance the strength of the peace Democrats. He was aware, of course, that the Confederate Constitution bestowed sole authority to conclude peace on the national government, but he did not believe that the cumbersome and arduous task of amending the Constitution was required before the states could meet.[85] He did recognize, however, that if an individual state opened negotiations without the consent of the Confederate government, the state would first have to reassume its sovereign powers— that is, secede. The vice-president believed that a state could take such action as "a perfect right" and "commit no breach of faith in doing so either expressed or implied."[86]

The vice-president decided to announce his position through a public response "to numerous letters almost daily received" that commented on the subjects of peace and the Northern election.[87] Stephens was particularly struck by a letter from Isaac Scott, J. R. Ross, and I. H. R. Washington of Macon, Georgia, that declared: "Already a powerful peace party has been organized at the North, and we hold it to be the duty of all good and patriotic men at the South to take such steps as will encourage them and convince them that we are not unwilling to adjust the differences and difficulties between the two sections upon honorable terms." The correspondents importuned Stephens to inaugurate a "peace movement at the South" and assured him that the weary and suffering people of Georgia would follow his lead.[88] He prepared an open letter in reply with the objective of expressing his support for the Democratic platform, particularly a convention of the states, and in the belief that such an expression "might aid the advocates of McClellan if given in time to bear upon the approaching election."[89] Stephens determined to publicize his convictions even though he recognized that his ideas ran contrary to the position of the president.[90]

Stephens gave his letter to the press, and various Confederate newspapers printed the document.[91] Omitting any reference to Confederate independence, he expressed an "ardent desire" to end the "unnatural and merciless war upon honorable and just terms. . . . The easy and perfect solution to all our present troubles. . . . is nothing more than the simple recognition of the . . . ultimate absolute sovereignty of the States. . . . It is the only keynote to peace—permanent lasting peace—consistent with the security of public liberty." Echoing the logic of Northern Copperheads, he labeled the attempt to maintain the Union by force as "preposterous" and warned that subjugation of the South would necessarily entail the overthrow of constitutional liberty in the North. Stephens praised the sentiments of the peace resolution adopted by the Georgia legislature the previous spring and heralded that resolution as the trail blazer down the true path to peace for the weary people of both sections.

The writer launched into a eulogy celebrating the platform of the Chicago convention as "a ray of light" in an otherwise dark and foreboding night. Praising the

plan for a cessation of hostilities and a convocation of the
states, Stephens said: "To such a convention of the States
I should have no objection as a peaceful conference and
interchange of views between equal and sovereign
Powers—just as the convention of 1787 was called and
assembled." He suggested that the duly constituted authorities at Richmond and Washington could give the
meeting legal standing by according it their sanction.
Stephens added, however, a significant qualification to
his endorsement: "I should be opposed to leaving the
questions at issue to the absolute decision of such a body.
Delegates might be clothed with powers to consult and
agree if they could upon some plan of adjustment to be
submitted for subsequent ratification by the sovereign
States whom it affected, before it should be obligatory or
binding, and then binding only on such as should so
ratify." He ended his letter by urging Southerners to
remain firm in their determination to prosecute a defensive war to preserve their rights.[92]

As Alexander Stephens had anticipated, his declaration provoked a varied response in the Confederacy.
Among his critics was the editor of the Richmond *Examiner,* who argued that the vice-president misunderstood
the peace Democracy. The Chicago platform, for all its
rhetoric, argued the *Examiner,* was not truly committed
to the dogma of state rights because it failed to acknowledge the validity of the right to secession.[93] Following a
different line of attack, the Charleston *Mercury* charged
that Stephens's letter "clearly means a reconstruction of
our Union with the Yankee States, or it means nothing."[94] The *Dispatch* denounced the sentiments expressed
by the vice-president and endorsed Davis's position.[95]

Alexander Stephens had defenders who responded to
his critics. The vice-president received personal letters
from friends who expressed support for his position and

regret for the attacks upon him by opponents.[96] Answering the charge that Stephens's letter was a veiled call for reconstruction, an editor in Georgia insisted that Stephens favored an armistice and convention of the states "for no other purpose than that of bringing the war to a speedy and honorable close" on terms that guarantee "that right of self-government which Mr. Davis says is the only object of the war on our part."[97] The letter also brought laudatory remarks from Southern reconstructionists who believed that Stephens was, in fact, advocating a restoration of the old Union.[98]

Senator Herschel V. Johnson was another Southern politician who had been studying the Democratic position and pondering the appropriate course for the Confederacy. Although recognizing that a convention of the states was a "mode of negotiation never contemplated by the framers of the Constitution," the senator saw no reason to quarrel over constitutional niceties if such a convention would lead to "an honorable & just peace." Although anxious to end the fighting, he did not believe that the Chicago platform was acceptable to the Confederacy because it, in his interpretation, offered negotiation not simply for peace "but peace *on the basis of Union.*" To accept the Democratic proposal, said Johnson, "is to surrender the idea of independence and to accept negotiation only as to the terms of return to the old Union." Although willing to enter negotiations without prior recognition of the Confederacy, the senator believed that the South should not commence peace talks if the other side laid down preconditions.[99] Believing, however, that a change of administration at Washington was in the best interest of the Confederacy, the senator was ready to promote the political defeat of Lincoln.

Johnson received a letter from Isaac Scott and his colleagues that was identical to the one they had sent to

Stephens, and Johnson's reply, which was also published in the Confederate press, was directed as much to the North as to his correspondents.[100] He argued that peace overtures from the South were futile because of the belligerent and uncompromising attitude of the existing Federal administration and because such initiatives would be interpreted in the North as an indication of Confederate weakness. In a lengthy discussion of the Southern position, Johnson contended that the South was fighting for the ideals of state rights and individual liberty that were the cornerstones of the original Constitution. He insisted that the South and the "thousands of Constitutional men at the North" really stood for the same principles and warned that subjugation of the South would also bring despotism in the rival section. "The North can have peace at any moment," said Johnson. "All that they need to do is to let us alone—cease to fight us; or if they prefer, agree to negotiate on terms honorable to both parties."

The Confederate senator called upon the people of the North to "change their ruler, . . . repudiate the avowed policies of subjugation, . . . return to a practical recognition of the true principles which underlie the whole structure of American Government . . . [and] the door will soon be opened for an honorable and lasting peace. . . . For although the Chicago platform falls below the great occasion, and the nominee still lower, yet the triumph of the Democratic party of the North will certainly secure a temporary suspension of hostilities and an effort to make peace by an appeal to reason." He pledged that if the Federal government passed into new hands and disavowed the program of subjugation, he would urge the Confederate government either to accept or to propose negotiations.[101] Compared to the statements of William W. Boyce and Alexander Stephens, the comments of Herschel Johnson were less equivocal on the matter of peace terms and more restrained in endorsing the Democrats.

A Southern politician who stood in the company of Jefferson Davis on the opposite end of the spectrum from Stephens and Boyce was Thomas J. Semmes, Confederate States senator from Louisiana. In a speech at Mobile, Alabama, the senator insisted that the South still possessed the means to secure its independence, and he vigorously condemned the idea of reconstruction. He declared that restoration of the Union would be a breach of faith with the Confederate dead and warned that a return to the Union with guarantees for state and civil rights was impossible. "We can never bury the animosities," said Semmes, "that the course of the Northern States and this war have produced."

Careful to express respect for persons of differing opinions and to assert a great desire for peace, Senator Semmes declared: "This idea of the Convention of the States is filled with danger. It is impracticable in itself, and is nothing but an apple of discord thrown among us to divide us." He pointed out that neither the states nor the authorities at Richmond could constitutionally accept an invitation for a gathering of the states because the Constitution lodged diplomatic authority with the central government while explicitly forbidding the states to make treaties or alliances with foreign powers. As further evidence of the impracticality of the plan, Semmes noted that the Federal Constitution imposed similar restrictions on the United States.

Turning to the divisive nature of a convention, the senator contended that "any State desiring to go into the Convention cannot do so and remain a member of the

Confederacy. It can do so only by seceding from the Confederacy, and assuming the attitude of a sovereign and independent power." He argued that even if the constitutional impediments were overcome, the very nature of the consultations would be disruptive to the South. Semmes stressed his conviction that the Democratic proposal rested on the precondition that the purpose of the meeting was to negotiate terms of reunion with resumption of the war as the alternative. If even one or two of the Southern states found the terms of reunion acceptable, "Such an event would necessarily produce a dissolution of the [Confederate] government." He argued that the South could negotiate effectively through agents of the national government and called for continued war to convince the North that subjugation of the South was impossible. Semmes urged Southerners to "stand by the Government that has been formed, and rely [on the principle] that peace can only be obtained by heavy blows from armed forces."[102]

Even as prominent Confederates ignored and defied the president's plea for unity and concentration on military activity, Confederates of lesser status were not content. Some took matters into their own hands. Although Southern editors probably often had a Northern audience in mind when they composed their editorials, they sometimes explicitly addressed their remarks to the North. The *Examiner,* for example, once began an editorial with a thinly veiled request that its comments be reproduced in the Northern press.[103] On another occasion the editor took issue with Northern newspapers that had been insisting that Southern interest in the election was proof that the South still considered itself part of the Union.[104] Some Confederates apparently determined to use fraudulent ballots or force in the election. A panicky provost marshal in Indiana wrote to a superior officer: "A very large number of men are coming to this State from Kentucky and further South. . . . and every circumstance tends to the conclusion that many of them come here upon invitation and for the purpose of voting the Democratic ticket."[105] A Union officer in Kentucky notified Joseph Holt, the judge-advocate general at Washington, that Confederate cavalry was planning to scatter through the state to obstruct the election and that Confederate guerrillas in some districts were actively interfering with the campaign travels of Union party workers.[106]

Northern apprehensions intensified when General Sterling Price led a Southern army into Missouri from Arkansas on September 19, 1864. Although Price hoped that the invasion would influence the election, his orders made no reference to Northern politics but instructed him to exploit the reported dissatisfaction and disaffection among Missourians by holding the state, if possible, and by attracting badly needed recruits for the Confederate army.[107] Nevertheless, General William S. Rosecrans, in St. Louis, concluded that Price's objective was to control the election in Missouri and to prevent balloting in Kansas.[108] Northern newspapers declared that the primary purpose of the invasion was political.[109] Through press reports, Southerners learned of the consternation the invaders aroused among Missourians loyal to the Federal cause.[110] The path of the invaders took them as far to the northeast as the outskirts of St. Louis and to the northwest as far as Independence before they retreated southward into Arkansas.[111]

During the final weeks of the presidential campaign, Southerners made assessments of the candidates and the probable consequences of the election. A recurrent theme in Confederate discussions of Lincoln was the assertion that he was resorting to all manner of outrageous fraud, graft, corruption, violence, suppression, bribery, deception, and the like to secure his reelection.[112] Another commonly repeated motif was the idea that, as the *Sentinel* said, "The Presidential contest in the United States will be decided by the result of military operations in the Confederate States."[113] Confederate observers called for special vigilance at the front, and some tried to gauge the ebb and flow of Republican confidence by the intensity of Federal military activity.[114] Predictions were frequently voiced that Lincoln would win the election, and the conviction remained firm that his political victory would mean a continuation of the war. Robert H. Smith, a former member of the Confederate Congress from Alabama, wrote to his wife, "If Lincoln shall be re-elected as I think from present appearances he will be the United States will attempt our subjugation with renewed energy and I fear the worst results."[115]

The recognition that Lincoln's reelection would herald renewed Northern commitment to the war caused many, if not most, Confederates to pray for the election of McClellan even though the Democratic position was equivocal. In defining the difference between the Democrats and the Republicans, the *Examiner* said: "Both parties profess to aim at the common object of preserving the Union in its original territorial limits; but the Lincoln party insists on affecting this by abolition; subjugation; and confiscation; while their opponents propose to employ military coercion only after the failure of peaceful and conciliatory measures. One faction offers the sword alone; the other holds out the olive branch and the sword."[116] The possibility of peace through Democratic political success was enough to evoke desperate hope for McClellan's election.

A deserter from a Confederate unit at Camp Isle Hope to the southeast of Savannah, Georgia, told Federal authorities: "The whole dependence of the South is upon the election, in the success of a man of peace principles, it being openly avowed in the streets of Savannah that if Lincoln is reelected they will of necessity at once have to yield, and they are only awaiting the election in the North."[117] Soldiers in the Western armies of the Confederacy were declaring in personal letters that they would lay down their arms if Lincoln won the election rather than face four more years of war.[118] A newspaper correspondent in Richmond reported, "Men in this vicinity still cling to McClellan, and rest their hopes of peace in the defeat of Lincoln."[119] In a letter to the *Sentinel,* "Gray Jacket" confided that he did "not know whether the McClellan ticket would help us any, if elected, yet I do not think it could be *harder* on us than the present 'regime,' and, therefore, I am in favor of it *on suspicion.*"[120] In a speech at Macon, Georgia, Senator Benjamin Hill declared, "If Lincoln is defeated and McClellan is elected in the coming election, we may have peace."[121] Arguing that McClellan "and his party are better men, and less inimical to the south, than Lincoln and his friends," George Fitzhugh, the well-known apologist for slavery, went on record in favor of the Democrats.[122] In addition to evaluating McClellan, Confederates estimated his chances, and some predicted his election.[123]

The sentiment regarding McClellan was mixed, however, with deep misgivings. As mentioned earlier, some Confederates were privately saying that if the Democrats won the White House and offered concessions to end the war and restore the Union, a vibrant reconstruction party would arise in the South and the Confederacy would disintegrate. Such comments also appeared on occasion in the public press. The *Examiner,* for example, declared: "Moreover, with a view to our ultimate and permanent separation from the Yankee people,

McClellan might be more perilous to us than Lincoln. If
the former were President, there might be some appearance again of 'Union men' amongst us. With Lincoln
there will be no danger. Every Southern man will fight
that base foe, while a brigade, a regiment, a company,
can hold together."[124] When presented in major journals
of the Confederacy, such comments were subject to a
variety of interpretations. Sometimes Confederate editors may have intended an endorsement of McClellan by
warning the North that Lincoln would inspire continued
Southern resistance whereas his opponent would elicit
conciliation and possible reunion from the South. Editors
were, most likely, also endeavoring to prepare Southerners for the possibility of McClellan's defeat by arguing
that Lincoln's reelection would probably be fortunate for
the Confederacy. When taken together with private expressions of similar sentiments, however, these public
statements of preference for Lincoln were representative
of a group of dedicated Confederates who honestly feared
the election of McClellan and sincerely favored the re-
election of Lincoln.

Southerners continued to nurture the hope that the
fiery campaign would ignite the tinder of resentment
against Lincoln and explode in a general conflagration at
the North. Reports reached the South that Federal soldiers had disrupted some gatherings of McClellan's supporters, and the *Sentinel* commented, "It is but the
shadowing of the storm, which the political canvass now
in progress at the North will witness more than once."[125]
An editor in North Carolina found an appealing quotation to the same effect from a Northern newspaper: "The
manner in which the rival claims of Mr. Lincoln and Gen.
McClellan are being pressed is a disgrace to the enlight-
enment of our country and a source of serious peril to the
public peace."[126] Some Confederates maintained that the

reelection of Lincoln would trigger the long-awaited rebellion in the Northwest because that section would be
unwilling to endure another four years of Republican
rule. A Confederate who had just returned from Memphis, Tennessee, where he talked with Northern supporters of McClellan, declared, "The election of Mr.
Lincoln would climax the revolutionary spirit and precipitate civil war in the border and Northwestern
States."[127] An editor in Richmond speculated on the possibility that an electoral dispute occasioned by Lincoln's
claim of victory on the basis of electoral votes from states
reconstructed under his direction might drive McClellan's supporters into armed resistance against the administration.[128]

In Canada, the Confederate agents continued their
activities to exploit the election. Clement Clay had been
preparing editorials for publication in support of McClellan when the general's letter of acceptance appeared in
the public press. With "mingled feelings of surprise,
indignation and regret," Clay read McClellan's statement and concluded that his candidacy offered no hope
for the South.[129] Laying aside the editorials, Clay penned
an impassioned letter pleading with George Pendleton to
refuse to run with McClellan because he had repudiated
the Chicago platform.[130] Clay and his colleagues watched
in despair as Northern morale revived and the prospect
of a Republican victory improved.[131]

Although the plans for an uprising at Chicago during
the Democratic convention had come to nothing, the
Confederate agents still clung to the belief that a potential for revolutionary violence existed among dissident
groups in the North. In a letter to the Confederate
secretary of state, Clay said: "All that a large portion of
the Northern people, especially in the Northwest, want
to resist the oppressions of the despotism at Washington

is a leader. They are ripe for resistance, and it may come soon after the Presidential election."[132] The Southern conspirators concocted elaborate plans for an insurrection to occur at certain strategic places in the North on election day. Using escaped Confederate prisoners of war as a core around which the Sons of Liberty would supposedly collect, the agents prepared for uprisings at Chicago and New York with diversionary activity in Boston and Cincinnati. The plan called for destruction and violence and the forcible release of Confederate soldiers held prisoner in camps near New York and Chicago. While the agents perfected their scheme, reports and rumors of organized violence scheduled for the day of the election reached highly placed Federal officials and filtered into the newspapers.[133]

On the day before the Federal balloting was to occur, President Davis responded to the furor in the South by presenting a defense of his position on the election in a message to Congress. Perhaps because he hoped to respond decisively to his critics and to rally his countrymen, he was particularly candid about his assessment of Northern politics. After reiterating his desire for negotiation of an acceptable peace, Davis restated his conviction that "the authorities who control the Government of our enemies" would offer peace only "on terms of our unconditional submission and degradation." He acknowledged "that individuals and parties in the United States have indicated a desire to substitute reason for force," but they, insisted Davis, were a distinct minority. Commenting on their motivation, he said, "Many are actuated by principle [devotion to state rights] and by disapproval and abhorrence of the iniquitous warfare that their Government is waging, while others are moved by the conviction that it is no longer to the interest of the United States to continue a struggle in which success is unattainable." He believed that the latter sentiment was particularly malleable to the Southern cause, but he rejected the notion that it could and should be intensified through diplomatic maneuvering from Richmond. The president flatly stated that war weariness and a readiness for peace "will be best and most certainly evoked . . . in the minds of a majority of the Northern people . . . by the demonstration on our part of ability and unshaken determination to defend our rights, and to hold no earthly price too dear for their purchase." The president urged that Confederates "resolutely continue to devote our united and unimpaired energies to the defense of our homes, our lives, and our liberties."[134]

The president had not altered his position. He was standing firm in his commitment to military action rather than a diplomatic offensive in the enemy section. His statement was essentially a defense of his past action. Although he had provided additional explanation of his reasoning, his remarks neither convinced nor mollified his political enemies, and the military effort he asked of his countrymen was now beyond their capacity. Davis may have hoped that his statement defending his position and actions would terminate the enervating controversy over electoral tactics, but such was not the case. One of the bitterest assaults on his approach to the election would come after Northerners had cast their ballots.

As Northerners went to the polls on November 8, 1864, Southerners anxiously awaited the outcome. The fall of Atlanta and McClellan's letter of acceptance had been serious blows to their hopes. While the agents continued their work in the North, Davis made belated efforts to mold public opinion on the home front. He called upon Southerners to disregard the election and to concentrate on fighting as the only sure means of securing Confederate nationhood. In a mood of despondency and desperation, Confederates rejected presidential leadership. Some called for endorsement of the Democrats, and public and private speculation regarding the election continued. Confederate preferences were largely for McClellan, but some feared that his election would present a dire challenge to the existence of the Confederacy. In any case, the uncertainty was almost concluded. As one Southerner put it, "This war will not be ended in Nov. but we may I think then safely take an observation & see where we stand."[135]

CHAPTER 7

Reelection of Lincoln and Defeat of the Confederacy:

"I . . . ask to what acts of mine you refer."

The protracted and turbulent presidential campaign came to an end on November 8, 1864, when voters finally went to the polling places and cast their votes. Davis's agents in Canada had hoped that this would be a day of violence and disruption, but the electorate went about its civic duty generally unmolested. When the returns reached the South, Confederates learned that Northerners had reelected Lincoln and had, thereby, reconfirmed their commitment to the war. The Confederacy would not achieve independence through Northern default. Southern despair deepened, and controversy related to the election continued while pressure increased for diplomatic feelers toward peace from the Confederacy. In desperation, Davis privately responded to public attacks on his conduct with respect to the election and adopted radical measures to revive the prospects of victory through military operations or foreign help, but the doom of the Confederacy was near.

During the days before the election, groups of Confederate soldiers slipped into the United States from Canada and traveled to Chicago and New York City with the intention of fomenting the violence Thompson and his colleagues had planned. Federal officials learned of the scheme and took countermeasures. Apprised of the plot, Colonel Benjamin Sweet, commandant of Camp Douglas near Chicago where some eight thousand Confederate prisoners of war were incarcerated, summoned reinforcements and engaged spies of his own who located the

conspirators and gained precise details of their plans.
Provided with this information, the wary colonel authorized raids that netted most of the ringleaders in Chicago,
and troops patrolled the streets of the city freely arrest-
ing suspicious persons until the day following the election. One who eluded capture was Captain Thomas
Hines, who finally made his way back to Richmond. The
Confederates in New York had reached their destination
well before the day of the election and completed the
detailed planning of their proposed operation with several prominent New Yorkers who had previously agreed
to cooperate. When the Federal government sent General
Benjamin Butler to the city with ten thousand soldiers
for the announced purpose of guarding against violence
during the election, however, the conspirators saw no
alternative but quietly to abandon their plans.[1] Reports
of the arrests in Chicago and the arrival of Butler in New
York appeared in Southern newspapers, but the Southern people did not generally know the full import of these
events.[2]

After the Northerners cast their ballots, the results of
the election were not known in the South for several
days. During the interim, Confederates studied the frag-
mentary returns and made prognostications of the outcome. Predictions that Lincoln would win were common
as electoral speculation became a widespread topic of
conversation in the Confederacy.[3] One day during the
waiting period, an interruption occurred in the routine
exchange of newspapers between the lines at Richmond,
and the delay "gave rise to an infinity of conjectures."[4]
Perhaps, thought some Confederates, the Federal government was suppressing news of Lincoln's defeat or
reports of the long-awaited riots and bloodshed in the
Northwest.[5] Such wishful thinking came to an end when
the normal exchange procedure resumed on the following

day, and Confederates learned that the election had passed without violence and that Lincoln had won re-election.

The Republican victory came as no surprise in the Confederacy because Southerners had understood that, since the reversal at Atlanta, Lincoln's prospects had improved markedly. The news was, nevertheless, disheartening. The Democrats had made a good showing, but Lincoln had a clear mandate to continue his policies. Of the total popular vote cast, the president received 2,206,938 to McClellan's 1,803,787, and Lincoln captured 212 electoral votes while the challenger garnered only 21. In addition, Lincoln's popular total for 1864 was an increase of slightly more than one-third million over the figure for 1860. As Confederates recognized, the Northern majority had voted to continue the war. The *Examiner* announced, "Conquest and subjugation were formally decreed against the South, after a second hearing, on the eighth day of November."[6] An observer of public affairs in Richmond privately wrote: "Lincoln has been re-elected President of the United States by overwhelming majorities. There is no use of disguising the fact that our subjugation is popular at the North."[7]

The decision of the Northern electorate was yet another blow to the already staggering morale of the Confederacy. Robert G. H. Kean confided to his diary: "The Yankee election was evidently a damper on the spirits of many of our people, and is said to have depressed the army a good deal. Lincoln's triumph was more complete than most of us expected. Most judicious persons believed that he would be reelected but nearly all, while thinking that his reelection would be better for us than McClellan's hoped that it would be closely contested, possibly attended with violence."[8] The outcome of the election aggravated the problem of desertion in the Confederate

army as weary soldiers left their posts rather than con-
front the demoralizing prospect of prolonged war. When
twenty Confederate deserters arrived within Federal
lines, the provost marshal general for the Army of the
Potomac said of the men, "They . . . assign as the principal reason for coming over the fact of Mr. Lincoln's
re-election and no prospect of the war ending."[9] Confederate journalists were generally busy boosting morale, but
the *Sentinel* did let slip a public admission of the consequences of Lincoln's reelection for Confederate spirits:
"There was a sadness, indeed, on the part of us all, when
the people who lately called us brethren showed themselves so insatiable for our blood."[10]

Much of the Confederate press immediately sought to
mitigate the impact of Lincoln's reelection by presenting
a variety of arguments to convince Southerners that the
Republican victory was not as calamitous as it appeared.
Editors argued that the election figures were not a reli-
able reflection of Northern sentiment because Lincoln
had manufactured votes through manipulation and
fraud.[11] Taking a different tack, some journalists contended that although Lincoln had won the election, he
faced a large and determined opposition. "He is elected,"
said the *Sentinel*, "but the powerful minority which op-
poses him, chills the joy of triumph and throws shadows
over his path."[12] Another newspaper in Richmond called
upon Southerners to meet the renewed vow of the North
"to destroy us, to seize our lands and homes, to beggar
our children, and brand our names forever as the names
of felons and traitors" with a fresh determination "to
drive back the foul invaders of our homes and make them
expiate their crime with their own base blood." The
editor insisted that although the North had rededicated
itself to continued, unsparing battle, "It by no means
follows that there are to be four years more of war."

Determined military effort, said the journalist, would place Confederates "on the safe shore from whence at our ease we may look at the absurd Yankee nation going to utter wreck in the storm it had conjured up for our destruction."[13]

Newspapers of the South found reasons why Lincoln's reelection was in the best interest of the Confederacy. The *Examiner* contended that Northerners elected Lincoln in the enthusiastic belief that his victory would crush the heart of the South. When they learn that the South will carry on regardless of who is elected, declared the newspaper, this enthusiasm will end in despair.[14] Some Confederate editors reported that the "Yankee privates are very much depressed at the result of the Presidential election, declaring there was not a free expression of opinion allowed them, and that they are hopeless of a speedy termination of the war."[15] The *Sentinel* argued that the election results provided "much ground for encouragement" to the South because the sizable number of true peace men who had been pledged to support McClellan were now free to continue their opposition to the war. The editor of the *Dispatch* sounded the theme that Lincoln's reelection would preserve the Confederacy because his harsh policies would provoke furious Southern resistance, whereas McClellan's conciliatory approach might have inspired reconstructionist sentiment in the South.[16]

Some Confederate newspapers also carried a few additional comments in the matter of the Southern approaches to the election. In two editorials, the Augusta *Constitutionalist* attacked Alexander Stephens for his public letter praising the Chicago platform. While endorsing the plan for a convention of the states, said the editor, Stephens "almost committed himself to reconstruction."[17] The Savannah *News* came to the support of

Vice-President Stephens, contending that he had been misunderstood and misrepresented by the *Constitutionalist*.[18] Alexander Stephens was not one to leave his defense in the hands of others, and he sent a letter to the *Constitutionalist* explaining his tactics during the campaign. He had originally written this letter to Thomas J. Semmes as a private response to the senator's speech at Mobile in which Semmes denounced proposals for a convention of the states and mentioned Stephens by name. The vice-president arranged for deletion of materials he deemed irrelevant before sending the document to the newspaper, but be left intact comments that later embroiled him in a personal and bitter exchange with Jefferson Davis.[19]

In a typically long declaration, Stephens gave the reasons for his endorsement of McClellan's candidacy and the proposal for a gathering of the states. While vigorously denying that he was a reconstructionist, Stephens struck at those who opposed his views and actions. He disagreed with critics who argued that peace overtures from the South depressed Confederate morale and were interpreted in the North simply as an indication of Southern weakness. "Nothing would give us more strength at home and abroad," declared the Georgian, than to employ "the moral power" of Confederate peace terms by frequently presenting them to the world. Rejecting the notion that the South should accept negotiation only after recognition of the Confederacy, Stephens said: "The doors to treat, to negotiate, to confer, to reason, should always be kept widely open. Those who have the right on their side should never shun or avoid reason."

The vice-president also took to task those Confederates who feared the possible consequences of McClellan's election. Stephens declared:

> I know there are many persons amongst us whose opinions are entitled to high consideration, who do not agree

with me on the question of McClellan's election. They prefer Lincoln to McClellan. Perhaps the President belongs to that class. Judging from his acts, I should think that he did. Those of the class to whom I refer with whom I have met, think that if what they term a conservative man should be elected, or any on the Chicago platform even, that such terms for a restoration of the Union would be offered as our people would accept. The ghost of the Union haunts them. The specter of reconstruction rears its ghastly head at every corner of their imagination.

Scoffing at such apprehensions, Stephens said, "These fears of *voluntary* reconstruction are but chimeras of the brain."

As the acerb Georgian continued in his defense, he laid blame for McClellan's defeat and Lincoln's election on Jefferson Davis. Stephens stressed that he had always thought that the Confederacy should encourage the growth of "the State Rights party at the North" with a view to dividing the enemy and to securing a Federal administration amenable to the Confederacy. He contended:

If the proper line of policy had been pursued by our authorities toward that element of popular sentiment at the North from the beginning, . . . I believe an out and out States Rights man might and would have been nominated at Chicago, and elected. But the policy of our authorities seems to me, as far as I can judge of it, to have been directed with a view to weaken, cripple and annihilate that party. So far from acting even upon the policy of dividing the enemy, their object seems to have been to unite and inflame them. I do moreover, verily believe that if President Davis, even after McClellan's nomination, had made a favorable response to the Chicago resolution looking to a convention of the States, as a mode of inaugurating negotiations of peace, that it would greatly have aided his election. It might have secured it.[20]

The animosity toward Davis's approach to the election,

which Stephens had long been nurturing, had finally
exploded into public view.

The vice-president's letter threw into sharp relief the
chasm between himself and Davis on the issue of the
Northern election. Various Southern newspapers printed
Stephens's declaration, and the document came to the
attention of the president.[21] Believing that he had done
nothing to warrant the allegations, Davis was outraged.
He feared that the charges would have a detrimental
effect on Northern peace advocates and suspected that
Stephens's true purpose was "to disparage" the president
and "to inspire distrust" in him among the Southern
people.[22] In a short yet acrid note to Stephens, Davis
demanded, "I . . . ask to what acts of mine you refer."[23]
When the president's letter reached Stephens, he was in
Richmond attending the session of Congress that had
begun in early November. After reading the note, he
determined to compose "a full, plain & pointed answer."[24]
Resolving to make the response "as short as possible,"
Stephens held himself to twenty-six pages. Still unable to
contain his anger, he showed a draft of his reply to
several members of Congress but enjoined them to keep
the matter confidential.[25]

In the letter to Davis, Stephens cited two instances in
which he believed the president had shown a clear preference for Lincoln: the case of David F. Cable and Davis's
speech at Columbia, South Carolina, following the disaster at Atlanta. After rehearsing the tedious history of the
correspondence regarding Cable, Stephens charged that
Davis had acted capriciously to prevent an interview
between Stephens and the prisoner because Davis opposed the vice-president's plan to encourage the peace
Democracy through assurances of Confederate support
and cooperation. With regard to the address in South

Carolina, Stephens alleged that the president had purposely damaged the Northern peace movement. Had Davis remained silent on the election, said Stephens, his course would have been at least benign, but the president chose instead to work actively against McClellan's candidacy by denouncing a convention of the states and calling for more war. "The tone and substance" of such a speech, declared the angry vice-president, "could have no effect at the North but to weaken and cripple the peace party."[26]

After reading Stephens's lengthy statement, the president responded with his own interpretation of events. He insisted that he had not opposed a conference between the vice-president and Cable and denied any devious conduct in the affair. Dismissing Stephens's inferences from the speech at Columbia as "strained and unnatural," Davis argued that he was simply warning Confederates against placing undue faith in the belief that the Northern election would bring peace. In conclusion, Davis told Stephens, "I . . . [have] never done an act or uttered a word that could justify you in attributing to me a preference for Lincoln over McClellan."[27] The contradictory approaches of Stephens and Davis to the Northern election had finally brought the two men to a direct confrontation, but their exchange of views was both superficial and futile. In a context of bitterness and acrimony, neither one had adequately addressed the fundamental differences of philosophy and approach that separated them.

While Davis bickered with Stephens behind the scenes, Southerners were taking stock of their situation. The prospect for Confederate independence through decisive military victory or foreign intervention seemed to have eluded the Confederacy by the end of 1863. Now, at the

close of 1864, the possibility of success through Northern
default also seemed to have disappeared, and Confederates responded to the state of affairs in a variety of ways.
William A. Graham, Confederate States senator from
North Carolina, blindly hoped that the North would
reconsider its position and conclude that the price of
victory was too great and offer peace terms by the first
months of 1865.[28] In desperation, a writer in the *Sentinel*
suggested that the Confederate states "ought to repeal
the old Declaration of Independence, and voluntarily
revert to their original proprietors—England, France,
and Spain, and by them be protected from the North."[29]
William W. Holden, the war-weary editor of the North
Carolina *Standard*, declared in a fit of utter despair: "But
it is now apparent to everyone that there is no hope of
foreign intervention; that the war is to be waged against
us indefinitely, and with undiminished vigor; that mere
fighting cannot close the war, if we may judge of the
future by the past; and that the only reasonable ground
for an early, and honorable, and permanent peace, is
through and by negotiations."[30]

Convictions similar to those of Holden provoked action
at Richmond, where a powerful group in the Congress
was laboring to find a way to commence negotiations.
Pressure for peace talks was particularly intense in the
House of Representatives, where twenty-six members
favored diplomatic efforts to obtain a cessation of hostilities. The disposition for peace was strongest among members who had been Whigs before the war, who had shown
Unionist sympathies at the time of secession, who had
been elected to Congress in 1863, and who represented
districts that were still under Confederate control and
would, therefore, bear the brunt of any sacrifices required by congressional legislation. Josiah Turner of
North Carolina, who once said that he would rather

"plough and feed hogs than legislate for the Confederacy," offered a resolution requesting Davis to appoint thirteen commissioners "to tender to the Government of the United States a conference for negotiating an honorable peace."[31] Henry Foote, the indefatigable votary of negotiations, introduced a resolution calling for a convention of Southern states to offer "advisory suggestions" to the Confederate government regarding "the further prosecution of the war" or "the establishment of peace."[32] In the Senate six members firmly supported peace diplomacy, and Senators William C. Rives of Virginia and William A. Graham drafted a secret resolution proposing reconstruction, which they never formally introduced.[33] Sentiment for peace negotiations was also powerful in the legislatures of Georgia and Alabama.[34]

While some Confederates talked of negotiations, others cast about for ways to revive the possibility of Confederate victory through European diplomacy or military action. A state supreme court justice in Raleigh, North Carolina, wrote: "Lincoln's election by so large a majority means war—war to the uttermost. . . . France made the former Revolution successful and I am afraid it will require her aid to make the present one so."[35] Other Southerners favored strengthening the Confederate army by drawing upon a vast reservoir of manpower hitherto untapped for combat duty: the slaves. Commenting upon both the foreign and military possibilities, John B. Jones said: "Intervention on the part of European powers is the only hope of many. Failing that, no doubt a Negro army will be organized—and it might be too late."[36]

Jefferson Davis recognized the desperate plight of the Confederacy, and he was prepared to adopt radical measures. Reports from the agents who were sent to Canada confirmed that there would be no Northern collapse in the foreseeable future. Commenting on the situation, James Holcombe said: "The northwest is not now, and without the systematic and possibly long-continued application of the agencies which control the popular mind may never be, ripe for revolution. But it is fermenting with the passions out of which revolutions have been created. In Illinois, Indiana, and possibly Ohio, a majority of the population are hostile to the present administration." Holcombe urged that rather than abandon efforts in the Northwest, the Confederate government should "employ money and talent without stint to give this brooding resentment the proportions of anarchy and civil strife."[37] Jacob Thompson concurred in this recommendation and reported that a new and more vigorous secret order was forming in the North to oppose the policies of the Lincoln administration.[38]

Although the agents did not enjoy the success they had desired, they did not rate their mission an unqualified failure. They argued that the threat of insurrection in the Northwest had forced the Federal government to garrison large numbers of troops in that region that might otherwise have served at the front. Although the complex plans for a Northwestern revolution did not materialize, Confederates had staged raids on the Great Lakes, at New York City, and at St. Albans, Vermont, all of which contributed to the consternation and agitation in the North. Holcombe contended that the diplomatic endeavor that produced Lincoln's "To Whom It May Concern" was a success because the president's declaration had "permanently weakened and distracted the war party at the North and there is much reason to hope that before many months intervene it will wholly deprive it of Democratic support."[39] Jacob Thompson insisted that the efforts to foment revolution in the Northwest would "satisfy the large class of discontents at home of the readiness and willingness of the administration to avail itself of every proffered assistance in our great struggle for independence."[40]

With the election, however, the operations from Canada were almost concluded. Holcombe decided that his original mission was completed, and he returned to the Confederacy by mid-November 1864.[41] Davis recalled Clay shortly thereafter, and Clay's mission ended when his ship ran aground off the coast of South Carolina and he waded ashore at Charleston.[42] Thompson remained in Canada and participated in further intrigues until the war ended; then he sailed to Europe.[43]

Even before receiving the reports from the commissioners regarding the situation in the Northwest, Jefferson Davis had resolved to take drastic action on both the military and diplomatic fronts. In his address of November 7, 1864, to the Confederate Congress, Davis asked for authority to have the Confederate government purchase forty thousand male slaves for duty as laborers for the army with emancipation as the reward for faithful service. Perhaps being intentionally vague, he implied that these blacks would be committed to combat if the military situation became extremely precarious. The concept of arming the blacks for military action was not new, and some Confederates were already publicly discussing the idea when the president made his proposal to Congress. High-ranking officers in the Army of Tennessee had suggested combat roles for Negroes as early as January 1864, but Davis had then ordered an end to these considerations because he knew that such proposals would provoke a public furor. Now, however, the president was prepared to run the gauntlet of public opinion because the depleted armies of the Confederacy were in dire need of additional soldiers to meet the continuation of the war which Lincoln's reelection made inevitable. In September 1864, General Lee had called upon Davis to take "immediate and vigorous measures to increase the strength of our armies. . . . As matters now stand, we have no troops disposable to meet movements of the enemy or strike where opportunity presents without taking them from the trenches and exposing some important point."[44] Such was the dilemma that inspired the president to take action.

Davis's request touched off a debate that raged in the halls of Congress and the newspapers of the Confederacy. Some Confederates regarded combat service and emancipation for blacks as a disaster for Southern society more abhorrent than defeat at the hands of the North, while other Confederates argued that no price was too high for Southern independence. After protracted discussion and faced with the seemingly irresistible numbers in the Federal armies, the Confederate Congress passed a bill allowing the president to secure the services of blacks for combat duty but made emancipation contingent upon the consent of the owners and states involved. Davis signed the measure into law and added the executive stipulation that no Negro could enter the Confederate service without prior manumission by the owner.[45]

While controversy swirled around the plan to arm the blacks, Davis sent Duncan F. Kenner, a distinguished member of the Confederate Congress from Louisiana, to Europe with a momentous diplomatic proposal. The emissary carried a letter of introduction from Secretary Benjamin to James Mason and John Slidell assuring them that Kenner's verbal communication came by and with the authority of the Confederate government.[46] Upon arriving in Europe, Kenner informed Mason and Slidell that the Confederacy was willing to offer emancipation of the slaves, among other concessions, in return for recognition. Southern diplomats had long been reporting that the moral stigma of slavery was a major obstacle to European recognition, and now Davis was ready to abandon slavery altogether if that would expedite foreign acknowledgment of Confederate independence. Recognition of the Confederacy by a major European power would add immense prestige to the Southern cause and might bring intervention in behalf of the fledgling republic. The commissioners accordingly made arrangements to present the proposal to the governments of France and England.[47]

The desperate efforts to revive the failing fortunes of the Confederacy proved futile. The drive for negotiations culminated in the Hampton Roads conference of February 1865. On board the *River Queen,* Alexander Stephens, Robert M. T. Hunter, and John A. Campbell met with Abraham Lincoln and William H. Seward and learned that the only terms of peace acceptable to the Federal government were reunion and emancipation.[48] Recruitment of Negro troops began, especially in Virginia, in compliance with the act of Congress and the presidential order, but these soldiers were not able to complete their brief training before the war ended.[49] When the Confederate diplomats in Europe laid the Kenner proposal before the appropriate authorities at London and Paris, both governments rejected the offer.[50]

With the reelection of Lincoln, the Federal armies continued their merciless pounding of the Confederacy while the navy tightened its stranglehold on Southern ports. After destroying the supply line feeding into Atlanta, Hood marched his veterans north in a vain effort to lure Sherman's ravaging army out of the Southern hinterland. In Tennessee, Federal forces under General George H. Thomas, "the Rock of Chickamauga," shattered Hood's army, and Joseph Johnston once again took command with the assignment to stop Sherman, who was cutting a swath of destruction through the Carolinas. In Virginia, Grant finally drove the Confederate defenders from their positions at Petersburg, and Richmond fell to the conquering invaders. Barely a month after Lincoln's inauguration for a second term, Lee surrendered at Appomattox, and capitulation of the remaining forces of the Confederacy followed in short order.

Devising and implementing Confederate policy for the Northern election would have posed a major challenge for even an exceptionally talented leader because significantly influencing the course of Northern political affairs was difficult. Although angry and frustrated, the majority of peace Democrats were not grasping for peace at any price. The immensity of the national debt was unprecedented and caused serious misgivings among Northerners, but the Federal government had not really overextended itself. Although the rate of inflation was reason for concern, the North was experiencing considerable economic growth. Conscription was exceedingly unpopular and Northwestern resentment of Eastern political power was genuine, but these tensions lacked sufficient focus to produce chaos. The Emancipation Proclamation stirred opposition, but most Northerners came to accept emancipation either as a virtuous war aim or a necessary, if undesirable, measure to win the war. For Southern purposes, the most vulnerable weakness of the North was its faulty perception of the military situation. Because Confederate military operations appeared more successful than they really were, many Northerners overlooked the fact that they were winning the war— until the fall of Atlanta. The Southern task was to consolidate and to intensify the varieties of Northern tension, misapprehension, anxiety, and discontent.

The magnitude of the problem Davis faced in dealing with public opinion in the South would also have taxed a particularly capable politician. Some of the president's enemies, Alexander Stephens for example, were virtually implacable. By 1864, the ranks of Davis's enemies were formidable and often unwilling to accept his leadership. As a consequence, the initiatives he did undertake with regard to the election were often undercut. While he was busily breathing defiance, working behind the scenes through secret agents, and urging a vigorous war, some of his opponents were calling for peace negotiations, demanding overt endorsement of the Democrats, and advocating restricted and defensive military action.

The Northern election also brought into sharp focus a fundamental paradox of the Confederacy: the tension between state rights and Confederate nationalism. For nationalists like Davis, the prospect of reunion through negotiations was a recurring nightmare. The possibility, particularly after the fall of Atlanta and McClellan's letter of acceptance, that the election might bring negotiations for reunion based on Northern concessions was anathema to the president. For advocates of state sovereignty, like William Boyce and others, Democratic offers of protection for state rights and slavery made the prospects of the election in the fall of 1864 still encouraging. The result was acceleration of the prolonged and debilitating controversy over state sovereignty in the Confederacy.

A last point in Davis's defense is that in devising a policy for the election he confronted the obstacles that traditionally hamper government policy makers. The pressures of conducting the war had become particularly great by 1864 and required a great deal of presidential time. Davis's ill health and the death of his son in the late spring only added to his burdens. Lack of information was also a problem. Slowness in communicating with the agents in Canada made coordination more difficult. When Davis devised his strategy in the spring of 1864, he could not anticipate the situation that would exist by fall.

The external and internal aspects of the problems generated by the election were especially difficult for Davis because of his limitations as a leader. Even so, he recognized early in 1864 the latent potential of the Northern political situation. At best the election provided the South with a unique chance to deflect the North from its commitment to the war, and at least the contest offered the opportunity to weaken the North through exacerbating heightened internal stresses. He understood that some peace advocates opposed the war out of a conviction that the Constitution did not authorize the Federal government to coerce a sovereign state. He also knew that much peace sentiment rested upon despair of ever conquering the South. Although he received exaggerated reports of organization among opponents of the war, he apparently did not place undue credence in such information.

The basic outline of Davis's strategy for influencing the election was reasonable. His approach involved both military action and diplomacy, but the implementation of the strategy was unimaginative and contradictory. He was probably correct in concluding that the military policy of the offensive-defensive would intensify Northern despair and electoral tensions, but he emphasized military affairs to the neglect, and sometimes contradiction, of diplomatic efforts by Thompson, Clay, and Holcombe. The Confederate president had concentrated on military action for so long that he was apparently unable to wage an effective diplomatic offensive against the North. Preoccupation with the military apparently caused Davis to overlook an opportunity in late August to aggravate Northern distress and perhaps to strengthen the position of the peace Democrats through a carefully drawn proposal for negotiations. The heavy reliance upon the military to influence Northern electoral sentiment made the loss of Atlanta all the more serious.

Both Davis and his agents sought to capitalize on war weariness and peace sentiment among Northern Democrats, but their tactics were contradictory. Clay and Holcombe in particular courted Northern peace men by allowing them to believe that the South might someday be wooed back into the Union after restoration of peace. Davis expected to intensify Northern war weariness through defiant statements of Southern unwillingness ever to accept reunion and through demonstration of Confederate invincibility. He hurled defiance against the enemy at the time of the Gilmore-Jaquess mission and his speaking tour in September. To some extent, Davis's forceful declarations of unyielding commitment to Confederate nationhood were counterproductive because they supported Lincoln's contention that negotiations with the South would prove futile. In addition, the show of unity and impregnability that Davis demanded was beyond the capacity of the South.

Davis's strategy for the external challenge was not, however, devoid of positive results. Military operations, particularly the Early raid and the slowed progress of Sherman before Atlanta, caused consternation in the North. The agents managed to intrigue with Northerners and to reap political benefits from the encounters with Greeley and Lincoln's dictum, "To Whom It May Concern." Nevertheless, the agents never found the key to the riddle of Northwestern sentiment that was sometimes antiwar, often anti-Lincoln, but seldom pro-Confederate.

The president's response to the external challenge was

weak, and his treatment of aroused expectations among
Confederates was haphazard and inconsistent. At first,
he offered encouragement to the belief that the Northern
election would redound to the benefit of the South, but
then he gave no public indication that the government
was interested in influencing the election, and he
vaguely disagreed with opponents who proposed a course
of action. The president's policy was largely to ignore
public concern regarding the election, even when government policies such as the Early raid, the removal of
Johnston, and the diplomatic encounters of midsummer
touched on Confederate expectations for the election.
With little presidential leadership, public debate was
uncertain, unclear, and uninformed, and speculation on
prospects for the election reached unrealistic heights in
August.

Davis went public on the election issue only after the
loss of Atlanta caused Confederate morale to plummet.
Because the military situation in the South and the
condition of morale in the North had drastically changed,
the time was past for a diplomatic initiative from Richmond designed to influence the election. Davis's position
was, therefore, better suited to the occasion than were
the proposals of his rivals. Because the president waited
until Confederates generally were despondent and his
political enemies were in an ugly mood, his belated effort
to assert leadership in the formation of public opinion on
the election was unsuccessful.

In the final analysis, the problems and opportunities of
Northern politics in 1864 taxed Davis where his talents
were weakest. The electoral challenges required him to
mold public opinion in both the North and the South, and
influencing public opinion was not Davis's forte. His
evaluation of the potential of the election was reasonably

accurate, but implementation of his strategy for influencing the contest was weak, and his response to aroused
expectations in the Confederacy was seriously deficient.

Notes

Chapter 1

1. Richmond *Dispatch*, July 2, 1863.
2. Augusta *Chronicle & Sentinel*, April 20, 1864. For similar comments see Richmond *Sentinel*, April 21, 1864; Charleston *Mercury*, April 12, 1864; Galveston *Tri-Weekly News*, January 8, 22, February 15, 1864; Atlanta *Confederacy* in Galveston *Tri-Weekly News*, May 19, 1864; Mobile *Daily Advertiser and Register*, January 20, 24, February 2, 1864; Montgomery *Mail* in Mobile *Daily Advertiser and Register*, February 4, 1864; Lawrence M. Keitt to Susanna S. Keitt, January 13, 1864, in Lawrence M. Keitt Papers, Duke University; Judah P. Benjamin to A. Dudley Mann, February 1, 1864, in *Official Records of the Union and Confederate Navies in the War of the Rebellion* (Washington, D.C.: U.S. Government Printing Office, 1894–1927), Ser. II, Vol. III, pp. 1015–16, hereinafter cited as *Official Records, Navies*; John B. Jones, *A Rebel War Clerk's Diary*, ed. Howard Swiggett (2 vols.; New York: Old Hickory Bookshop, 1935), II, 149.
3. Richmond *Sentinel*, February 9, 1864; Richmond *Examiner*, February 29, 1864; Charleston *Mercury*, March 19, 1864; Augusta *Constitutionalist*, April 6, 1864; Galveston *Tri-Weekly News*, January 8, March 9, 1864; Mobile *Daily Advertiser and Register*, February 6, 24, April 7, 1864.
4. Frank G. Ruffin to James A. Seddon, February 8, 1864, in *The War of the Rebellion: A Compilation of the Official Records of the Union and Confederate Armies* (Washington, D.C.: U.S. Government Printing Office, 1880–1901), Ser. IV, Vol. III, p. 87, hereinafter cited as *Official Records, Armies*.
5. Charleston *Courier* in Augusta *Constitutionalist*, May 6, 1864. For similar comments see Richmond *Dispatch*, April 23, 1864; Mobile *Daily Advertiser and Register*, April 28, 1864.
6. Chicago *Tribune* in Augusta *Constitutionalist*, May 1, 1864. See also Augusta *Chronicle & Sentinel*, February 19, 1864; Mobile *Daily Advertiser and Register*, February 26, 1864.

7. Augusta *Chronicle & Sentinel*, March 29, 1864.

8. Richmond *Examiner*, April 5, 1864; Augusta *Constitutionalist*, April 16, 1864; Galveston *Tri-Weekly News*, May 8, 1864.

9. I. B. Cohen to Alexander H. Stephens, April 21, 1864, in Alexander H. Stephens Papers, Library of Congress. For another prediction of violence see Robert G. H. Kean, *The Diary of Robert Gurlick Hill Kean*, ed. Edward Younger (New York: Oxford University Press, 1957), p. 153.

10. New York *Daily News* in Richmond *Sentinel*, February 6, 1864; New York *Metropolitan Record* in ibid., April 22, 1864; New York *Metropolitan Record* in Augusta *Constitutionalist*, May 10, 1864; New York *Sunday Mercury* in Mobile *Daily Advertiser and Register*, January 16, 1864; New York *Daily News* in ibid., March 30, 1864; New York *Daily News* in Galveston *Tri-Weekly News*, January 22, 1864; Paris (Illinois) *Times* in ibid., April 22, 1864.

11. New York *News* in Augusta *Constitutionalist*, April 17, 1864.

12. New York *News* in Augusta *Constitutionalist*, April 28, 1864.

13. Augusta *Chronicle & Sentinel*, January 6, 1864. See also Richmond *Examiner*, January 18, 1864.

14. Augusta *Chronicle & Sentinel*, January 6, 1864. See also ibid., January 23, 1864; Mobile *Daily Advertiser and Register*, January 13, February 20, 1864; Galveston *Tri-Weekly News*, January 18, February 10, March 2, 1864; Richmond *Sentinel*, January 19, 22, 25, 1864.

15. Galveston *Tri-Weekly News*, January 25, 1864.

16. Richmond *Examiner*, March 28, 1864; Augusta *Constitutionalist*, April 1, 1864; Mobile *Daily Advertiser and Register*, April 5, 1864.

17. Alexander H. Long, Address before the United States House of Representatives, April 8, 1864, *Congressional Globe*, 38th Cong., 1st sess., pp. 1499–1503. The quotations are on pp. 1502 and 1503.

18. Benjamin G. Harris, Address before the United States House of Representatives, April 9, 1864, ibid., p. 1515.

19. Frank L. Klement, *The Copperheads in the Middle West*, (Chicago: University of Chicago Press, 1960), pp. 229–30.

20. Richmond *Sentinel*, April 29, May 7, 1864; Augusta *Constitutionalist*, April 22, 28, May 19, 1864; Augusta *Chronicle & Sentinel*, April 21, 1864; Mobile *Daily Advertiser and Register*, April 23, 26, 30, 1864; Galveston *Tri-Weekly News*, May 22, 23, 1864; Kean, *Diary*, p. 153; Jones, *Diary*, II, 187.

21. Henry Hotze to Judah P. Benjamin, May 7, 1864, in *Official Records, Navies*, Ser. II, Vol. III, p. 1117.

22. Mobile *Daily Advertiser and Register*, April 29, 1864. See also Augusta *Chronicle & Sentinel*, May 3, 1864.

23. Galveston *Tri-Weekly News*, May 1, 1864.

24. Augusta *Chronicle & Sentinel*, April 28, 1864. See also Richmond *Sentinel*, April 21, 1864; Mobile *Daily Advertiser and Register*, May 1, 1864.

25. Richmond *Examiner*, January 25, 1864. See also Mobile *Daily Advertiser and Register,* March 2, 9, April 15, 23, 1864; Galveston *Tri-Weekly News*, February 24, April 6, 1864.

26. Augusta *Chronicle & Sentinel*, January 31, 1864; Augusta *Constitutionalist*, March 19, February 5, April 5, 13, 1864; Richmond *Sentinel*, March 14, 1864.

27. Richmond *Sentinel*, January 22, March 14, 1864; Augusta *Constitutionalist*, January 22, February 5, April 15, 1864; Augusta *Chronicle & Sentinel*, January 31, 1864; Mobile *Daily Advertiser and Register*, January 23, March 29, April 20, 1864; Galveston *Tri-Weekly News*, April 20, 27, 1864.

28. Augusta *Constitutionalist*, January 9, March 5, 15, 1864; Richmond *Sentinel*, March 7, 1864; Mobile *Daily Advertiser and Register*, February 6, March 25, 29, April 2, 1864; Galveston *Tri-Weekly News*, April 1, May 11, 19, 1864.

29. Augusta *Chronicle & Sentinel*, March 5, 1864. See also Mobile *Daily Advertiser and Register*, March 8, 19, 1864; Galveston *Tri-Weekly News*, March 23, 1864.

30. Augusta *Chronicle & Sentinel*, January 31, February 9, 1864; Richmond *Sentinel*, March 12, 1864; Augusta *Constitutionalist*, March 19, 22, 29, 1864; Mobile *Daily Advertiser and Register*, February 4, March 30, 1864; Galveston *Tri-Weekly News*, January 8, 20, February 10, April 4, 27, 1864.

31. Charleston *Courier* in Augusta *Chronicle & Sentinel*, April 19, 1864; Richmond *Sentinel*, March 12, 25, 1864.

32. Richmond *Sentinel*, May 19, 1864; Augusta *Constitutionalist*, March 3, 29, 1864; Charleston *Courier* in Augusta *Chronicle & Sentinel*, April 19, 1864; Richmond *Examiner*, March 23, 1864; Mobile *Daily Advertiser and Register*, March 31, 1864; Galveston *Tri-Weekly News*, January 8, April 1, May 14, 1864.

33. Augusta *Chronicle & Sentinel*, January 31, 1864.

34. Louisville *Journal* in Richmond *Sentinel*, January 8, 1864; New York *Metropolitan Record* and New York *Freeman's Journal* in Augusta *Constitutionalist*, April 13, 1864; Augusta *Chronicle & Sentinel*, January 27, 1864; Cincinnati *Enquirer* in Mobile *Daily Advertiser and Register*, February 4, 1864; Montgomery *Mail* in Mobile *Daily Advertiser and Register*, February 27, 1864; Chicago *Times* in Galveston *Tri-Weekly News*, January 8, 1864.

35. Charleston *Mercury*, March 14, 1864.

36. Richmond *Sentinel*, March 25, 1864. See also Mobile *Daily Advertiser and Register*, March 30, 1864.

37. North Carolina *Standard*, January 20, 1864.

38. Richmond *Examiner*, January 25, 1864.

39. Augusta *Chronicle & Sentinel*, April 19, 1864. See also Richmond *Examiner*, January 25, 1864; Mobile *Daily Advertiser and Register*, January 6, February 26, 1864; Jones, *Diary*, II, 115.

40. James M. Barr to Rebecca Ann D. Barr, April 12, 1864, in James M. Barr, *Confederate War Correspondence of James Michael Barr and Wife Ann Dowling Barr*, ed. Ruth B. McDaniel (Taylors, S.C.: Faith Printing Company, 1963), p. 213. For a similar comment by a soldier, see Edwin H. Fay to Sarah S. Fay, January 9, 1864, in Edwin H. Fay, *"This Infernal War,"* ed. Bell I. Wiley (Austin: University of Texas Press, 1958), p. 385. See also Joseph C. Bradley to Linton Stephens, April 8, 1864, in Alexander H. Stephens Papers, Library of Congress; Augusta *Constitutionalist*, March 10, 1864.

41. Richmond *Examiner*, March 10, 1864. See also Charleston *Mercury*, March 14, 1864; Mobile *Daily Advertiser and*

Register, January 23, April 20, 1864; David M. Carter to William A. Graham, March 16, 1864, in William A. Graham Papers, North Carolina Department of Archives and History, Raleigh, N.C.

42. Savannah *News* in Mobile *Daily Advertiser and Register*, February 4, 1864. See also Richmond *Examiner*, March 23, 1864.

43. Richmond *Examiner*, March 19, 1864.

44. Augusta *Constitutionalist*, March 10, 1864. See also letter of William F. Samford in Augusta *Chronicle & Sentinel*, January 21, 1864; Galveston *Tri-Weekly News*, April 13, 1864.

45. London *Times*, March 25, 1864, in Augusta *Constitutionalist*, May 1, 1864.

46. John Slidell to Judah P. Benjamin, April 7, 1864, in *Official Records, Navies*, Ser. II, Vol. III, p. 1078.

47. New York *Sunday Mercury* in Richmond *Sentinel*, April 15, 1864. This excerpt also appeared in Augusta *Constitutionalist*, April 21, 1864. For similar comments see New York *Herald* in Augusta *Constitutionalist*, January 22, 1864; New York *Times* in Mobile *Daily Advertiser and Register*, January 22, 1864; New York *Daily News* in ibid., January 26, 1864.

48. Augusta *Chronicle & Sentinel*, March 11, 1864; Richmond *Examiner*, January 26, 1864; Atlanta *Confederacy* in Augusta *Chronicle & Sentinel*, May 6, 1864; Charleston *Courier* in Augusta *Constitutionalist*, June 10, 1864; Augusta *Constitutionalist*, March 29, 1864; Mobile *Daily Advertiser and Register*, January 7, 16, 24, February 13, 16, 26, March 4, 1864; Galveston *Tri-Weekly News*, February 28, March 23, April 29, 1864; Savannah *News* in Mobile *Daily Advertiser and Register*, February 4, 1864; Cohen to Stephens, April 21, 1864; Kean, *Diary*, p. 143.

49. Augusta *Constitutionalist*, January 22, 1864.

50. Augusta *Chronicle & Sentinel*, May 22, 1864.

51. Augusta *Constitutionalist*, May 26, 1864.

52. New York *Herald* in Augusta *Constitutionalist*, April 21, 1864. See also New York *Sunday Mercury* in ibid., April 21, 1864.

53. Robert E. Lee to Jefferson Davis, May 18, 1864, in Robert E. Lee, *Lee's Dispatches*, ed. Douglas S. Freeman (New York: G. P. Putnam's Sons, 1915), p. 185; Charleston *Courier*

in Augusta *Chronicle & Sentinel*, June 10, 1864; Augusta *Chronicle & Sentinel*, February 6, 1864; Richmond *Examiner*, June 10, 1864; Charleston *Mercury*, June 6, 1864; Jones, *Diary*, II, 225–26.

54. Augusta *Chronicle & Sentinel*, April 20, 1864; Augusta *Constitutionalist*, April 13, 1864; Macon *Telegraph*, in Mobile *Daily Advertiser and Register*, February 18, 1864; Galveston *Tri-Weekly News*, March 13, 1864; Josiah Gorgas, *The Civil War Diary of General Josiah Gorgas*, ed. Frank E. Vandiver (University, Ala.: University of Alabama Press, 1947), p. 84.

55. Galveston *Tri-Weekly News*, February 24, 1864.

56. Richmond *Examiner*, March 12, April 15, 1864.

57. Frank G. Ruffin to James A. Seddon, February 8, 1864, in *Official Records, Armies*, Ser. IV, Vol. III, pp. 84–89. For the rudiments of another plan submitted to Seddon for influencing the election see Jones, *Diary*, II, 128.

58. Benjamin H. Hill, Speech at LaGrange, Georgia, March 1, 1864, in Augusta *Chronicle & Sentinel*, March 18, 1864. Hill also communicated his ideas to Alexander H. Stephens. See Benjamin H. Hill to Alexander H. Stephens, March 14, 1864, in *The Correspondence of Robert Toombs, Alexander H. Stephens, and Howell Cobb*, ed. Ulrich B. Phillips in American Historical Association, *Annual Report* (Washington, D.C., 1913), II, 635–36.

59. William F. Samford to Alexander H. Stephens, January 1, 1864, in Alexander H. Stephens Papers, Library of Congress.

Chapter 2

1. Jefferson Davis, *Rise and Fall of the Confederate Government* (2 vols.; London: Longmans, Green and Company, 1881), II, 611.

2. Jefferson Davis to Robert E. Lee, Braxton Bragg, and E. Kirby Smith [September 7, 1862], in Jefferson Davis, *Jefferson Davis: Constitutionalist, His Letters, Papers, and Speeches*, ed. Dunbar Rowland (10 vols.; New York: J. J. Little & Ives Company, 1923), V, 338–39.

3. Jefferson Davis, Speech at Jackson, Mississippi, Jackson *Mississippian*, December 26, 1862.

4. Oscar A. Kinchen, *Confederate Operations in Canada and the North* (North Quincy, Mass.: Christopher Publishing House, 1970), p. 29.

5. Letter from R. A. Alston in Jones, *Diary*, II, 155.

6. Leonidas Polk to Jefferson Davis, February 27, 1864, in *Official Records, Armies*, Ser. IV, Vol. III, p. 174.

7. J. W. Tucker to Jefferson Davis, March 14, 1864, in *Jefferson Davis*, ed. Rowland, VI, 206.

8. Herschel V. Johnson to Alexander H. Stephens, September 28, 1864, in Herschel V. Johnson Papers, Duke University. See also Herschel V. Johnson to Alexander H. Stephens, October 12, 1865, ibid.

9. Jefferson Davis to Robert M. T. Hunter, April 14, 1864, in *Official Records, Armies*, Ser. IV, Vol. III, p. 304.

10. Johnson to Stephens, September 28, 1864.

11. Herschel V. Johnson to Alexander H. Stephens, July 11, 1864, in Herschel V. Johnson Papers, Duke University.

12. Thomas H. Hines, "The Northwestern Conspiracy," *Southern Bivouac*, New Series II (1886), 443.

13. Johnson to Stephens, September 28, 1864.

14. Ibid.

15. Alexander H. H. Stuart in Alexander F. Robertson, *Alexander Hugh Holmes Stuart* (Richmond: William Byrd Press, 1925), pp. 207–8. See also Alexander H. H. Stuart to Robert C. Winthrop, December 25, 1889, in Robert C. Winthrop Papers, Massachusetts Historical Society, Boston, Mass.

16. L. Quinton Washington in Pierce Butler, *Judah P. Benjamin* (Philadelphia: Jacobs & Co., 1906), p. 348.

17. Davis, *Rise and Fall*, II, 611.

18. Judah P. Benjamin to John Slidell, April 30, 1864, in *Official Records, Navies*, Ser. II, Vol. III, pp. 1105–6.

19. John Hunt Morgan to James A. Seddon, January 27, 1864, in *Official Records, Armies*, Ser. I, Vol. XXXII, Pt. II, pp. 621–22.

20. James Longstreet to A. R. Lawton, March 5, 1864, ibid., Pt. III, p. 588.

21. Jefferson Davis to Zebulon B. Vance, January 8, 1864, in ibid., Ser. I, Vol. LI, Pt. II, p. 810.

22. William N. Pendleton, "Memorandum of Conference Held at Request of President Davis & Under His Instructions, with General J. E. Johnston, April 15, 1864," in William N. Pendleton Papers, Duke University.

23. Jefferson Davis to Samuel J. Person, December 15, 1864, in *Jefferson Davis*, ed. Rowland, VI, 420.

24. Stephen R. Mallory to James D. Bulloch, March 21, 1864, in *Official Records, Navies*, Ser. II, Vol. II, p. 613. See also Stephen R. Mallory to Samuel Barron, February 22, 1864, ibid., p. 593.

25. Alexander H. Stephens to Jefferson Davis, April 9, 1864, in Georgia Portfolio, II, 50, Duke University.

26. David F. Cable to Alexander H. Stephens, February 28, 1864, in Alexander H. Stephens Papers, Library of Congress.

27. Jefferson Davis to Alexander H. Stephens, April 19, 1864, in *Jefferson Davis*, ed. Rowland, VI, 231.

Chapter 3

1. Jefferson Davis, Address to the Confederate States Army, February 10, 1864, in *Official Records, Armies*, Ser. I, Vol. XXXII, Pt. II, p. 172.

2. Augustus R. Wright, "Resolution," in U.S. Congress, Senate, *Journal of the Congress of the Confederate States of America*, S. Doc. 234, 58th Cong., 2d sess., 1904, VI, 738.

3. Jones, *Diary*, II, 143.

4. North Carolina *Standard*, February 24, 1864; Selma *Daily Reporter*, February 10, 1864.

5. Augusta *Constitutionalist*, February 11, 1864.

6. Congress to the People of the Confederacy [February 17, 1864], in *Official Records, Armies*, Ser. IV, Vol. III, pp. 129–37.

7. Congress, "Joint Resolution in Reference to the Adoption and Publication of an Address to the People of the Confederate States," February 17, 1864, in ibid., pp. 139–40; *Journal of the Congress of the Confederate States of America*, VI, 849–50.

8. Augusta *Chronicle & Sentinel*, March 6, 1864.

9. Lawrence M. Keitt to Susanna S. Keitt, February 26, 1864, in Lawrence M. Keitt Papers, Duke University.

10. Klement, *Copperheads*, 118.

11. Alexander H. Stephens to Herschel V. Johnson, April 8, 1864, in *Official Records, Armies,* Ser. IV, Vol. III, p. 279.

12. Alexander H. Stephens to Jefferson Davis, June 12, 1863, in James D. Richardson, comp. and ed., *A Compilation of the Messages and Papers of the Confederacy* (2 vols.; Nashville: United States Printing Company, 1906), I, 340.

13. Alexander H. Stephens to Herschel V. Johnson, March 12, 1864, in Autograph Letters and Portraits of the Signers of the Constitution of the Confederate States, p. 74, Duke University. See also James Z. Rabun, "Alexander H. Stephens and Jefferson Davis," *American Historical Review,* LVIII (1953), 307.

14. Stephens to Johnson, March 12, 1864, p. 74.

15. Alexander H. Stephens to Linton Stephens, June 3, 1864, Alexander H. Stephens, "A Letter for Posterity," ed. James Z. Rabun, in Emory University Publications, *Sources & Reprints* (Atlanta, 1954), Ser. VIII, No. 3, 17–18: Alexander H. Stephens to Linton Stephens, April 28, 1864, in Alexander H. Stephens Papers, Manhattanville College of the Sacred Heart, Purchase, N.Y.

16. Alexander H. Stephens to Linton Stephens, May 7, 1864, in Alexander H. Stephens Papers, Manhattanville College. For a general statement of the military strategy favored by Stephens for the campaign of 1864, see Alexander H. Stephens to Jefferson Davis, January 22, 1864, in Alexander H. Stephens Papers, Duke University.

17. Linton Stephens to Alexander H. Stephens, June 7, 1864, in Alexander H. Stephens Papers, Manhattanville College.

18. E. Merton Coulter, *The Confederate States of America* (Baton Rouge: Louisiana State University Press, 1950), pp. 500–501.

19. Augusta *Chronicle & Sentinel,* January 24, April 8, 1864.

20. Ibid., January 20, 1864.

21. Ibid., January 16, 20, 30, 1864.

22. Ibid., March 6, 1864.

23. Joseph E. Brown to General Assembly of Georgia, March 10, 1864, in Allen D. Chandler, comp., *The Confederate Records of Georgia* (5 vols.; Atlanta: Charles P. Byrd, 1909), II, 649–55.

24. Stephens to Johnson, April 8, 1864, p. 279; General Assembly of Georgia, "Resolutions Declaring the Ground on which the Confederate States Stand in this War, and the Terms on which Peace Ought to Be Offered to the Enemy," March 19, 1864, in *Official Records, Armies*, Ser. IV, Vol. III, pp. 235–37.

25. Speaking of the purpose for offering negotiations, Linton Stephens privately said: "The object is to break down Lincoln by having him to *reject*, not offers of communication, but offers of *peace* on the principle of 1776—by manifesting to his own people that he stands convicted by a breach of his pledge to entertain and consider any proposition of peace which be made by our government, and to hold him up as responsible for the continuance of the war." See Linton Stephens to Alexander H. Stephens, June 6, 1864, in Alexander H. Stephens Papers, Manhattanville College. For a similar comment by Brown, see Joseph E. Brown to R. E. Colston, April 14, 1864, in Augusta *Constitutionalist*, April 20, 1864.

26. Stephens to Johnson, April 8, 1864, p. 279.

27. Joseph E. Brown to Alexander H. Stephens, April 5, 1864, in Toombs, Stephens, and Cobb, *Correspondence*, pp. 639–40; Joseph E. Brown to Alexander H. Stephens, April 12, 1864, ibid., pp. 640–41.

28. Augusta *Constitutionalist*, March 12, 22, 1864; North Carolina *Standard*, April 6, 1864; Charleston *Mercury*, March 24, 25, 1864.

29. Richmond *Examiner*, March 21, 1864.

30. Ibid., March 30, 1864. See also James Gardner to E. Starnes, March 21, 1864, in Augusta *Constitutionalist*, March 25, 1864.

31. Richmond *Examiner*, March 21, 30, 1864.

32. Savannah *Republican* in Richmond *Sentinel*, April 21, 1864. For a similar comment see Richmond *Examiner*, April 8, 1864.

33. Augusta *Constitutionalist*, May 15, 1864.

34. Letter from Honorable P. Clayton, March 13, 1864, in Augusta *Chronicle & Sentinel*, March 19, 1864.

35. Augusta *Chronicle & Sentinel*, March 12, 15, 16, 19, April 2, 1864.

36. Joseph E. Brown to George T. Anderson, May 2, 1864, in Augusta *Constitutionalist*, May 15, 1864.

37. Brown to Colston, April 14, 1864.

38. North Carolina *Democrat* in Augusta *Chronicle & Sentinel*, March 27, 1864.

39. Joseph C. Bradley to Linton Stephens, April 8, 1864, in Alexander H. Stephens Papers, Library of Congress.

40. Herschel V. Johnson to Alexander H. Stephens, April 11, 1864, in Herschel V. Johnson Papers, Duke University.

41. Henry Cleveland to Alexander H. Stephens, June 8, 1864, in Alexander H. Stephens Papers, Library of Congress.

42. Jefferson Davis to Congress, May 2, 1864, in *Journal of the Congress of the Confederate States of America*, VII, 8–10.

43. North Carolina *Standard*, January 20, 27, February 10, 1864.

44. Zebulon B. Vance to Jefferson Davis, December 30, 1863, in *Official Records, Armies*, Ser. I, Vol. LI, Pt. II, p. 807; Jefferson Davis to Zebulon B. Vance, January 8, 1864, ibid., pp. 808–10.

45. Vance to Davis, December 30, 1863, p. 807.

46. Davis to Vance, January 8, 1864, pp. 808–10.

47. A. H. Arrington et al. to Zebulon B. Vance, January 25, 1864, in *Official Records, Armies,* Ser. I, Vol. LI, Pt. II, p. 813; Zebulon B. Vance to Jefferson Davis, January 27, 1864, ibid., p. 814; Jefferson Davis to Zebulon B. Vance, January 30, 1864, ibid.; Zebulon B. Vance to Jefferson Davis, February 4, 1864, ibid., p. 817; Jefferson Davis to Zebulon B. Vance, February 17, 1864, ibid., Ser. IV, Vol. III, p. 153.

48. Richmond *Sentinel*, May 30, 1864.

49. Richmond *Examiner* in Augusta *Constitutionalist*, June 8, 1864. See also Augusta *Constitutionalist*, June 5, 1864; North Carolina *Standard*, June 15, 1864.

50. Alexander H. Stephens to Linton Stephens, June 3, 1864, in Stephens, "Letter for Posterity," pp. 12–24. The quotations are from pp. 17 and 22.

51. William F. Zornow, "The Cleveland Convention, 1864, and Radical Democrats," *Mid-America*, XXXVI (1954), 39–53.

52. Radical Democratic Party Platform of 1864, in Edward McPherson, ed., *The Political History of the United States of America during the Great Rebellion* (New York: D. Appleton & Co., 1864), p. 473.

53. John C. Frémont to Worthington G. Snethen et al., June 4, 1864, in ibid., p. 414.

54. Richmond *Sentinel*, April 20, 1864; Augusta *Constitutionalist*, April 20, June 11, 1864; Richmond *Dispatch*, June 21, 1864; Augusta *Chronicle & Sentinel*, June 16, July 22, 1864; North Carolina *Standard*, June 17, 1864.

55. Augusta *Chronicle & Sentinel*, June 15, 1864.

56. Richmond *Examiner*, June 7, 1864.

57. Alexander H. Stephens to Linton Stephens, September 3, 1864, in Alexander H. Stephens Papers, Manhattanville College.

58. Richmond *Examiner*, June 7, 1864.

59. Richmond *Dispatch*, June 8, 1864. See also Augusta *Chronicle & Sentinel*, June 23, 1864.

60. William F. Zornow, "The Union Party Convention at Baltimore in 1864," *Maryland Historical Magazine*, XLV (1950), 178–200.

61. Union Party Platform of 1864, in Kirk H. Porter and Donald B. Johnson, eds., *National Party Platforms, 1840–1968* (Urbana: University of Illinois Press, 1970), pp. 35–36.

62. Abraham Lincoln to William Dennison et al., June 27, 1864, in McPherson, ed., *Political History*, p. 409.

63. Richmond *Dispatch*, June 9, 1864; Augusta *Constitutionalist*, June 9, 1864.

64. Richmond *Dispatch*, June 14, 1864, July 5, 1864; Charleston *Mercury*, July 9, 1864; Augusta *Chronicle & Sentinel*, July 8, 1864.

65. Augusta *Constitutionalist*, April 12, 13, 1864.

66. Richmond *Dispatch*, July 5, 1864.

67. Richmond *Examiner*, June 13, 1864.

68. Augusta *Chronicle & Sentinel*, January 31, 1864. See also Richmond *Examiner*, January 25, 1864.

69. Richmond *Examiner*, June 13, 1864. See also Charleston *Mercury*, June 22, July 2, 1864; Augusta *Constitutionalist*, June 4, 1864; Richmond *Sentinel*, June 28, 1864.

70. Jones, *Diary*, II, 299. See also I. B. Cohen to Alexander H. Stephens, April 21, 1864, in Alexander H. Stephens Papers, Library of Congress.

71. Augusta *Chronicle & Sentinel*, June 15, 1864.

72. Richmond *Sentinel*, July 6, 1864.

73. Judah P. Benjamin to John Slidell, June 23, 1864, in *Official Records, Navies*, Ser. II, Vol. III, p. 1156.

74. Stephen R. Mallory to James D. Bulloch, July 5, 1864, ibid., Ser. II, Vol. II, pp. 680–81.

75. Richard E. Yeats, "Governor Vance and the Peace Movement," *North Carolina Historical Review*, XVII (1940), 109.

76. Raleigh *Conservative*, April 27, 1864.

77. Zebulon B. Vance to the General Assembly of North Carolina, May 17, 1864, in North Carolina, *Executive and Legislative Documents* (Raleigh, 1864), May Session, Document No. 1, p. 15; North Carolina General Assembly, Adjourned Session of 1864, "Resolutions in Reference to a Basis of Peace," May 28, 1864, *Public Laws* (Raleigh, 1864), p. 20. This resolution appeared in Augusta *Chronicle & Sentinel*, June 3, 1864.

78. Thomas B. Alexander and Richard E. Beringer, *The Anatomy of the Confederate Congress* (Nashville: Vanderbilt University Press, 1972), pp. 44–46, 337, 340; Wilfred B. Yearns, *The Confederate Congress* (Athens: University of Georgia Press, 1960), pp. 49–59.

79. James T. Leach, "Resolution," May 23, 1864, in Southern Historical Society, *Papers* (Richmond, 1958), LI, 130. See also Josiah Turner, Jr., to Sophia D. Turner, May 7, 1864, in Josiah Turner Papers, Southern Historical Collection, University of North Carolina Library, Chapel Hill.

80. Richmond *Examiner*, May 24, 1864.

81. *Journal of the Congress of the Confederate States of America*, IV, 143; VII, 112, 113, 150–51.

82. Charleston *Mercury*, June 6, 1864.

83. Confederate States Congress, "Joint Resolution Declaring the Dispositions, Principles and Purposes of the Confederate States in Relation to the Existing War with the United States," June 14, 1864, in *Official Records, Armies*, Ser. IV, Vol. III, pp. 486–88; Richmond *Sentinel*, June 13, 1864; Augusta *Chronicle & Sentinel*, June 17, 1864; North Carolina *Standard*, June 22, 1864. See also James M. Mason to Judah P. Benjamin, November 10, 1864, in *Official Records, Navies*, Ser. II, Vol. III, p. 1231.

84. Alexander H. Stephens to Linton Stephens, August 28, 1864, in Alexander H. Stephens Papers, Manhattanville College; Alexander H. Stephens to I. H. R. Washington et al., September 22, 1864, in Augusta *Constitutionalist*, October 4, 1864.

Chapter 4

1. Augusta *Chronicle & Sentinel*, July 26, 1864.

2. Richmond *Examiner*, July 13, 1864. See also Richmond *Dispatch*, July 19, 1864.

3. Robert E. Lee to Jefferson Davis, July 10, 1864, in Robert E. Lee, *The Wartime Papers of R. E. Lee*, ed. Clifford Dowdey and Louis H. Manarin (Boston: Little, Brown and Company, 1961), p. 818.

4. Richmond *Dispatch*, July 13, 1864.

5. Richmond *Examiner*, July 30, 1864.

6. Ibid., in Augusta *Constitutionalist*, August 7, 1864; Augusta *Constitutionalist*, July 26, 1864.

7. "Tyrone Powers," July 18, 1864, in Augusta *Constitutionalist*, July 26, 1864.

8. Henry Cleveland to Alexander H. Stephens, July 15, 1864, in Alexander H. Stephens Papers, Library of Congress. See also Kean, *Diary*, p. 164.

9. Charleston *Mercury*, July 22, 1864.

10. Joseph E. Brown to James A. Seddon, September 12, 1864, in *Official Records, Armies*, Ser. I, Vol. LII, Pt. II, p. 737; Alexander H. Stephens to Linton Stephens, August 28, 1864, in Alexander H. Stephens Papers, Manhattanville College of the Sacred Heart, Purchase, N.Y.

11. Jefferson Davis to Herschel V. Johnson, September 18, 1864, in *Official Records, Armies*, Ser. I, Vol. XLII, Pt. II, pp. 1258–59. See also Jefferson Davis, Speech at Macon, Georgia, September 28, 1864, in *Jefferson Davis*, ed. Rowland, VI, 343–44.

12. Clement C. Clay to Judah P. Benjamin, August 11, 1864, in *Official Records, Armies*, Ser. IV, Vol. III, p. 584.

13. Ibid.; Clement C. Clay to Judah P. Benjamin, July 25, 1864, in Clement C. Clay Papers, Duke University; James P. Holcombe to Judah P. Benjamin, November 16, 1864, in *Official Records, Navies*, Ser. II, Vol. III, p. 1235; Hines, "Northwestern Conspiracy," p. 500.

14. Clement C. Clay to Jacob Thompson, July 11, 1864, in U.S. Congress, House, *Assassination of Lincoln*, House Report 104, 39th Cong., 1st sess., 1866, p. 17.

15. Clement C. Clay to James M. Mason and John Slidell, August 24, 1864, in Clement C. Clay Letterbook, Duke University; Clement C. Clay and James P. Holcombe to Jefferson Davis, July 25, 1864, in Clement C. Clay Papers, Duke University.

16. Clay to Benjamin, August 11, 1864, p. 584.

17. Ibid., p. 585.

18. Clay to Mason and Slidell, August 25, 1864.

19. Edward C. Kirkland, *The Peacemakers of 1864* (New York: The Macmillan Company, 1927), pp. 68–72. Clay to Benjamin, August 11, 1864, pp. 584–87. The quotation is on p. 585.

20. William C. Jewett to Horace Greeley, July 5, 1864, in Don C. Seitz, *Horace Greeley* (Indianapolis: Bobbs-Merrill Company, 1926), p. 247.

21. Clay to Benjamin, August 11, 1864, p. 585.

22. Horace Greeley to Abraham Lincoln, July 7, 1864, in Seitz, *Greeley*, pp. 248–50.

23. John G. Nicolay and John Hay, *Abraham Lincoln* (10 vols.; New York: The Century Company, 1886), IX, 187.

24. Abraham Lincoln to Horace Greeley, July 9, 1864, in *The Collected Works of Abraham Lincoln*, ed. Roy P. Basler (10 vols.; New Brunswick, N.J.: Rutgers University Press, 1953), VII, 435.

25. Kirkland, *Peacemakers*, pp. 78–80; Horace Greeley to Clement C. Clay, Jacob Thompson, and James P. Holcombe, July 17, 1864, in New York *Tribune*, July 22, 1864.

26. Clay to Benjamin, August 11, 1864, p. 585; Holcombe to Benjamin, November 16, 1864, p. 1236.

27. Clay and Holcombe to Davis, July 25, 1864; Holcombe to Benjamin, November 16, 1864, pp. 1237–38.

28. Kinchen, *Confederate Operations*, p. 80; Hines, "Northwestern Conspiracy," p. 502.

29. Clement C. Clay and James P. Holcombe to Horace Greeley, July 18, 1864, in New York *Tribune*, July 22, 1864.

30. Clay and Holcombe to Davis, July 25, 1864.

31. Nicolay and Hay, *Lincoln*, IX, 192–93.

32. Abraham Lincoln to "To Whom It May Concern," July 18, 1864, in New York *Tribune*, July 22, 1864.

33. Clay and Holcombe to Greeley, July 18, 1864.

34. Clay and Holcombe to Davis, July 25, 1864.

35. New York *Tribune*, July 22, 1864.

36. Judah P. Benjamin to James M. Mason, August 25, 1864, in *Official Records, Navies*, Ser. II, Vol. III, p. 1194; Richmond *Examiner*, July 26, 1864; Richmond *Dispatch*, July 27, 1864; Richmond *Sentinel*, July 27, 1864; Augusta *Constitutionalist*, July 30, 1864; Charleston *Mercury*, August 1, 1864.

37. Stephen R. Mallory to Virginia C. Clay, August 1, 1864, in Clement C. Clay Papers, Duke University.

38. Richmond *Sentinel,* July 26, 1864. See also Richmond *Examiner*, July 27, 1864.

39. Richmond *Examiner*, July 26, 1864. See also ibid., July 28, 1864; Richmond *Dispatch*, July 26, 1864.

40. Charleston *Mercury*, August 1, 1864.

41. Richmond *Dispatch*, August 22, 1864.

42. Charleston *Mercury*, August 1, 1864.

43. Richmond *Dispatch*, July 26, 1864.

44. Augusta *Constitutionalist*, July 28, 1864.

45. Henry Hotze to Judah P. Benjamin, August 6, 1864, in *Official Records, Navies*, Ser. II, Vol. III, p. 1186. See also A. Dudley Mann to Judah P. Benjamin, October 15, 1864, ibid., pp. 1223–24.

46. Richmond *Sentinel*, July 26, 1864. See also Augusta *Constitutionalist*, July 28, 1864.

47. Richmond *Sentinel*, July 27, 1864.

48. Augusta *Constitutionalist*, July 30, 1864.

49. Mallory to Virginia C. Clay, August 1, 1864.

50. Clay to Benjamin, August 11, 1864, pp. 585–86.

51. Holcombe to Benjamin, November 16, 1864, p. 1238.

52. Clay and Holcombe to Davis, July 25, 1864; Clay to Mason and Slidell, August 24, 1864; Clay to Benjamin, August 11, 1864, pp. 584-87; Holcombe to Benjamin, November 16, 1864, pp. 1235–39.

53. Columbus (Ohio) *Crisis*, August 3, 1864.

54. Nicolay and Hay, *Lincoln*, IX, 194.

55. William S. Rosecrans, "List of Special Mentions," January 7, 1864, in *Official Records, Armies*, Ser. I, Vol. XXX, Pt. I, p. 84.

56. Kirkland, *Peacemakers*, pp. 85–90.

57. Ibid., pp. 90–92; James G. Randall and Richard N. Current, *Lincoln the President* (4 vols.; New York: Dodd, Mead & Company, 1945–1955), IV, 165–66.

58. James R. Gilmore and James Jaquess to Judah P. Benjamin, July 17, 1864, in James R. Gilmore [Edmund Kirke], "Our Visit to Richmond," *Atlantic Monthly*, XIV (1864), 376. This document also appears in Benjamin to Mason, August 25, 1864, p. 1191.

59. Benjamin to Mason, August 25, 1864, p. 1191.

60. Gilmore, "Visit," p. 382.

61. Ibid., pp. 372–83.

62. Davis, *Rise and Fall*, II, 611; Larry E. Nelson, " 'Independence or Fight,' " *Civil War Times Illustrated*, XV (June 1976), 10–14.

63. Kirkland, *Peacemakers*, p. 96.

64. Boston *Evening Transcript*, July 22, 1864.

65. Charleston *Mercury*, August 29, 30, 1864; Richmond *Dispatch*, August 25, 26, 1864; Richmond *Sentinel*, July 26, August 26, 1864; Augusta *Constitutionalist*, August 30, 1864.

66. Benjamin to Mason, August 25, 1864, pp. 1190–95. The quotation is on p. 1193. See also James M. Mason to Judah P. Benjamin, September 29, 1864, in *Official Records, Navies*, Ser. II, Vol. III, p. 1219.

67. Richmond *Examiner*, August 26, 1864; Augusta *Chronicle & Sentinel*, August 3, 1864; Charleston *Mercury*, August 30, 1864; Richmond *Dispatch*, August 25, 26, 30, 1864.

68. Alexander H. Stephens to Linton Stephens, August 29, 1864, in Alexander H. Stephens Papers, Manhattanville College; Augusta *Chronicle & Sentinel*, August 1, 1864.

69. Richmond *Sentinel*, August 26, 1864.

70. Charleston *Mercury*, August 30, 1864.

71. Richmond *Examiner*, August 2, 1864.

72. Augusta *Constitutionalist*, August 2, 1864.

73. Ibid., August 30, 1864. See also Richmond *Examiner*, August 27, 1864; Charleston *Mercury*, August 30, 1864.

74. Richmond *Dispatch*, August 30, 1864.

75. Richmond *Sentinel*, August 26, 1864. See also Richmond *Dispatch*, August 30, 1864.

76. Clay and Holcombe to Davis, July 25, 1864.

77. Clay to Benjamin, August 11, 1864, p. 585.

78. Augusta *Constitutionalist*, May 1, 1864. See also Augusta *Chronicle & Sentinel*, May 6, June 3, 1864.

79. Benjamin H. Hill to James A. Seddon, July 14, 1864, in *Official Records, Armies*, Ser. I, Vol. LII, Pt. II, p. 706.

80. Joseph E. Johnston, *Narrative of Operations* (Bloomington: Indiana University Press, 1956), pp. 362–63.

81. James A. Seddon to Benjamin H. Hill, July 11, 1864, in *Official Records, Armies*, Ser. I, Vol. LII, Pt. II, pp. 693–95; Hill to Seddon, July 14, 1864, pp. 704–7; letter by Benjamin H. Hill, October 12, 1878, in Davis, *Rise and Fall*, II, 557–61.

82. Benjamin H. Hill to Joseph E. Johnston, July 14, 1864, in *Official Records, Armies*, Ser. I, Vol. XXXVIII, Pt. V, p. 879.

83. James A. Seddon to Benjamin H. Hill, July 13, 1864, in ibid., Ser. I, Vol. LII, Pt. II, pp. 693–95; Hill to Seddon, July 14, 1864, pp. 704–7.

84. Richmond *Whig*, July 20, 1864. See also ibid., July 22, 1864.

85. Augusta *Chronicle & Sentinel*, July 21, 1864. See also Richmond *Examiner*, July 20, 25, 1864.

86. Richmond *Sentinel*, July 21, 1864. See also ibid., July 20, 23, 1864; Richmond *Dispatch*, July 21, 25, 1864; Richmond *Enquirer*, July 19, 25, 1864.

Chapter 5

1. James M. Mason to Judah P. Benjamin, July 14, 1864, in *Official Records, Navies*, Ser. II, Vol. III, pp. 1173–74.

2. Jacob Thompson to John Slidell and James M. Mason, August 23, 1864, in Hines, "Northwestern Conspiracy," pp. 508–9; Hines, "Northwestern Conspiracy," pp. 502, 505–6; Klement, *Copperheads*, p. 173. For a discussion of whether Vallandigham accepted money from Thompson, see Frank L. Klement, *Limits of Dissent: Clement L. Vallandigham and the Civil War* (Lexington: University Press of Kentucky, 1970), p. 271, footnote 37.

3. Hines, "Northwestern Conspiracy," pp. 503–4. See also James P. Holcombe to Judah P. Benjamin, November 16, 1864, in *Official Records, Navies*, Ser. II, Vol. III, p. 1238.

4. Hines, "Northwestern Conspiracy," pp. 506–7.

5. Klement, *Limits of Dissent*, pp. 138–212, 257–78.

6. Hines, "Northwestern Conspiracy," p. 506; Kinchen, *Confederate Operations*, pp. 51–54.

7. Jacob Thompson to Judah P. Benjamin, December 3, 1864, in *Official Records, Armies*, Ser. I, Vol. XLIII, Pt. II, p. 931; Hines, "Northwestern Conspiracy," pp. 507–8; Kinchen, *Confederate Operations*, pp. 54–64.

8. Thompson to Slidell and Mason, August 23, 1864, p. 509. See also Thompson to Benjamin, December 3, 1864, pp. 930–31.

9. Jacob Thompson to [Judah P. Benjamin, ?], July [?], 1864, in Hines, "Northwestern Conspiracy," p. 507.

10. Hines, "Northwestern Conspiracy," pp. 500, 568–69.

11. Thompson to Benjamin, December 3, 1864, p. 933.

12. For examples of publication of the speech see Richmond *Dispatch*, June 22, 1864; Augusta *Constitutionalist*, July 1, 1864.

13. Augusta *Chronicle & Sentinel*, July 5, 19, 1864; Gorgas, *Diary*, p. 124; Charleston *Mercury*, July 9, 1864.

14. Augusta *Chronicle & Sentinel*, August 18, 1864; Richmond *Dispatch*, August 18, 1864.

15. Richmond *Sentinel*, August 30, 1864; Augusta *Chronicle & Sentinel*, August 17, 19, 1864; Alexander H. Stephens to Herschel V. Johnson, September 5, 1864, in Alexander H. Stephens Papers, Library of Congress.

16. New York *New Nation* in Augusta *Chronicle & Sentinel*, July 26, 1864.

17. Richmond *Dispatch*, July 21, 1864; Augusta *Chronicle & Sentinel*, July 14, 1864; Richmond *Examiner*, July 9, 1864. See also Augusta *Chronicle & Sentinel*, July 27, 1864; Ruhl J. Bartlett, *John C. Frémont and the Republican Party* (Columbus: Ohio State University Press, 1930), p. 111.

18. Richmond *Examiner*, July 5, 9, 25, August 3, 1864; Richmond *Sentinel*, July 25, 1864; Charleston *Mercury*, July 9, 1864; Augusta *Chronicle & Sentinel*, July 30, 1864.

19. Richmond *Dispatch*, August 8, 1864.

20. Richmond *Sentinel*, June 28, 1864; Augusta *Constitutionalist*, June 28, 1864; Augusta *Chronicle & Sentinel*, July 1, 1864.

21. Augusta *Chronicle & Sentinel*, July 1, 1864.

22. Richmond *Examiner*, July 25, 1864; Richmond *Sentinel*, July 20, 1864; Augusta *Chronicle & Sentinel*, July 1, 13, 15, 24, 1864; Augusta *Constitutionalist*, June 30, 1864.

23. Augusta *Chronicle & Sentinel*, July 27, 1864.

24. Ibid., July 16, 1864. See also Mobile *Daily Advertiser and Register* in Augusta *Constitutionalist*, July 1, 1864.

25. Richmond *Sentinel*, July 15, 1864; Augusta *Chronicle & Sentinel*, July 8, 1864. See also Richmond *Dispatch*, July 23, 1864.

26. Richmond *Sentinel*, July 15, 1864.

27. Augusta *Chronicle & Sentinel*, July 8, 1864.

28. Richmond *Examiner*, July 9, 1864.

29. New York *Times*, July 14, 1864.

30. Augusta *Constitutionalist*, August 3, 1864. See also Augusta *Chronicle & Sentinel*, August 2, 1864; Richmond *Dispatch*, July 30, 1864; Richmond *Sentinel*, July 29, 1864; Mobile *Daily Advertiser and Register* in Augusta *Constitutionalist*, July 1, 1864.

31. Augusta *Chronicle & Sentinel*, July 31, 1864. See also Richmond *Examiner*, July 25, 1864.

32. Richmond *Sentinel*, July 29, 1864.

33. Augusta *Chronicle & Sentinel*, August 6, 1864.

34. Richmond *Dispatch*, July 30, 1864; Augusta *Chronicle & Sentinel*, August 6, 1864.

35. Klement, *Limits of Dissent*, pp. 257–78.

36. North Carolina *Standard*, July 13, 1864; Richmond *Sentinel*, June 22, 25, 30, 1864; Augusta *Chronicle & Sentinel*, June 26, July 6, 1864; Augusta *Constitutionalist*, June 23, 1864.

37. Augusta *Chronicle & Sentinel*, August 7, 16, 21, 1864; Richmond *Sentinel*, June 7, 1864; Augusta *Constitutionalist*, August 20, 1864; Charleston *Mercury*, June 22, 1864.

38. Augusta *Chronicle & Sentinel*, July 10, 1864; Richmond *Dispatch*, July 16, 1864.

39. Edwin H. Faye to Sarah H. Faye, July 17, 1864, in Fay, "Infernal War," p. 399.

40. Chicago *Times* in Richmond *Examiner*, July 6, 1864; New York *Herald* in Richmond *Examiner*, July 23, 1864; Richmond *Examiner*, June 28, July 22, 1864; Charleston *Mercury*, July 2, 1864; Augusta *Chronicle & Sentinel*, July 26, 1864; Augusta *Constitutionalist*, July 17, 1864; Jones, *Diary*, II, 239; Kean, *Diary*, p. 163.

41. Jack F. Leach, *Conscription in the United States* (Rutland, Vt.: Charles E. Tuttle Publishing House, 1952), p. 420.

42. Richmond *Sentinel*, July 22, 23, August 5, 1864; Richmond *Dispatch*, July 23, 1864; Richmond *Examiner*, July 23, 1864; Augusta *Chronicle & Sentinel*, July 26, 1864; New York *Record* in Augusta *Constitutionalist*, August 11, 1864; Jones, *Diary*, II, 239.

43. Richmond *Examiner*, July 7, 1864; Richmond *Sentinel*, June 9, July 7, August 26, 1864; Augusta *Constitutionalist*, June 14, 1864; Augusta *Chronicle & Sentinel*, July 23, 27, August 14, 1864; Charleston *Courier*, in Augusta *Chronicle & Sentinel*, June 10, 1864; Charleston *Mercury*, August 30, 1864; Richmond *Dispatch*, August 24, 1864.

44. Richmond *Dispatch*, June 10, 1864; Richmond *Sentinel*, June 23, 1864; Augusta *Chronicle & Sentinel*, July 23, 1864.

45. Wilkes (New York) *Spirit of the Times* in Richmond *Dispatch*, June 11, 1864. For a similar comment see Concord (New Hampshire) *Standard* in Augusta *Chronicle & Sentinel*, August 24, 1864.

46. Augusta *Chronicle & Sentinel*, July 26, 1864; Richmond *Examiner*, July 13, 1864; Augusta *Constitutionalist*, July 5, 1864; Jones, *Diary*, II, 238; Richmond *Dispatch*, August 25, 1864.

47. Richmond *Dispatch*, July 6, 19, 21, 1864; Richmond *Sentinel*, July 7, August 1, 1864; Charleston *Mercury*, July 13, 1864; Richmond *Examiner*, July 13, 1864; Augusta *Chronicle & Sentinel*, August 6, 1864.

48. Richmond *Sentinel*, July 8, 1864; Richmond *Dispatch*, July 9, 1864; Richmond *Examiner*, July 9, 1864.

49. Klement, *Copperheads*, pp. 175–86.

50. Richmond *Sentinel*, August 3, 1864; Augusta *Chronicle & Sentinel*, August 7, 1864; North Carolina *Standard*, August 10, 1864; Charleston *Mercury*, August 31, 1864.

51. Abraham Lincoln, Secret Memorandum, August 23, 1864, in Lincoln, *Collected Works*, VII, 514.

52. Linton Stephens to Alexander H. Stephens, September 4, 1864, in Alexander H. Stephens Papers, Manhattanville College of the Sacred Heart, Purchase, N.Y.

53. C. C. Andrews to Abraham Lincoln, August 1, 1864, in *Official Records, Armies*, Ser. I, Vol. XLI, Pt. II, p. 502. See also C. C. Andrews to Abraham Lincoln, July 18, 1864, ibid., p. 234.

54. Statement of C. G. Reed to T. B. Stevenson, August 6, 1864, ibid., Ser. I, Vol. XXXV, Pt. II, p. 220.

55. Statement of Charles Harris, September 7, 1864, in *Official Records, Navies*, Ser. I, Vol. XV, p. 678. See also

Ulysses S. Grant to Edwin M. Stanton, September 13, 1864, ibid., *Armies*, Ser. III, Vol. IV, p. 713.

56. John W. Graham, who was serving with the Army of Northern Virginia at Petersburg wrote, "Scarcely anyone I meet speaks of peace at all likely to take place soon, and the men expect to spend the winter at Petersburg." See John W. Graham to William A. Graham, August 28, 1864, in William A. Graham Papers, Southern Historical Collection, University of North Carolina Library, Chapel Hill.

57. Richmond *Examiner*, August 27, 1864.

58. Augusta *Chronicle & Sentinel*, August 19, 1864. For additional predictions that Northern developments portended an early and acceptable peace, see Josephus Anderson to Howell Cobb, August 29, 1864, in Toombs, Stephens, and Cobb, *Correspondence*, p. 650; Richmond *Sentinel*, August 5, 8, 12, 22, 24, 1864; Augusta *Constitutionalist*, July 30, August 12, 17, 1864; Richmond *Examiner*, August 12, 27, 1864; Augusta *Chronicle & Sentinel*, August 21, 1864.

59. Jones, *Diary*, II, 247, 268–69.

60. Gorgas, *Diary*, p. 138. See also David Schenck, Diary, August 20, September 1, 1864, in Southern Historical Collection, University of North Carolina Library, Chapel Hill.

61. Richmond *Dispatch*, August 18, 1864. See also Augusta *Chronicle & Sentinel*, September 1, 1864.

62. Augusta *Constitutionalist*, August 29, 1864.

63. Richmond *Examiner*, July 26, 1864. For a similar comment see North Carolina *Standard*, August 3, 1864.

64. Augusta *Chronicle & Sentinel*, August 3, 1864; Richmond *Sentinel*, July 27, 1864. See also New York *Tribune*, July 22, 1864.

65. Augusta *Constitutionalist*, August 28, 1864; Richmond *Examiner*, August 15, 1864; Augusta *Chronicle & Sentinel*, August 14, 26, 30, September 2, 3, 1864; Francis A. Shoup, Journal of Operations, August 25, 1864, in *Official Records, Armies*, Ser. I, Vol. XXXVIII, Pt. III, p. 693. See also Richmond *Dispatch*, August 27, 1864; Richmond *Examiner*, August 17, 1864; A. Dudley Mann to Judah P. Benjamin, August 26, 1864, in *Official Records, Navies*, Ser. II, Vol. III, pp. 1194–95.

66. Augusta *Constitutionalist*, August 28, 1864. See also Richmond *Examiner*, August 17, 1864.

67. Augusta *Constitutionalist*, August 28, 1864. See also Augusta *Chronicle & Sentinel*, August 30, 1864.

68. Richmond *Sentinel*, August 1, 1864.

69. Richmond *Sentinel* in Charleston *Mercury*, August 15, 1864.

70. Charleston *Mercury*, August 5, 1864. See also Augusta *Constitutionalist*, August 7, 1864.

71. Charleston *Mercury*, August 15, 1864.

72. Augusta *Chronicle & Sentinel*, August 14, 1864.

73. Ibid., August 14, 17, 1864.

74. Richmond *Sentinel*, August 12, 1864.

75. Ibid., August 20, 1864.

76. Richmond *Enquirer* in North Carolina *Standard*, August 3, 1864; Augusta *Constitutionalist*, July 30, 1864; Richmond *Examiner*, August 26, 1864; Charleston *Mercury*, August 31, 1864.

77. Charleston *Mercury*, August 24, 25, 1864. See also Richmond *Dispatch*, August 31, 1864.

78. Augusta *Chronicle & Sentinel*, August 31, 1864.

79. Richmond *Dispatch*, August 22, 1864.

80. Ibid.; Richmond *Examiner*, August 23, 1864.

81. Augusta *Constitutionalist*, August 3, 1864. See also Richmond *Sentinel*, August 1, 1864.

82. Richmond *Examiner*, August 30, 1864.

83. Richmond *Sentinel*, August 2, 1864.

84. Alexander H. Stephens to Jefferson Davis, May 7, 1864, in Alexander H. Stephens Papers, Duke University.

85. David F. Cable to Alexander H. Stephens, June 21, 1864, in Jefferson Davis Papers, Duke University.

86. Alexander H. Stephens to Jefferson Davis, July 5, 1864, in Alexander H. Stephens Papers, Duke University. See also Herschel V. Johnson to Alexander H. Stephens, July 11, 1864, in Herschel V. Johnson Papers, Duke University.

87. Alexander H. Stephens to R. M. Johnston, August 26, 1864, in Alexander H. Stephens Papers, Library of Congress. See also Alexander H. Stephens to Linton Stephens, August 7,

1864, in Alexander H. Stephens Papers, Manhattanville College.

88. Alexander H. Stephens to Linton Stephens, August 28, 1864, in Alexander H. Stephens Papers, Manhattanville College. See also Alexander H. Stephens to Linton Stephens, August 29, 1864, ibid.; Linton Stephens to Alexander H. Stephens, September 2, 1864, ibid.

89. Thompson to Mason and Slidell, August 23, 1864, p. 509; Clement C. Clay to James M. Mason and John Slidell, August 24, 1864, in Clement C. Clay Letterbook, Duke University; Clement C. Clay to Judah P. Benjamin, September 12, 1864, in *Official Records, Armies*, Ser. IV, Vol. III, pp. 636–37; Hines, "Northwestern Conspiracy," pp. 501–2; Kinchen, *Confederate Operations*, pp. 87–90.

90. Clay to Mason and Slidell, August 24, 1864; Thompson to Mason and Slidell, August 23, 1864, pp. 508–10. See also Louis B. Sanders to Virginia C. Clay, August 12, 1864, in Clement C. Clay Papers, Duke University.

91. Richmond *Sentinel*, September 1, 1864. For statements of similar reasoning and conclusions see ibid., August 6, 18, 22, September 3, 1864; Richmond *Examiner*, July 30, August 10, 12, 20, 23, 25, 30, 31, 1864; Richmond *Dispatch*, August 8, 18, 1864; Augusta *Chronicle & Sentinel*, July 30, August 19, 20, 1864; Augusta *Constitutionalist*, August 23, 1864; Alexander H. Stephens to Linton Stephens, August 28, 1864; Thompson to [Benjamin ?], July [?], 1864, p. 507.

92. Richmond *Dispatch*, August 18, September 2, 1864; Augusta *Constitutionalist*, August 26, 1864.

93. Augusta *Constitutionalist*, August 23, 1864; See also Jones, *Diary*, II, 276.

94. Charleston *Mercury*, August 17, 1864; Richmond *Examiner*, August 12, 15, 1864; Augusta *Constitutionalist*, August 12, 1864; North Carolina *Standard*, August 31, 1864; Augusta *Chronicle & Sentinel*, August 19, 27, 1864; Richmond *Sentinel*, August 22, 1864; Alexandria (Virginia) *Gazette*, August 1, 1864; Clay to Slidell and Mason, August 24, 1864; Thompson to Mason and Slidell, August 23, 1864, p. 509; Hines, "Northwestern Conspiracy," p. 573.

95. Alexander H. Stephens to Linton Stephens, August 29, 1864. See also Richmond *Examiner*, August 29, 1864; Richmond *Sentinel*, August 29, 1864.

96. Edmund Ruffin, Diary, August 29, 1864, Library of Congress.

97. Hines, "Northwestern Conspiracy," pp. 567–74; Kinchen, *Confederate Operations*, pp. 66–72.

98. Democratic Party Platform of 1864, in Porter and Johnson, eds., *National Party Platforms*, pp. 34–35.

99. William F. Zornow, *Lincoln and the Party Divided* (Norman, Okla.: University of Oklahoma Press, 1954), pp. 129–40.

100. Richmond *Dispatch*, September 1, 3, 1864; Richmond *Sentinel*, September 1, 3, 1864; Augusta *Chronicle & Sentinel*, September 9, 1864; North Carolina *Standard*, September 7, 1864; Augusta *Constitutionalist*, September 7, 1864. See also A. S. Pendleton to John C. Breckinridge, September 3, 1864, in *Official Records, Armies*, Ser. I, Vol. XLIII, Pt. II, p. 863; Jones, *Diary*, II, 276.

101. Alexander H. Stephens to Linton Stephens, September 2, 1864, in Alexander H. Stephens Papers, Manhattanville College. See also Alexander H. Stephens to Linton Stephens, September 3, 1864, in ibid.

102. Richmond *Dispatch*, September 1, 1864. See also J. Schneider to Edwin Y. Lansing, September 1, 1864, in *Official Records, Armies*, Ser. I, Vol. XLIII, Pt. II, p. 7.

103. Jones, *Diary*, II, 275.

104. Ibid., p. 276.

105. Richmond *Examiner*, September 5, 1864; Charleston *Mercury*, September 5, 1864. See also Richmond *Dispatch*, September 5, 1864; Richmond *Sentinel*, September 5, 1864.

106. Josiah Gorgas to George W. Rains, September 3, 1864, in George W. Rains Papers, Southern Historical Collection, University of North Carolina Library, Chapel Hill.

107. "Sethon" to Editor, September 4, 1864, in Augusta *Constitutionalist*, September 9, 1864.

108. Richmond *Dispatch*, September 5, 1864.

109. Jones, *Diary*, II, 275.

110. Gorgas to Rains, September 3, 1864.

111. Richmond *Sentinel*, September 3, 1864. See also Jones, *Diary*, II, 276.

112. Richmond *Sentinel*, September 2, 1864.

113. Alexander H. Stephens to Linton Stephens, September 4, 1864, in Alexander H. Stephens Papers, Manhattanville College. See also Alexander H. Stephens to Linton Stephens, September 3, 1864. For Linton Stephens's views on the convention, see Linton Stephens to Alexander H. Stephens, September 2, 4, 1864, ibid.

114. Stephens to Johnson, September 5, 1864.

Chapter 6

1. Chesnut, *Diary*, p. 434.

2. Alexander H. Stephens to Linton Stephens, September 3, 1864, in Alexander H. Stephens Papers, Manhattanville College of the Sacred Heart, Purchase, N.Y. See also Alexander H. Stephens to Linton Stephens, September 4, 1864, ibid.; Linton Stephens to Alexander H. Stephens, September 4, 1864, ibid.

3. Augusta *Chronicle & Sentinel*, September 4, 1864. See also Richmond *Dispatch*, September 3, 4, 1864; Richmond *Sentinel*, September 5, 1864; Jones, *Diary*, II, 276.

4. Jones, *Diary*, II, 277.

5. Thomas L. Connelly, *Autumn of Glory* (Baton Rouge: Louisiana State University Press, 1971), pp. 402–3, 421.

6. Augusta *Constitutionalist*, September 6, 1864.

7. David Schenck, Diary, September 15, 1864, in Southern Historical Collection, University of North Carolina Library, Chapel Hill. This entry contrasts vividly with the optimistic and confident entry of September 1, 1864.

8. George to "Brother," September 8, 1864, in Augusta *Constitutionalist*, September 15, 1864. See also John W. Graham to William A. Graham, September 5, 1864, in William A. Graham Papers, Southern Historical Collection, University of North Carolina Library, Chapel Hill; Chesnut, *Diary*, p. 436; Joseph E. Brown to Alexander H. Stephens, September 30, 1864, in Toombs, Stephens, and Cobb, *Correspondence*, p. 653.

9. Augusta *Chronicle & Sentinel*, September 8, 1864; Richmond *Sentinel*, September 5, 1864; North Carolina *Standard*, September 7, 1864.

10. John W. Graham to William A. Graham, September 5, 1864; Gorgas, *Diary*, p. 140; George to "Brother," September 8, 1864.

11. Richmond *Examiner*, September 5, 1864.

12. Ibid., September 6, 1864. For similar comments, see ibid., September 29, 1864; Augusta *Chronicle & Sentinel*, September 10, 1864; Richmond *Dispatch*, September 5, 1864; "Roundabout" to Editor, September 6, 1864, in Augusta *Constitutionalist*, September 11, 1864.

13. For general comments on the mood of the South following the disaster at Atlanta see James A. Seddon, Official Report, *Official Records, Armies*, Ser. IV, Vol. III, pp. 757–58; Herschel V. Johnson, "From the Autobiography of Herschel V. Johnson," *American Historical Review*, XXX (1925), 334; Gorgas, *Diary*, pp. 141–42; Richmond *Examiner*, September 14, October 1, 1864.

14. Richmond *Sentinel*, September 16, 1864.

15. Augusta *Chronicle & Sentinel*, September 22, 1864. See also Richmond *Dispatch*, September 8, 1864; North Carolina *Standard*, October 5, 1864; David Schenck, Diary, September 15, 1864.

16. Charleston *Courier*, September 9, 1864.

17. Richmond *Dispatch*, September 16, 1864.

18. Charleston *Mercury*, September 20, October 15, 1864; Richmond *Examiner*, September 5, 6, 12, 13, 20, 24, 26, 28, 29, 1864; Augusta *Constitutionalist*, September 13, 29, October 2, 1864; Augusta *Chronicle & Sentinel*, September 8, 1864; Richmond *Dispatch*, September 5, 6, 15, 1864; Richmond *Sentinel*, September 6, 7, 8, 10, 13, 16, October 3, 4, 22, 1864.

19. Charles R. Wilson, "McClellan's Changing Views on the Peace Plank of 1864," *American Historical Review*, XXXVIII (1933), 498–510.

20. George B. McClellan to Horatio Seymour et al., September 8, 1864, in New York *Times*, September 9, 1864.

21. Richmond *Dispatch*, September 13, 1864; Augusta *Chronicle & Sentinel*, September 13, 1864; Charleston *Mer-*

cury, September 13, 1864; North Carolina *Standard,* September 21, 1864.

22. John Slidell tọ Judah P. Benjamin, September 26, 1864, in *Official Records, Navies,* Ser. II, Vol. III, p. 1217.

23. Richmond *Sentinel,* September 13, 1864. See also ibid., September 16, 20, 1864; Richmond *Dispatch,* September 13, 1864; Augusta *Constitutionalist,* September 17, 1864.

24. Richmond *Examiner,* September 16, 1864. See also Jones, *Diary,* II, 285.

25. Richmond *Sentinel,* September 16, 1864. See also North Carolina *Standard,* September 28, 1864; Charleston *Mercury,* September 15, 1864; Augusta *Chronicle & Sentinel,* September 28, 1864; Augusta *Constitutionalist,* September 17, 1864; John Mullaly to Editor of New York *Times,* September 9, 1864, in Augusta *Constitutionalist,* September 20, 1864; Richmond *Examiner,* September 16, 20, 1864.

26. New York *Times* in Augusta *Chronicle & Sentinel,* September 21, 1864. See also Charleston *Mercury,* September 20, 1864.

27. Richmond *Sentinel,* September 20, 1864; Augusta *Chronicle & Sentinel,* September 20, 1864; Richmond *Sentinel,* September 22, 1864.

28. Zornow, *Lincoln,* p. 138; Richmond *Dispatch,* October 22, 1864.

29. George H. Pendleton to John B. Haskin, October 17, 1864, in Richmond *Sentinel,* October 26, 1864. See also New York *Herald* in Charleston *Mercury,* November 1, 1864.

30. Clement L. Vallandigham, Address at Sidney, Ohio, September 24, 1864, in Richmond *Sentinel,* October 10, 1864. See also Augusta *Constitutionalist,* October 14, 1864.

31. Fernando Wood, Address at New York City, September 24, 1864, in Augusta *Chronicle & Sentinel,* September 30, 1864.

32. Richmond *Sentinel,* September 21, 24, October 4, 1864; Augusta *Chronicle & Sentinel,* September 17, October 1, 1864; Augusta *Constitutionalist,* September 24, 1864; Charleston *Mercury,* September 30, 1864; Richmond *Examiner,* September 24, 1864.

33. Columbia *South Carolinian*, September 29, 1864.

34. Richmond *Examiner*, September 20, 1864; Augusta *Chronicle & Sentinel*, September 10, 1864; Richmond *Sentinel*, September 13, 19, 1864.

35. Richmond *Examiner*, September 20, 1864; Augusta *Chronicle & Sentinel*, September 29, 1864.

36. Bartlett, *Frémont*, pp. 121–33.

37. Charleston *Mercury*, September 30, 1864. For examples of publication of Frémont's letter in the Confederate press, see Richmond *Dispatch*, September 28, 1864; Richmond *Sentinel*, September 28, 1864; Augusta *Chronicle & Sentinel*, September 30, 1864; Augusta *Constitutionalist*, October 2, 1864; North Carolina *Standard*, October 5, 1864.

38. Allan Nevins, *Ordeal of the Union* (8 vols., New York: Charles Scribner's Sons, 1947–71), VII, 97–143; Zornow, *Lincoln*, pp. 141–221; Wood Gray, *The Hidden Civil War* (New York: Viking Press, 1942), pp. 189–205.

39. S. J. Anderson to Jefferson Davis, August 30, 1864, in *Jefferson Davis*, ed. Rowland, VI, 324–26.

40. L. [?] Ditzler to Jefferson Davis, September 15, 1864, in Jefferson Davis Papers, Duke University.

41. Clement C. Clay to Judah P. Benjamin, September 12, 1864, in Clement C. Clay Papers, Duke University.

42. Jefferson Davis to A. R. Wright et al., November 17, 1864, in *Jefferson Davis*, ed. Rowland, VI, 403–6; Herschel V. Johnson to Alexander H. Stephens, October 12, 1864, in Herschel V. Johnson Papers, Duke University.

43. David M. Carter to William A. Graham, March 16, 1864, in William A. Graham Papers, North Carolina Department of Archives and History, Raleigh.

44. J. Smith to Alexander H. Stephens, September 21, 1864, in Alexander H. Stephens Papers, Library of Congress.

45. E. Kirby Smith to Jefferson Davis, January 20, 1864, in *Official Records, Armies*, Ser. I, Vol. XXXIV, Pt. II, p. 896.

46. Kean, *Diary*, p. 174. See also A. Dudley Mann to Judah P. Benjamin, October 28, 1864, in *Official Records, Navies*, Ser. II, Vol. III, pp. 1227–28; Jones, *Diary*, II, 289. For an example of a Southerner expressing willingness to accept reconstruction on the basis of concessions implied by McClellan and the

Democrats, see George Brooks to William A. Graham, September 14, 1864, in William A. Graham Papers, Southern Historical Collection, University of North Carolina Library, Chapel Hill.

47. Judah P. Benjamin to Henry Hotze, September 15, 1864, in *Official Records, Navies*, Ser. II, Vol. III, p. 1207; Judah P. Benjamin to James M. Mason, September 20, 1864, ibid., p. 1217; Jones, *Diary*, II, 290.

48. After seeing and hearing Davis give a speech at Charlotte, North Carolina, an admirer said of the president's delivery and appearance: "He uses no common place phrases or terms, but explains everything in the best English. Much in the style of McCauley or Chalmers—No emotion or excitement seems to disturb his ideas, though impromptu all was perfect and might be printed without correction and defy criticism. The chief peculiarity that was exhibited in his countenance was fierceness and determination. His sharp features seemed to indicate impatience under opposition and a determination to overcome it." See David Schenck, Diary, September [?], 1864.

49. Jefferson Davis, Speech at Macon, Georgia, in Richmond *Examiner*, September 29, 1864.

50. Jefferson Davis, Speech at Augusta, Georgia, in Richmond *Dispatch*, October 10, 1864.

51. Jefferson Davis, Speech at Columbia, South Carolina, in Charleston *Courier*, October 6, 1864.

52. Ibid.

53. Davis, Speech at Augusta, Georgia.

54. Ibid.

55. Davis, Speech at Columbia, South Carolina.

56. Ibid.

57. Ibid.

58. Davis, Speech at Augusta, Georgia.

59. Davis, Speech at Columbia, South Carolina.

60. Jefferson Davis, Speech at Montgomery, Alabama, in Charleston *Courier*, October 3, 1864.

61. H. L. Flash to Jefferson Davis, October 7, 1864, in Jefferson Davis Papers, Duke University.

62. Johnson to Stephens, October 12, 1864.

63. Davis, Speech at Macon, Georgia.

64. Charleston *Mercury*, September 27, October 21, 1864; North Carolina *Standard*, October 5, 1864; Gorgas, *Diary*, p. 147; Augusta *Chronicle & Sentinel*, September 28, 1864. See also Richmond *Sentinel*, October 7, 1864.

65. "A Georgian" to Jefferson Davis, September 22, 1864, in Jefferson Davis Papers, Duke University.

66. William T. Sherman to Ulysses S. Grant, September 27, 1864, in *Official Records, Armies*, Ser. I, Vol. XXXIX, Pt. II, p. 488; Washington *Chronicle* in Charleston *Mercury*, October 21, 1864.

67. Richmond *Sentinel*, October 13, 26, 31, 1864; Richmond *Examiner*, October 14, 1864; Charleston *Mercury*, October 5, 1864; Jones, *Diary*, II, 287–88; Augusta *Chronicle & Sentinel*, September 24, October 2, 11, 16, November 4, 1864; North Carolina *Standard*, September 7, 1864; Raleigh *Progress* in North Carolina *Standard*, October 12, 1864; Raleigh *Progress*, November 4, 1864.

68. Richmond *Sentinel*, September 7, 1864; Jones, *Diary*, II, 289.

69. Raleigh *Progress* in North Carolina *Standard*, October 12, 1864.

70. Augusta *Chronicle & Sentinel*, October 15, 1864. See also Walter L. Fleming, "The Peace Movement in Alabama during the Civil War," *South Atlantic Quarterly*, II (1903), 119–20.

71. May S. Ringold, *The Role of the State Legislatures in the Confederacy* (Athens: University of Georgia Press, 1966), p. 99.

72. William W. Boyce to James H. Hammond, October 5, 1864, "Boyce-Hammond Correspondence," ed. Rosser H. Taylor, *Journal of Southern History*, III, (1937), 354.

73. William W. Boyce to Jefferson Davis, September 29, 1864, in Columbia *Guardian*, October 3, 1864.

74. Augusta *Constitutionalist*, October 21, 1864.

75. North Carolina *Standard*, October 12, 25, November 2, 1864; Charleston *Mercury*, October 20, 1864; Augusta *Constitutionalist*, October 21, 1864; Augusta *Chronicle & Sentinel*, October 8, 1864. See also Jason Niles, Diary, October 25, 1864,

in Southern Historical Collection, University of North Carolina Library, Chapel Hill.

76. Richmond *Sentinel*, October 13, 1864; Fayetteville (N.C.) *Observer* in North Carolina *Standard*, October 19, 1864; Augusta *Constitutionalist*, October 30, 1864; Charleston *Mercury*, November 7, 1864. See also Chesnut, *Diary*, p. 448.

77. Charleston *Mercury*, October 13, 1864.

78. Carolina *Spartan* in Augusta *Chronicle & Sentinel*, November 4, 1864; Athens *Watchman* in Augusta *Chronicle & Sentinel*, October 22, 1864; North Carolina *Standard*, October 26, 1864; Raleigh *Progress* in North Carolina *Standard*, October 12, 1864; Augusta *Chronicle & Sentinel*, November 2, 3, 1864.

79. Butler's Brigade, South Carolina Cavalry, Army of Northern Virginia, Resolutions, October 31, 1864, in North Carolina *Standard*, November 16, 1864.

80. Augusta *Chronicle & Sentinel*, October 27, 1864.

81. Alexander H. Stephens to Linton Stephens, October 9, 1864, in Alexander H. Stephens Papers, Manhattanville College.

82. Alexander H. Stephens to Herschel V. Johnson, September 11, 1864, in Herschel V. Johnson Papers, Duke University; Alexander H. Stephens to Herschel V. Johnson, October 9, 1864, ibid.; Alexander H. Stephens to Linton Stephens, October 15, 1864, in Alexander H. Stephens Papers, Manhattanville College; Alexander H. Stephens, *A Constitutional View of the Late War between the States* (2 vols., Philadelphia: National Publishing Co., 1868–70), II, 584.

83. Stephens to Johnson, September 11, 1864.

84. Alexander H. Stephens to Thomas J. Semmes, November 5, 1864, in Thomas J. Semmes Papers, Duke University. Portions of this letter appeared in Augusta *Constitutionalist*, November 16, 1864.

85. Alexander H. Stephens to Linton Stephens, October 9, 1864.

86. Alexander H. Stephens to Linton Stephens, October 15, 1864.

87. Alexander H. Stephens to Herschel V. Johnson, October 2, 1864, in Herschel V. Johnson Papers, Duke University. The views of Linton Stephens on a convention of the states were essentially the same as those of his brother. See Linton Stephens to Alexander H. Stephens, October 13, 1864, in James D. Waddell, *Biographical Sketch of Linton Stephens* (Atlanta: Dodson & Scott, 1877), pp. 284–86.

88. Isaac Scott et al. to Alexander H. Stephens, September 14, 1864, in Alexander H. Stephens Papers, Library of Congress. This letter also appeared in Augusta *Constitutionalist*, November 10, 1864.

89. Alexander H. Stephens to Herschel V. Johnson, October 9, 1864, in Herschel V. Johnson Papers, Duke University. See also Alexander H. Stephens to Linton Stephens, October 15, 1864.

90. Alexander H. Stephens to Linton Stephens, October 9, 1864.

91. Augusta *Chronicle & Sentinel*, October 2, 1864; Augusta *Constitutionalist*, October 4, 1864; Charleston *Courier*, October 4, 1864; Charleston *Mercury*, October 5, 1864; Columbia *South Carolinian*, October 6, 1864; North Carolina *Standard*, October 12, 1864; Richmond *Dispatch*, October 11, 1864.

92. Alexander H. Stephens to Isaac Scott et al., September 22, 1864, in Augusta *Constitutionalist*, October 4, 1864. Governor Brown also went on record in favor of a convention of the states on terms similar to those expressed by Stephens. See Joseph E. Brown to General Assembly. November 3, 1864, in Chandler, comp., *Confederate Records*, II, 740–52.

93. Richmond *Examiner*, October 21, 1864.

94. Charleston *Mercury*, October 5, 1864. See also ibid., October 6, 1864.

95. Richmond *Dispatch*, October 11, 1864.

96. J. Smith to Alexander H. Stephens, October 16, 1864, in Alexander H. Stephens Papers, Library of Congress; Iverson Harris to Alexander H. Stephens, October 4, 1864, ibid.

97. Columbus *Sun* in Augusta *Chronicle & Sentinel*, October 28, 1864.

98. "Omega" to Editor of Raleigh *Progress* in North Carolina *Standard*, November 2, 1864.

99. Johnson to Stephens, October 12, 1864.

100. Herschel V. Johnson to Isaac Scott et al., September 25, 1864, in Charleston *Courier*, October 14, 1864. See also Augusta *Chronicle & Sentinel*, October 7, 1864; Augusta *Constitutionalist*, October 7, 1864; Johnson, "Autobiography," p. 334.

101. Johnson to Scott et al., September 25, 1864.

102. Thomas J. Semmes, Address at Mobile, Alabama, October 28, 1864, in Augusta *Constitutionalist*, November 3, 1864.

103. Richmond *Examiner*, October 24, 1864.

104. Ibid., October 28, 1864.

105. James G. Jones to James B. Fry, September 12, 1864, in *Official Records, Armies*, Ser. III, Vol. IV, p. 711.

106. S. G. Burbridge to Joseph Holt, October 16, 1864, ibid., Ser. I, Vol. XXXIX, Pt. III, p. 321. See also Lewis M. Clark to S. G. Burbridge, October 31, 1864, ibid., Pt. I, pp. 882–83.

107. W. R. Boggs to Sterling Price, August 4, 1864, ibid., Ser. I, Vol. XLI, Pt. II, pp. 1040–41; E. Kirby Smith to Jefferson Davis, November 21, 1864, Jefferson Davis Papers, Duke University; Robert L. Kirby, *Kirby Smith's Confederacy* (New York: Columbia University Press, 1972), pp. 335–36; Robert E. Shalhope, *Sterling Price: Portrait of a Southerner* (Columbia: University of Missouri Press, 1971), pp. 262, 266–67, 274.

108. William S. Rosecrans to Abraham Lincoln, November 15, 1864, in *Official Records, Armies*, Ser. I, Vol. XLI, Pt. IV, p. 576.

109. North Carolina *Standard*, October 26, 1864.

110. Augusta *Chronicle & Sentinel*, October 1, 1864; Gorgas, *Diary*, pp. 145, 149; John W. Brown, Diary, November 3, 1864, in Southern Historical Collection, University of North Carolina Library, Chapel Hill.

111. Sterling Price to E. Kirby Smith, December 28, 1864, in *Official Records, Armies*, Ser. I, Vol. XLI, Pt. I, pp. 625–40.

112. Richmond *Sentinel*, September 1, November 1, 3, 1864; Richmond *Examiner*, September 3, October 7, 10, November 1, 1864; Richmond *Dispatch*, September 5, November 7, 1864; Charleston *Courier*, October 15, 1864; Charleston *Mercury*,

October 15, 1864; North Carolina *Standard*, September 7, 1864.

113. Richmond *Sentinel*, October 3, 1864.

114. Richmond *Dispatch*, September 9, 17, 26, October 17, 1864; Richmond *Sentinel*, September 10, 1864; Mobile *Daily Advertiser and Register* in Richmond *Sentinel*, September 16, 1864; Richmond *Examiner*, October 26, 29, 1864; Charleston *Mercury*, September 20, 1864; Stephens to Johnson, September 11, 1864; John W. Graham to William A. Graham, September 25, 1864, in William A. Graham Papers, Southern Historical Collection, University of North Carolina Library, Chapel Hill; James A. Seddon to Jefferson Davis, November 3, 1864, in *Official Records, Armies*, Ser. IV, Vol. III, p. 756; Jones, *Diary*, II, 324, 325.

115. Robert H. Smith to Helen H. Smith, September 19, 1864, in Robert H. Smith Papers, Southern Historical Collection, University of North Carolina Library, Chapel Hill; Johnson to Stephens, October 12, 1864; Gorgas, *Diary*, p. 149; Jones, *Diary*, II, 323, 326–27; Richmond *Examiner*, October 18, 24, November 2, 1864.

116. Richmond *Examiner*, November 2, 1864. See also Richmond *Dispatch*, September 19, 1864; Augusta *Chronicle & Sentinel*, September 18, 1864.

117. J. G. Foster to H. W. Halleck, October 3, 1864, in *Official Records, Armies*, Ser. I, Vol. XXXV, Pt. II, p. 307.

118. C. C. Andrews to Abraham Lincoln, November 20, 1864, ibid., Ser. I, Vol. XLI, Pt. IV, p. 626; Robert S. Hudson to Jefferson Davis, November 25, 1864, ibid., Pt. I, p. 1247.

119. Charleston *Mercury* in Augusta *Chronicle & Sentinel*, September 24, 1864.

120. "Grey Jacket" to Editor, Richmond *Sentinel*, September 19, 1864. A North Carolinian who felt the same dilemma said: "I hardly know whether to wish the election of McClellan or Lincoln, & the only preference I have is that I think it better to deal with a miserable man than a fool. God give us safe deliverance." See Thomas P. Devereux to William A. Graham, September 14, 1864, in William A. Graham Papers, Southern Historical Collection, University of North Carolina Library,

Chapel Hill. For a similar statement by an Arkansan, see John W. Brown, Diary, November 11, 1864.

121. Benjamin H. Hill, Speech at Macon, Georgia, September 23, 1864, in Augusta *Chronicle & Sentinel*, September 28, 1864.

122. George Fitzhugh to Editor, September 26, 1864, in Richmond *Sentinel*, September 28, 1864.

123. Augusta *Constitutionalist*, September 27, 1864; Augusta *Chronicle & Sentinel*, September 30, 1864; Richmond *Dispatch*, October 6, 11, 1864; Richmond *Examiner*, September 20, 26, October 24, 1864; J. B. Magruder to Robert W. Johnson, November 5, 1864, in *Official Records, Armies*, Ser. I, Vol. XLI, Pt. IV, p. 1030; Henry S. Burrage, "The Effect of President Lincoln's Re-election upon the Waning Fortunes of the Confederate States," Military Historical Society of Massachusetts, *Civil War and Miscellaneous Papers* (Boston, 1918), XIV, 216.

124. Richmond *Examiner*, October 10, 1864. For similar expressions, see ibid., September 3, October 10, 15, 17, November 2, 1864; Richmond *Sentinel*, September 29, 1864; Richmond *Dispatch,* October 18, November 7, 1864; Charleston *Mercury*, October 15, 1864.

125. Richmond *Sentinel*, September 24, 1864. See also ibid., October 4, 1864; Jones, *Diary*, II, 277, 299; Gorgas, *Diary*, p. 149.

126. New York *Herald* in North Carolina *Standard*, October 19, 1864.

127. H. A. M. Henderson to Editor of Jackson *Mississippian,* October 10, 1864, in Richmond *Sentinel*, October 21, 1864. See also John S. Ford to J. E. Dwyer, October 9, 1864, in *Official Records, Armies*, Ser. I, Vol. LIII, p. 1021; Benjamin H. Hill to Herschel V. Johnson, October 13, 1864, in Herschel V. Johnson Papers, Duke University; Jones, *Diary*, II, 313; Edmund Ruffin, Diary, October 11, 1864, Library of Congress.

128. Richmond *Sentinel*, September 19, 1864.

129. Clement C. Clay to George H. Pendleton, September 16, 1864, in Clement C. Clay Letterbook, Duke University. See also Kinchen, *Confederate Operations*, p. 95.

130. Clay to Pendleton, September 16, 1864.

131. Clement C. Clay to James P. Holcombe, September 14, 1864, in Clement C. Clay Papers, Duke University.

132. [Clement C. Clay] to Judah P. Benjamin, November 1, 1864, in *Official Records, Armies*, Ser. I, Vol. XLIII, Pt. II, p. 917.

133. Kinchen, *Confederate Operations*, pp. 148–51; Jones, *Diary*, II, 326.

134. Jefferson Davis to Congress, November 7, 1864, *Jefferson Davis*, ed. Rowland, VI, 397–98.

135. Robert H. Smith to Helen H. Smith, September 19, 1864.

Chapter 7

1. Kinchen, *Confederate Operations*, pp. 148–50; Gray, *Hidden Civil War*, pp. 206–7; Nevins, *Ordeal*, VII, 133–34.

2. Richmond *Sentinel*, November 9, 19, 1864; Richmond *Examiner*, November 10, 1864; Augusta *Chronicle & Sentinel*, November 11, 1864.

3. Augusta *Chronicle & Sentinel*, November 10, 11, 12, 1864; Richmond *Sentinel*, November 12, 14, 1864; Richmond *Dispatch*, November 14, 1864; Jones, *Diary*, II, 327, 328; James D. White to J. B. Magruder, November 8, 1864, in *Official Records, Armies*, Ser. I, Vol. XLI, Pt. IV, p. 1035; M. M. Parsons to Sterling Price, November 16, 1864, ibid., p. 1055; D. Herndon Lindsey to Sterling Price, November 28, 1864, ibid., p. 1081; John W. Brown, Diary, November 11, 1864, in Southern Historical Collection, University of North Carolina Library, Chapel Hill; Jason Niles, Diary, November 13, 1864, ibid.; Edmund Ruffin, Diary, November 8, 1864, in Library of Congress.

4. Richmond *Dispatch*, November 14, 1864.

5. Ibid., November 12, 1864; Richmond *Sentinel*, November 12, 1864; Augusta *Constitutionalist*, November 13, 1864.

6. Richmond *Examiner*, November 25, 1864. See also ibid., November 15, 1864; Richmond *Sentinel*, November 11, 1864; North Carolina *Standard*, November 16, 1864.

7. Gorgas, *Diary*, p. 150. See also William H. Battle to
Kemp Battle, November 15, 1864, in Battle Family Papers,
Southern Historical Collection, University of North Carolina
Library, Chapel Hill.

8. Kean, *Diary*, p. 177.

9. J. McEntee to Andrew A. Humphreys, November 22,
1864, in *Official Records, Armies*, Ser. I, Vol. XLII, Pt. III, p.
681. See also J. G. Foster to H. W. Halleck, November 21, 1864,
ibid., Ser. I, Vol. XLIV, p. 517; N. T. Dana to O. O. Howard,
November 16, 1864, ibid., Ser. I, Vol. XLI, Pt. IV, p. 586; Frank
W. Marston to C. T. Christenson, December 29, 1864, ibid., p.
955; Burrage, "Lincoln's Re-election," p. 217.

10. Richmond *Sentinel*, December 18, 1864. See also Augusta *Constitutionalist*, December 17, 1864; Jones, *Diary*, II,
330.

11. Richmond *Dispatch*, November 9, 1864; Richmond *Sentinel*, December 10, 1864.

12. Richmond *Sentinel*, November 15, 1864.

13. Richmond *Examiner*, November 11, 1864. See also ibid.,
November 18, 1864.

14. Ibid., November 9, 1864.

15. Richmond *Sentinel*, in Augusta *Constitutionalist*, November 19, 1864.

16. Richmond *Sentinel*, November 19, 1864; Richmond *Dispatch*, November 12, 1864.

17. Augusta *Constitutionalist*, November 10, 1864. See also
ibid., November 8, 1864.

18. Savannah *News* in Augusta *Chronicle & Sentinel*, November 23, 1864.

19. Alexander H. Stephens to Editor, November 14, 1864, in
Augusta *Constitutionalist*, November 16, 1864; Alexander H.
Stephens to Jefferson Davis, December 13, 1864, in *Official
Records, Armies*, Ser. IV, Vol. III, p. 934.

20. Alexander H. Stephens to Thomas J. Semmes, November 5, 1864, in Augusta *Constitutionalist*, November 16,
1864. The original of this letter is in Thomas J. Semmes
Papers, Duke University.

21. Augusta *Chronicle & Sentinel*, November 18, 1864; Richmond *Dispatch*, November 21, 1864; Richmond *Sentinel*, November 21, 1864.

22. Jefferson Davis to Alexander H. Stephens, January 6, 1865, in *Official Records, Armies*, Ser. IV, Vol. III, p. 1004.

23. Jefferson Davis to Alexander H. Stephens, November 21, 1864, ibid., p. 840.

24. Alexander H. Stephens to Linton Stephens, December 10, 1864, in Alexander H. Stephens Papers, Manhattanville College of the Sacred Heart, Purchase, N.Y.

25. Ibid. See also Alexander H. Stephens to Linton Stephens, December 16, 1864, in Alexander H. Stephens Papers, Manhattanville College.

26. Stephens to Davis, December 13, 1864, pp. 934–40. The quotation is on pp. 938–39.

27. Davis to Stephens, January 6, 1865, pp. 1000–1004. The quotations are on pp. 1003 and 1004.

28. William A. Graham to Zebulon B. Vance, November 29, 1864, in Zebulon B. Vance Papers, North Carolina Department of Archives and History, Raleigh. For a similar expression, see Jones, *Diary*, II, 324.

29. Jones, *Diary*, II, 355.

30. North Carolina *Standard*, November 23, 1864.

31. Josiah Turner to Sophia D. Turner, May 2, 1864, in Josiah Turner Papers, Duke University; Josiah Turner, Resolution, December 16, 1864, in *Journal of the Congress of the Confederate States of America*, VII, 360.

32. Henry S. Foote, Resolution, November 30, 1864, in *Journal of the Congress of the Confederate States of America*, VII, 312–13.

33. Alexander and Beringer, *Anatomy*, pp. 263–99; Yearns, *Confederate Congress*, pp. 171–83.

34. T. Conn Bryan, *Confederate Georgia* (Athens: University of Georgia Press, 1953), p. 97; Fleming, "Peace Movement in Alabama," pp. 121–22.

35. William H. Battle to Kemp P. Battle, November 15, 1864.

36. Jones, *Diary*, II, 368.

37. James P. Holcombe to Judah P. Benjamin, November 16, 1864, in *Official Records, Navies*, Ser. II, Vol. III, pp. 1234–39. The quotation is on p. 1238.

38. Ibid., p. 1238. See also Jacob Thompson to Judah P. Benjamin, December 3, 1864, ibid., *Armies*, Ser. I, Vol. XLIII, Pt. II, pp. 930–31, 935.

39. Holcombe to Benjamin, November 16, 1864, p. 1238.

40. Thompson to Benjamin, December 3, 1864, p. 930.

41. Holcombe to Benjamin, November 16, 1864, pp. 1239–40.

42. Clement C. Clay, Diary, [February, 1865], in Clement C. Clay Papers, Duke University; Kinchen, *Confederate Operations*, p. 185.

43. Kinchen, *Confederate Operations*, pp. 185–214.

44. Robert E. Lee to Jefferson Davis, September 2, 1864, in Lee, *Wartime Papers*, p. 847.

45. Robert F. Durden, *The Gray and the Black: The Confederate Debate on Emancipation* (Baton Rouge: Louisiana State University Press, 1972), pp. 54–63, 66, 104–6, 202–3, 268–69.

46. Judah P. Benjamin to John Slidell, December 27, 1864, in *Official Records, Navies*, Ser. II, Vol. III, pp. 1253–56.

47. Frank L. Owsley, *King Cotton Diplomacy* (Chicago: University of Chicago Press, 1931), pp. 552–58.

48. Ludwell H. Johnson, "Lincoln's Solution to the Problem of Peace Terms, 1864–1865," *Journal of Southern History*, XXXIV (1968), 580–83.

49. Durden, *Gray and Black*, pp. 274–83.

50. James M. Mason to Judah P. Benjamin, March 31, 1865, in *Official Records, Navies*, Ser. II, Vol. III, pp. 1270–76; Owsley, *Diplomacy*, pp. 558–61.

Bibliography

I. Primary Sources
Manuscripts

Duke University, Durham, North Carolina
  Autograph Letters and Portraits of the Signers of the Constitution of the Confederate States
  Clement C. Clay Papers
  Jefferson Davis Papers
  Lawrence M. Keitt Papers
  Georgia Portfolio
  Herschel V. Johnson Papers
  William N. Pendleton Papers
  Thomas J. Semmes Papers
  Alexander H. Stephens Papers
  Josiah Turner Papers
Library of Congress, Washington, D.C.
  Edmund Ruffin Diary
  Alexander H. Stephens Papers
Manhattanville College of the Sacred Heart, Purchase, New York
  Alexander H. Stephens Papers
Massachusetts Historical Society, Boston, Massachusetts
  Robert C. Winthrop Papers
North Carolina Department of Archives and History, Raleigh, North Carolina
  William A. Graham Papers
  Zebulon B. Vance Papers
University of Kentucky, Lexington, Kentucky
  Thomas H. Hines Papers
University of North Carolina, Southern Historical Collection, Chapel Hill, North Carolina
  Battle Family Papers
  John W. Brown Diary
  William A. Graham Papers
  Jason Niles Diary
  George W. Rains Papers
  James G. Ramsey Papers
  David Schenck Diary

Robert H. Smith Papers
Josiah Turner Papers

Newspapers

Alexandria *Gazette*, August 1864
Atlanta *Southern Confederacy*, July 1861
Augusta *Chronicle & Sentinel*, 1864
Augusta *Constitutionalist*, 1864
Boston *Evening Transcript*, July 1864
Charleston *Courier*, 1864
Charleston *Mercury*, 1864
Chattanooga *Daily Rebel*, March 1863
Chicago *Times*, December 1862
Columbia *Guardian*, October 1864
Columbia *South Carolinian*, September 1864
Columbus *Crisis*, August 1864
Detroit *Free Press*, January 1861
Galveston *Tri-Weekly News*, 1864
Jackson *Mississippian*, December 1862
Knoxville *Daily Register*, 1862, 1863
Mobile *Daily Advertiser and Register*, 1864
New York *Times*, May 1861; September 1864
New York *Tribune*, July 1864
North Carolina *Standard*, 1864
Raleigh *Conservative*, April 1864
Raleigh *Progress*, November 1864
Richmond *Dispatch*, 1862; 1863; 1864
Richmond *Enquirer*, April 1863; July 1864
Richmond *Examiner*, 1863; 1864
Richmond *Sentinel*, 1864
Richmond *Whig*, July 1864
Selma *Daily Register*, February 1864

Government Documents

*An Act for Enrolling and Calling Out the National Forces, and
    for other Purposes. Statutes at Large.* Vol. XII (1863).
Chandler, Allen D., comp. *The Confederate Records of Georgia.*
    5 vols. Atlanta: Charles P. Byrd, 1909.

North Carolina. General Assembly. *Executive and Legislative Documents*. May Session, 1864. Doc. No. 1.

———. General Assembly. "Resolutions in Reference to a Basis of Peace." *Public Laws*, 1864.

U.S. Congress. House. *Assassination of Lincoln*. H. Rep. 104. 39th Cong., 1st sess., 1866.

———.Congress. House. Representative Alexander H. Long, Address, April 8, 1864. *Congressional Globe*, 38th Cong., 1st sess., 1864, pp. 1499–1503.

———.Congress. House. Representative Benjamin G. Harris, Address, April 9, 1864. *Congressional Globe*, 38th Cong., 1st sess., 1864, pp. 1515–16.

———.Congress. House. Representative Clement L. Vallandigham, Address, January 14, 1863. *Congressional Globe*, 37th Cong., 3d sess., 1863, appendix, pp. 52–60.

———. Congress. Senate. *Biographical Directory of the American Congress, 1774–1971*. S. Doc. 92–8, 92d Cong., 1st sess., 1971.

———. Congress. Senate. *Journal of the Congress of the Confederate States of America*. S. Doc. 234, 58th Cong., 2d sess., 1904.

———. War Department. *War of the Rebellion: A Compilation of the Official Records of the Union and Confederate Armies*. Washington, D.C.: U.S. Government Printing Office, 1880–1901.

———. Navy Department. *Official Records of the Union and Confederate Navies in the War of the Rebellion*. Washington, D.C.: U.S. Government Printing Office, 1894–1927.

Books, Articles, and Pamphlets

Adams, Charles F. *A Cycle of Adams Letters, 1861–1865*. Edited by Worthington C. Ford. Boston: Houghton Mifflin Company, 1920.

Barr, James M. *Confederate War Correspondence of James Michael Barr and Wife Rebecca Ann Dowling Barr*. Edited by Ruth B. McDaniel. Taylors, S.C.: Faith Printing Company, 1963.

Boyce, William W., and James H. Hammond. "Boyce-Hammond Correspondence." Edited by Rosser H. Taylor. *Journal
of Southern History*, III (August 1937), 348–54.

Burrage, Henry S. "The Effect of President Lincoln's Re-elec-
tion upon the Waning Fortunes of the Confederate States."
Military Historical Society of Massachusetts. *Civil War and
Miscellaneous Papers*, XIV. Boston, 1918.

Castleman, John B. *Active Service*. Louisville: Courier-Journal
Job Printing Company, 1917.

Chesnut, Mary Boykin. *A Diary from Dixie*. Edited by Ben
Ames Williams. Boston: Houghton Mifflin Company, 1961.

Cobb, Thomas R. R. "Thomas R. R. Cobb: Extracts from Letters
to His Wife." Southern Historical Society, *Papers*, XXVIII.
Richmond, 1900.

Davis, Jefferson. *Jefferson Davis: Constitutionalist, His Letters, Papers, and Speeches*. Edited by Dunbar Rowland. 10
vols. New York: J. J. Little and Ives Company, 1923.

————. *Rise and Fall of the Confederate Government*. 2 vols.
London: Longmans, Green and Company, 1881.

Duke, Basil. *History of Morgan's Cavalry*. Edited by Cecil F.
Holland. Bloomington, Ind.: Indiana University Press, 1960.

Fay, Edwin H. *"This Infernal War."* Edited by Bell I. Wiley.
Austin: University of Texas Press, 1958.

Gilmore, James R. [Edmund Kirke]. "Our Visit to Richmond."
Atlantic Monthly, XIV (September 1864), 372–83.

Gorgas, Josiah. *The Civil War Diary of General Josiah Gorgas*.
Edited by Frank E. Vandiver. University, Ala.: University of
Alabama Press, 1947.

Hines, Thomas H. "The Northwestern Conspiracy." *Southern
Bivouac*, New Series II (December 1886), 437–45; (January
1887), 500–510; (February 1887), 567–74; (April 1887), 699–
704.

Johnson, Herschel V. "From the Autobiography of Herschel V.
Johnson." *American Historical Review*, XXX (January
1925), 311–36.

Johnson, Robert Underwood, and Clarence Clough Buel, eds.
Battles and Leaders of the Civil War. 4 vols. New York: The
Century Company, 1884–88.

Johnston, Joseph E. *Narrative of Operations*. Bloomington, Ind.: Indiana University Press, 1956.

Jones, John B. *A Rebel War Clerk's Diary*. Edited by Howard Swiggett. 2 vols. New York: Old Hickory Bookshop, 1935.

Kean, Robert G. H. *The Diary of Robert Gurlick Hill Kean*. Edited by Edward Younger. New York: Oxford University Press, 1957.

Lee, Robert E. *Lee's Dispatches*. Edited by Douglas S. Freeman. New York: G. P. Putnam's Sons, 1915.

———. *The Wartime Papers of R. E. Lee*. Edited by Clifford Dowdey and Louis H. Manarin. Boston: Little, Brown and Company, 1961.

Lincoln, Abraham. *The Collected Works of Abraham Lincoln*. Edited by Roy P. Basler. 10 vols. New Brunswick, N.J.: Rutgers University Press, 1953.

Longstreet, James. *From Manassas to Appomattox*. Philadelphia: J. B. Lippincott Company, 1895.

McPherson, Edward, ed. *The Political History of the United States of America during the Great Rebellion*. New York: D. Appleton & Company, 1864.

Porter, Kirk H., and Donald B. Johnson, eds. *National Party Platforms, 1840–1968*. Urbana: University of Illinois Press, 1970.

Richardson, James D., ed. *A Compilation of the Messages and Papers of the Confederacy*. 2 vols. Nashville: United States Printing Company, 1906.

Russell, William H. *My Diary North and South*. Boston: T. G. H. P. Burnham, 1863.

Stephens, Alexander H. *A Constitutional View of the Late War between the States*. 2 vols. Philadelphia: National Publishing Company, 1868–70.

———. "A Letter for Posterity." Edited by James Z. Rabun. Emory University Publications. *Sources & Reprints*. Atlanta, 1954.

Toombs, Robert; Alexander H. Stephens; and Howell Cobb. *The Correspondence of Robert Toombs, Alexander H. Stephens, and Howell Cobb*. Edited by Ulrich B. Phillips. American Historical Association, *Annual Report*, II, 1911. Washington, D.C., 1913.

222   Bibliography

Vandiver, Frank E., ed. "Proceedings of the Second Confeder-
ate Congress." Southern Historical Society. *Papers*, LI. Rich-
mond, Va., 1958.
Welles, Gideon. *Diary of Gideon Welles*. 3 vols. Boston:
Houghton Mifflin Company, 1909.
Worth, Jonathan. *Correspondence of Jonathan Worth*. Edited
by J. G. de Roulhac Hamilton. Raleigh: Edwards &
Broughton Printing Co., 1909.

II. Secondary Sources
Books

Alexander, Thomas B., and Richard E. Beringer. *The Anatomy
of the Confederate Congress*. Nashville: Vanderbilt Univer-
sity Press, 1972.
Andrews, J. Cutler. *The South Reports the Civil War*. Prince-
ton: Princeton University Press, 1970.
Barrett, John G. *The Civil War in North Carolina*. Chapel Hill:
University of North Carolina Press, 1963.
Bartlett, Ruhl J. *John C. Frémont and the Republican Party*.
Columbus: Ohio State University Press, 1930.
Beale, Howard K. "The Election of 1864." In *Lincoln for the
Ages*, pp. 307–11, edited by Ralph G. Newman. Garden City,
N.Y.: Doubleday, 1960.
Benton, Elbert J. *The Movement for Peace without a Victory
during the Civil War*. Western Reserve Historical Society.
Publications, No. 99. Cleveland, 1918.
Bettersworth, John Knox. *Confederate Mississippi*. Baton
Rouge: Louisiana State University Press, 1943.
Bragg, Jefferson Davis. *Louisiana in the Confederacy*. Baton
Rouge: Louisiana State University Press, 1941.
Bryan, T. Conn. *Confederate Georgia*. Athens: University of
Georgia Press, 1953.
Butler, Pierce. *Judah P. Benjamin*. Philadelphia: Jacobs &
Company, 1906.
Capers, Gerald M. *Occupied City: New Orleans under the
Federals*. Lexington: University Press of Kentucky, 1965.
Carter, Hodding. *Their Words Were Bullets: The Southern
Press in War, Reconstruction, and Peace*. Athens: University
of Georgia Press, 1969.

Castle, Albert. *General Sterling Price and the Civil War in the West*. Baton Rouge: Louisiana State University Press, 1968.

Catton, Bruce. *This Hallowed Ground*. Garden City, N.Y.: Doubleday & Company, Inc., 1956.

Cauthen, Charles Edward. *South Carolina Goes to War, 1860–1865*. Chapel Hill: University of North Carolina Press, 1950.

Connelly, Thomas L. *The Army of the Heartland*. Baton Rouge: Louisiana State University Press, 1967.

———. *Autumn of Glory*. Baton Rouge: Louisiana State University Press, 1971.

Coulter, E. Merton. *Civil War and Readjustment in Kentucky*. Chapel Hill: University of North Carolina Press, 1926.

———. *The Confederate States of America*. Vol. VII of *A History of the South*, edited by Wendell H. Stephenson and E. Merton Coulter. 9 vols. Baton Rouge: Louisiana State University Press, 1947–.

Davis, Michael. *The Image of Lincoln in the South*. Knoxville: University of Tennessee Press, 1971.

Dorfman, Joseph. *The Economic Mind in American Civilization*. 5 vols. New York: Viking Press, 1946–59.

Dubose, John W. *The Life and Times of William Lowndes Yancey*. Birmingham, Ala.: Roberts & Sons, 1892.

Durden, Robert F. *The Gray and the Black: The Confederate Debate on Emancipation*. Baton Rouge: Louisiana State University Press, 1972.

Durkin, Joseph T. *Stephen R. Mallory*. Chapel Hill: University of North Carolina Press, 1954.

Eaton, Clement. *A History of the Southern Confederacy*. New York: The Macmillan Company, 1954.

Escott, Paul D. *After Secession: Jefferson Davis and the Failure of Confederate Nationalism*. Baton Rouge: Louisiana State University Press, 1978.

Faulkner, Harold U. *American Economic History*. New York: Harper & Brothers, 1960.

Fleming, Walter L. *Civil War and Reconstruction in Alabama*. New York: Columbia University Press, 1905.

Flippin, Percy S. *Herschel V. Johnson of Georgia*. Richmond: Press of the Dietz Printing Company, 1931.

Freeman, Douglas S. *R. E. Lee.* 5 vols. New York: Charles Scribner's Sons, 1934–35.

Gosnell, Harpur A. *Guns on the Western Waters.* Baton Rouge: Louisiana State University Press, 1949.

Gray, Wood. *The Hidden Civil War.* New York: Viking Press, 1942.

Griffith, Louis T., and John E. Talmadge. *Georgia Journalism, 1763–1950.* Athens: University of Georgia Press, 1951.

Hendrick, Burton J. *Statesmen of the Lost Cause: Jefferson Davis and His Cabinet.* Boston: Little, Brown and Company, 1939.

Holland, Cecil F. *Morgan and His Raiders.* New York: The Macmillan Company, 1942.

Horan, James D. *Confederate Agent: A Discovery in History.* New York: Crown Publishers, 1954.

Horn, Stanley F. *The Army of Tennessee.* New York: The Bobbs-Merrill Company, 1941.

Hyman, Harold M. "Election of 1864." In *History of American Presidential Elections, 1789–1968*, Vol. II, pp. 1155–78, edited by Arthur M. Schlesinger, Jr. and Fred L. Israel. New York: Chelsea House, 1971.

Johns, John E. *Florida during the Civil War.* Gainesville: University of Florida Press, 1963.

Jones, Archer. *Confederate Strategy from Shiloh to Vicksburg.* Baton Rouge: Louisiana State University Press, 1961.

Kinchen, Oscar A. *Confederate Operations in Canada and the North.* North Quincy, Mass.: Christopher Publishing House, 1970.

Kirby, Robert L. *Kirby Smith's Confederacy.* New York: Columbia University Press, 1972.

Kirkland, Edward C. *The Peacemakers of 1864.* New York: The Macmillan Company, 1927.

Klement, Frank L. *The Copperheads in the Middle West.* Chicago: University of Chicago Press, 1960.

_____. *Limits of Dissent: Clement L. Vallandigham and the Civil War.* Lexington: University Press of Kentucky, 1970.

Leach, Jack F. *Conscription in the United States.* Rutland, Vt.: Charles E. Tuttle Publishing Company, 1952.

McElroy, Robert. *Jefferson Davis: The Unreal and the Real.* 2 vols. New York: Harper & Brothers, 1937.

McWhiney, Grady. *Braxton Bragg and Confederate Defeat.* New York: Columbia University Press, 1969.

Meade, Robert D. *Judah P. Benjamin.* New York: Oxford University Press, 1943.

Merli, Frank J. *Great Britain and the Confederate Navy.* Bloomington, Ind.: Indiana University Press, 1970.

Murdock, Eugene C. *One Million Men: The Civil War Draft in the North.* Madison: The State Historical Society of Wisconsin, 1971.

Nevins, Allan. *Ordeal of the Union.* 8 vols. New York: Charles Scribner's Sons, 1947–71.

Nicolay, John G., and John Hay. *Abraham Lincoln.* 10 vols. New York: The Century Company, 1886.

Owsley, Frank L. *King Cotton Diplomacy.* Chicago: University of Chicago Press, 1931.

Parrish, William E. *Turbulent Partnership: Missouri and the Union, 1861–1865.* Columbia: University of Missouri Press, 1963.

Patrick, Rembert W. *Jefferson Davis and His Cabinet.* Baton Rouge: Louisiana State University Press, 1944.

Potter, David M. "Jefferson Davis and the Political Factors in Confederate Defeat." In *Why the North Won the Civil War*, pp. 91–114, edited by David Donald. Baton Rouge: Louisiana State University Press, 1960.

Randall, James G., and Richard N. Current. *Lincoln the President.* 4 vols. New York: Dodd, Mead & Company, 1945–55.

Randall, James G., and David Donald. *The Civil War and Reconstruction.* Lexington, Mass.: D. C. Heath and Company, 1969.

Ringold, May S. *The Role of the State Legislatures in the Confederacy.* Athens: University of Georgia Press, 1966.

Robertson, Alexander F. *Alexander Hugh Holmes Stuart.* Richmond: William Byrd Press, 1925.

Sass, Herbert R. *Outspoken: 150 Years of the Charleston News and Courier.* Columbia: University of South Carolina Press, 1953.

Seitz, Don C. *Horace Greeley*. Indianapolis: Bobbs-Merrill Company, 1926.

Shalhope, Robert E. *Sterling Price: Portrait of a Southerner*. Columbia: University of Missouri Press, 1971.

Strode, Hudson. *Jefferson Davis*. 3 vols. New York: Harcourt Brace, 1955–64.

Studenski, Paul, and Herman E. Kross. *Financial History of the United States*. New York: McGraw-Hill Book Company, 1963.

Tatum, Georgia Lee. *Disloyalty in the Confederacy*. Chapel Hill: University of North Carolina Press, 1934.

Thompson, William Y. *Robert Toombs of Georgia*. Baton Rouge: Louisiana State University Press, 1966.

Tucker, Glenn. *Zeb Vance*. Indianapolis: Bobbs-Merrill Company, 1965.

Vandiver, Frank E. *Jubal's Raid*. New York: McGraw-Hill Book Company, 1960.

———. *Rebel Brass*. Baton Rouge: Louisiana State University Press, 1956.

———. *Their Tattered Flags*. New York: Harper's Magazine Press, 1970.

Von Abele, Rudolph. *Alexander H. Stephens*. New York: A. A. Knopf, 1946.

Waddell, James D. *Biographical Sketch of Linton Stephens*. Atlanta: Dodson & Scott, 1877.

Warner, Ezra J., and W. Buck Yearns. *Biographical Register of the Confederate Congress*. Baton Rouge: Louisiana State University Press, 1975.

Wiley, Bell I. *The Road to Appomattox*. New York: Atheneum, 1956.

Winters, John D. *The Civil War in Louisiana*. Baton Rouge: Louisiana State University Press, 1963.

Yearns, Wilfred B. *The Confederate Congress*. Athens: University of Georgia Press, 1960.

Zornow, William F. *Lincoln and the Party Divided*. Norman, Okla.: University of Oklahoma Press, 1954.

Articles

Blumenthal, Henry. "Confederate Diplomacy: Popular Notions and International Realities." *Journal of Southern History,* XXXII (May 1966), 151–71.

Callahan, J. M. "The Diplomatic Relations of the Confederate States with England." American Historical Association. *Annual Report,* 1898. Washington, D.C., 1899.

Cooper, William J., Jr. "A Reassessment of Jefferson Davis as War Leader: The Case from Atlanta to Nashville." *Journal of Southern History,* XXXVI (May 1970), 189–204.

Curry, Richard O. "The Union As It Was: A Critique of Recent Interpretations of the Copperheads." *Civil War History,* XIII (March 1967), 25–39.

Dimick, Howard T. "Peace Overtures of July, 1864." *Louisiana Historical Quarterly,* XXIX (October 1946), 1241–58.

Dudley, Harold M. "The Election of 1864." *Mississippi Valley Historical Review,* XVIII (March 1932), 500–518.

Fleming, Walter L. "The Peace Movement in Alabama during the Civil War." *South Atlantic Quarterly,* II (April 1903), 114–24.

Gentry, Judith F. "A Confederate Success in Europe: The Erlanger Loan." *Journal of Southern History,* XXXVI (May 1970), 157–88.

Gloneck, James F. "Lincoln, Johnson, and the Baltimore Ticket." *Abraham Lincoln Quarterly,* VI (March 1951), 255–71.

Hay, Thomas R. "The Davis-Hood-Johnston Controversy." *Mississippi Valley Historical Review,* XI (June 1924), 54–84.

James, Alfred P. "General Joseph Eggleston Johnston, Storm Center of the Confederate Army." *Mississippi Valley Historical Review,* XIV (December 1927), 342–59.

Johnson, Ludwell H. "Beverly Tucker's Canadian Mission, 1864–1865." *Journal of Southern History,* XXIX (February 1963), 88–89.

———. "Lincoln's Solution to the Problem of Peace Terms, 1864–1865." *Journal of Southern History,* XXXIV (November 1968), 576–85.

Jones, Robert H. "Anglo-American Relations, 1861–1865, Reconsidered." *Mid-America*, XLV (January 1963), 36–49.

Kirkpatrick, Arthur R. "Missouri's Delegation in the Confederate Congress." *Civil War History*, V (June 1959), 188–98.

———. "Missouri's Secessionist Government, 1861–1865." *Missouri Historical Review*, XLV (January 1951), 124–37.

Klement, Frank L. "Clement L. Vallandigham's Exile in the Confederacy." *Journal of Southern History*, XXXI (May 1965), 149–63.

———. "Middle Western Copperheads and the Genesis of the Granger Movement." *Mississippi Valley Historical Review*, XXXVIII (March 1952), 679–94.

Malone, Henry T. "Atlanta Journalism during the Confederacy." *Georgia Historical Quarterly*, XXXVII (September 1953), 210–19.

———. "Charleston Daily Courier: Standard Bearer of the Confederacy." *Journalism Quarterly*, XXIX (Summer 1952), 307–15.

Merrill, Louis. "General Benjamin F. Butler in the Presidential Campaign of 1864." *Mississippi Valley Historical Review*, XXX (March 1947), 537–70.

McWhiney, Grady. "Controversy in Kentucky: Braxton Bragg's Campaign of 1862." *Civil War History*, VI (March 1960), 5–42.

Moore, Ross H. "The Vicksburg Campaign." *Journal of Mississippi History*, I (July 1939), 151–68.

Nelson, Larry E. " 'Independence or Fight.' " *Civil War Times Illustrated*, XV (June 1976), 10–14.

Oates, Stephen B. "Henry Hotze: Confederate Agent Abroad." *The Historian*, XXVII (February 1965), 131–54.

Osborn, George C. "The Atlanta Campaign, 1864." *Georgia Historical Quarterly*, XXXIV (December 1950), 271–87.

Owsley, Frank L. "Defeatism in the Confederacy." *North Carolina Historical Review*, III (July 1926), 446–56.

Owsley, Harriet C. "Peace and the Presidential Election of 1864." *Tennessee Historical Quarterly*, XVIII (March 1959), 3–19.

Parks, Joseph H. "State Rights in a Crisis: Governor Joseph E. Brown versus President Jefferson Davis." *Journal of Southern History*, XXXII (Februray 1966), 3–24.

Rabun, James Z. "Alexander Stephens and the Confederacy." *Emory University Quarterly*, VI (October 1950), 129–46.

————. "Alexander H. Stephens and Jefferson Davis." *American Historical Review*, LVIII (January 1953), 290–321.

Randall, James G. "The Newspaper Problem in Its Bearing upon Military Secrecy during the Civil War." *American Historical Review*, XXIII (January 1918), 303–23.

Raper, Horace W. "William W. Holden and the Peace Movement in North Carolina." *North Carolina Historical Review*, XXXI (October 1954), 493–516.

Sanger, Donald B. "The Atlanta Campaign: Its Political Background and Effect." *Infantry Journal*, XXXV (September 1929), 297–309.

Silver, James W. "Propaganda in the Confederacy." *Journal of Southern History*, II (November 1945), 487–503.

Thomas, David Y. "Missouri in the Confederacy." *Missouri Historical Review*, XVIII (April 1924), 382–91.

Trexler, Harrison A. "The Davis Administration and the Richmond Press." *Journal of Southern History*, XVI (May 1950), 177–95.

Wiley, Bell I. "Camp Newspapers of the Confederacy." *North Carolina Historical Review*, XX (March 1943), 327–35.

Wilson, Charles R. "McClellan's Changing Views on the Peace Plank of 1864." *American Historical Review*, XXXVIII (April 1933), 498–510.

Wilson, Quintus Charles. "Confederate Press Association, A Pioneer News Agency." *Journalism Quarterly*, XXVI (June 1949), 160–66.

Yearns, Wilfred B., Jr. "The Peace Movement in the Confederate Congress." *Georgia Historical Quarterly*, XLI (March 1957), 1–18.

Yeates, Richard E. "Governor Vance and the Peace Movement, Part I." *North Carolina Historical Review*, XVII (January 1940), 1–25.

———. "Governor Vance and the Peace Movement, Part II."
North Carolina Historical Review, XVII (April 1940), 89–
113.

Zornow, William F. "The Cleveland Convention, 1864, and
Radical Democrats." *Mid–America*, XXXVI (January 1954),
39–53.

———. "The Union Party Convention at Baltimore in 1864."
Maryland Historical Magazine, XLV (September 1950), 176–
200.

Dissertations

Arnold, Marcus L. "Jefferson Davis and His Critics." Ph.D.
dissertation, University of Texas, 1929.

Harbison, Winfred A. "The Opposition to President Lincoln
within the Republican Party." Ph.D. dissertation, University of Illinois, 1930.

Nelson, Larry E. "The Confederacy and the United States
Presidential Election of 1864." Ph.D. dissertation, Duke
University, 1975.

Robbins, John B. "Confederate Nationalism: Politics and Government in the Confederate South." Ph.D. dissertation, Rice
University, 1964.

Index